The End of Innocence

A Da Capo Press Reprint Series

FRANKLIN D. ROOSEVELT
AND THE ERA OF THE NEW DEAL

GENERAL EDITOR: FRANK FREIDEL
Harvard University

The End of Innocence

BY JONATHAN DANIELS

DA CAPO PRESS • NEW YORK • 1972

Library of Congress Cataloging in Publication Data

Daniels, Jonathan, 1902-
   The end of innocence.
   (Franklin D. Roosevelt and the era of the New Deal)
   1. U.S.—Politics and government—1913-1921.
  2. Daniels, Josephus, 1862-1948 3. Roosevelt,
Franklin Delano, Pres. U.S., 1882-1945. I. Title.
II. Series.
E766.D26 1972   973.91   73-37285
ISBN 0-306-70423-4

This Da Capo Press edition of *The End of Innocence*
is an unabridged republicaion of the
first edition published in Philadelphia and New York in 1954.
It is reprinted by special arrangement with the author.

Published by Da Capo Press, Inc.
A Subsidiary of Plenum Publishing Corporation
227 West 17th St., New York, New York 10011

The End of Innocence

Secretary of the Navy Josephus Daniels and his young assistant, FDR, photographed during World War I in the portico of the old Navy Department building which faces the White House. "You are saying to yourself, 'Some day I'll be living in that house,'" Mr. Daniels told the smiling Roosevelt. It was not prophecy but whimsy.

The End of Innocence

BY JONATHAN DANIELS

J. B. LIPPINCOTT COMPANY · *Philadelphia* · *New York*

To my brothers

JOSEPHUS, WORTH AND FRANK

Contents

Sources and Acknowledgments

AN AUTHOR SHOULD BE ABLE TO SET DOWN NEATLY AND PRECISELY
his debts and his sources. I regret that I cannot. I suspect this
book began to be written when I went to Washington at the
age of eleven, a solemn supporter of William Jennings Bryan
but a boy much more at home in the Washington woods
through which, not long before, the strenuous Theodore Roosevelt loved to lead the perspiring and bramble-scratched ambassadors. It was strange then how much nearer the woods seemed
in Washington than in North Carolina. In the supposedly
thriftless South, the farmers plowed the cotton fields right up
to the city limits. In Washington the landowners could more
confidently await the realtors. There were more birds. I had
no idea then that bird-watching was a fashion with statesmen,
TR, Lord Grey and, in lasting emulation, Franklin Roosevelt.

An inland child, wandering down that part of Rock Creek
which was still unlandscaped and unmotorized to the Potomac
edge, I was particularly fascinated with the gulls. I owe some
of the reconstruction of that recollection (as I owe help in other
memories to others, too) to a naturalist named Louis J. Halle,
Jr., who also watched them in Washington: the great black-
backed and herring gulls which sacrifice some deftness to size and
weight, and the little Bonaparte's gulls which are quickness and
grace itself but because they lack the momentum of heavier
birds must be continually flapping and flicking their wings to

9

sustain themselves. But the best are the ringbills with a capacity for a thousand slight, continuous adjustments of wing and tail to the air in which they move. A boy or a statesman may learn from the gulls; even gulls might learn from the best politicians.

I set them down as a source in writing about years which I confronted as much in terms of homesickness as of history. Their movements at least were clear in the writing of a book which has seemed often less an historical than an emotional enterprise. It remains such a book. Written about the two men I admired most and who loved each other well, I finish it far from fully satisfied with the picture drawn of either of them in those years in which the world changed so greatly about them and they were changed within it. Those have been described as tragic years. They were the years which seemed, after he was stricken so quickly beyond them, all the years allotted by fate to the usefulness of Franklin Roosevelt. They were years which ended in the defeat of much for which my father had hoped. They were still, as my father wrote to Roosevelt as they ended, "golden years." They remain "golden years" for me and, I think, guide years, too, for an America which has not yet fulfilled its hopes and its purposes.

Much of this book, of course, takes its color from a boy's memories and a man's observations. Some of it is the record of the things an old man told his son. Some of it comes from things the always romantic Roosevelt told me in easy moments about his youth. No documents defend such materials. This book, however, is at least as crowded with research as recollection. Not boastfully I can say that there is at least as much sweat as emotion in it. Also, there is in it the help of many people, living and dead, the evidently powerful and the apparently inconsequential. The period they knew has been much written about. Sometimes the shelves of books about the Wilson times seem endless like those of all the times in which America made war and made peace. Beyond such times and such books the letters and papers, diaries and documents pile up in new and old libraries.

My basic help in this book came from my father's unpublished diary. Parts of it were intelligible only by references to other works beside it. It was a good beginning to have beside it an index to all references to him in those years, prepared for him when they ended by *The New York Times*. That helped me in tracing the story not only in that great paper but in others, notably my father's own *News and Observer* of Raleigh. The contemporary record, however, is clarified and enlivened by materials only lately available; such as the papers of my father and other men of the period in the Library of Congress, Roosevelt's own papers and those of other men which he collected to leave in the Franklin D. Roosevelt Library at Hyde Park, and the fascinating and intimate story of Roosevelt himself set out in *F.D.R. His Personal Letters*, edited by Elliott Roosevelt (Little, Brown and Company). I owe much to the written and spoken recollections of others about the young Roosevelt—to the unpublished portions of the diaries of Colonel Edward M. House, to a lively journal kept by FDR's friend, Livingston Davis, to forgotten and neglected diplomatic cables. I am glad to admit a debt even to the gossips of the period and admit also an equal fascination for and wariness of the *Letters of Henry Adams, 1892-1918* (Houghton Mifflin Company) and such publications as *Town Topics* and *The Clubfellow and Washington Mirror*. The philosopher sometimes outdid the tatlers in his reports.

Among living people I owe debts to many, none more than to my friends, David Mearns and Frank Freidel. As assistant librarian and chief of the manuscripts division of the Library of Congress, Mearns' helpfulness and discernment are not even equaled by the great resources over which he presides. Certainly today no one can write about Roosevelt or his part in the Wilson period without grateful dependence upon the scholarship of Dr. Freidel as Roosevelt's chief biographer. I was also much helped by the perceptive editing which Carroll Kilpatrick gave to the correspondence between FDR and my father in his *Roosevelt and Daniels: A Friendship in Politics.* Dr. Herman Kahn of the Roosevelt Library at Hyde Park deserves my deepest appreciation. So does my brother, Dr. Worth B. Daniels, who gave me the benefit of his own emotion and his good sense, too, in suggesting revisions. George Stevens, editor of Lippincott, has been patient, critical and helpful. Many others have helped: Robert E. Williams, Eula Williamson, A. T. Dill. And my wife, Lucy Cathcart Daniels, deserves but does not ask thanks: "Let's get this book out of our house and our hair." Here it is.

JONATHAN DANIELS

The End of Innocence

The Image of Democracy

HE WOULD HAVE LAUGHED AT THE SUGGESTION BUT MY FATHER, Josephus Daniels, was a beautiful old man. In his post as Ambassador to Mexico he had the proper decorative setting for his hale, humorous, shrewd old age. At seventy-nine, in 1941, he had been fighting a long time. He found in old and peaceful, violent and brooding Mexico the perfect place to spend a golden twilight. Or so it seemed to me when I visited him in Mexico City. My father, who had never been convinced of the virtue of unnecessary physical exercise, had only to walk across the wide, walled garden from the embassy to the chancellery. On his way, I remember, he sometimes stopped to look at the white, sleeping volcanoes seeming nearer than they were. It pleased him that they never looked the same, yet were always unchanging. It was an almost personal tribute that he had learned to pronounce their names, Popocatepetl and Ixtacihuatl. He was never, however, more interested in mountains than in men. Sometimes he hurried across the garden without even looking over the wall.

He felt far off and left out during his last summer in Mexico. With world war approaching almost step by step as it had come before, he felt like an old firehorse far from the fire. Almost like yesterday's echo he had been hearing, in that summer before Pearl Harbor, the demands of self-confident critics that the President name a "superman" to clean out confusion and break the bottlenecks in defense production and preparations. Only the word "bottleneck" was new. As America had approached world war before, my father had heard almost identical demands, sometimes from a younger Franklin Roosevelt himself. My father was impatient but he was not disturbed. He sent the President not only his advice but his faith, writing in an uphill scrawl, not always easily decipherable, but with no faltering of his pen as he grew old. He included a quotation from a statement of Woodrow Wilson in the face of similar demands:

"... I have no gods at my disposal."

After nearly sixty years in the politics of the American democracy, the one thing of which my father was most certain was that no gods were ever available. If there had been any he would have had a chance to see them. He was more than half as old as the republic itself. He had been born in a small, Southern river town under Federal gunboat fire. He had been fatherless in Reconstruction. Not noticed but noticing everything, he had been a young Democratic editor at the inauguration of the stalwart Republican Garfield. More important, as the chief Democrat of his state in national party councils, he had been a lieutenant of William Jennings Bryan when that Nebraskan, just old enough to run for President, had become the first major party candidate in a generation to boldly make his own the cause of those Americans who knew that they were poor and felt that they were oppressed. He had helped bring the cause —and the men—of Bryan to Woodrow Wilson. As Secretary of the Navy in Wilson's Cabinet he had brought Franklin Roosevelt to Washington as Assistant Secretary. He had seen Bryan rejected, Wilson defeated, and young Franklin Roosevelt escape political destruction only by the skin of his teeth.

My father had fought for peace and made war. He had shared in many defeats and some victories. He could look back, at the last, and see confidently that the years of greatest effort and deepest disappointment had been a foundation time for faith. They proved the indestructibility of the old American promise for people as the most radical doctrine on earth. The instruction and encouragement of those years fitted like a glove—or a gauntlet—the needs of the time in which he was old and so many others were young.

He talked much to me about that doctrine, not always with his blue eyes blazing. More often they were twinkling. The radical American change as he remembered it was a serious business, but a humorous one, too. The strength of the mass of Americans who made it lay in the combination of humility and humor which are the qualities denied to men who present themselves as gods. Franklin Roosevelt may not have learned that from my father as I did, but I know that he learned it while he was working beside my father. Also, I know that it was the one thing which my father as an old man watching him with admiration, affection and wariness never meant to let him forget. It was the essence of the reminder, offered as weapon but as warning, too:

"... I have no gods at my disposal."

My father did not always trust the experts. He was scornful of any supposed elite. He kept an almost mystic faith in the people themselves. Strength was in them even when their stirring was imperceptible. Danger and difficulty had not recently been invented for them. Where they were, they had been before. And all the long years and increasingly with the years he noticed that no men made America in the image of democracy. Democracy made its image in them. It would not fail to do so. He was as sure of that as he was of his friends the mountains beyond the garden wall.

He was the most reticent man who ever wrote his memoirs. He wrote five big loving volumes of a happy life. He liked to say that he wrote not by the word but by the pound. But his memoirs were only a mellowed reflection of the diaries that he had kept, intermittently but with increasing care as the First World War came and passed. Sometimes they were dull and profuse. He recorded the punch lines of Wilson's jokes which the President seemed sometimes to use not to point his discussions with the Cabinet, but as barriers against discussion. They were not diaries lovingly prepared for publication from the outset, to prove to history that he was history—as were the diaries of Wilson's one-time friend, Colonel E. M. House. For the Wilson period the House diaries deserve a title like that which Mr. Dooley gave to Theodore Roosevelt's account of his activities in the Spanish War, "Alone in Cubia." Some of the Daniels entries amount to only a single scrawled word. Often he used only initials to identify persons. Sometimes he seemed almost whispering items to himself. The diaries were often obviously not expositions for the future but reminders only to himself.

What seemed, as I began to prepare the diaries for publication, to be a filial editing chore turned into an enterprise in deciphering, investigation, and recollection. Inevitably it has led to the recapture of my own education. My way has been lighted by a candle burning at both ends—a blessing for once— the illumination of my young memories and the klieg-lit experience of serving as one of Franklin Roosevelt's secretaries at the moment of his victory and his death. I remember not only the galloping young man, but his august agility and audacity at the last, even when it was my job to screen all the grisly pictures of him which had been flown back from Yalta and to release only those which seemed least marked by what afterward we understood was his dying.

Before I began to work on my father's diaries I had read, of course, the *Personal Letters* (1905-1928) of Roosevelt who apparently never threw away a letter or even an envelope. The sharp things which he wrote in some of those letters about my father prompted Elliott Roosevelt, who edited them for the family, to write that "the somewhat derogatory remarks about Josephus Daniels in the letters of this chapter are far more illustrative of the growth of F.D.R.'s personality than of Daniels' competence as a Secretary of the Navy." My father would have appreciated that. He himself wrote of Roosevelt that he "was young then and made some mistakes. Upon reflection, although I was older, I made mistakes, too." I doubt that my father would have appreciated so much Elliott's further gesture in dedicating the book jointly to "The memory of two great Americans, Josephus Daniels and Louis McHenry Howe"— FDR's boss and his man Friday in the Wilson days. In Roosevelt's whole life I think those two could be fairly described as the faithful and the fixer, though Howe gave to Roosevelt in those days a loyalty Roosevelt was not then able to give to anybody else. As the Roosevelt family felt, I think that the story of the differences between my father and Roosevelt is important to history. It is important not only because of Roosevelt's later eminence but because their conflicts, resolved in lasting affection, involve the material for understanding conflict within democracy.

Little as I knew in the Wilson years—much as I may misunderstand later—about the surprising questions which preoccupied the statesmen and the politicians, the admirals and the diplomats, I doubt if I could have understood any of them half so well if I had not, as a boy, seen the Washington in which they worked. Obviously, that may add prejudice to a picture. Certainly in view of such memories, early and late, this book can never pretend to be objective.

It is memory-ridden and emotion-torn. It will attempt to tell what I learned of democracy from seeing in action my father, Woodrow Wilson, and FDR. It is their story and my education. Sometimes, I hope, it may reflect the unabashed observations of a boy staring with bird-steady eyes.

That boy—and the man he became—was fortunately placed on the bridge that ran between the men and across the years. He was where he could see democracy realizing itself through different kinds of men—and none so different as the homespun democrat my father always seemed and the dissimilar aristocrats Woodrow Wilson and Franklin Roosevelt were. Democracy in action can be seen only in such different men. And the men only reflect the American people defining their will and getting what they want. That is not a game, though the symbols of card-playing have been popular with American philosophers and politicians from Henry Adams, who reported in his *Education* that no child born when he was born held better cards, to Franklin Roosevelt, who proposed and provided a new deal. Game or not, I held a ringside seat in the Wilson administration when so much happened which was to seem a rehearsal for later events. My memories have been fortified and refreshed by my father's diaries. The significance of what he scribbled then has sometimes suddenly and startlingly illuminated for me the democracy in militant phase which I saw as Roosevelt's assistant and secretary.

It seems to me more sad than strange that in the Wilson years *The Education of Henry Adams* related how the author, a son of the founders, came as an aristocrat in democracy only to pessimism and disdain. I am not abashed because my education as a democrat has led me to believe joyously and confidently in democracy. It pleased me to discover that Adams' book was finished in the first decade of the century, when Republicans and Democrats (Theodore Roosevelt as well as William Jennings Bryan) were in full surge of faith that democracy could fulfill its purposes, but only published in 1918 when it met a mass market for disillusionment. That year those wealthy reactionaries, who never have to learn disdain for democracy from a philosopher, already looked forward eagerly to the destruction of Wilson's reforms as long afterward they hoped to destroy those of President Franklin Roosevelt.

The democratic visionaries were clearly routed at the end of the Wilson years as they so often are. Much of the fault was certainly their own. Possibly the collision of high hope and "hard facts" was as inevitable as winter. Perhaps the idealists and reformers in a sort of summer elation failed to foresee it like the summer-dancing grasshoppers which, in contrast to the hoarding ants, have received so much castigation and contempt from Aesop to La Fontaine to Henry Adams. Mr. Adams had a special liking for that story. It has always seemed a particularly apt parable to those who, having a fixed store for themselves, not only presume their own wisdom but the improvidence of those less well provided for. Maybe those who embraced the coming of the great wars and were not saddened by the end of reform were the ants. They have seemed so to themselves, often to history. It could be, however, that they welcomed the winter while the grasshoppers kept faith in spring.

That is not a fable for a child or a philosopher. It was, however, part of what I began to learn when, as naïve newcomer, I arrived in Washington in 1913 as son of one of those Democrats whom Wilson led back into power for the first time in sixteen years. They included, in the persons of my father and his friend, Mr. Bryan, the kind of radical Democrats whom even Grover Cleveland had helped keep out of town in the revolutionary election of 1896. I lacked entirely the lineage, the investments and the Boston background with which Henry Adams was equipped when he came as an aristocrat to Washington near the beginning of his *Education*. But on his arrival in 1850 he was just one year and one month older than I was on mine. Adams was both appalled and fascinated by the vivid poverty and luxuriant disorder which slopped over into the capital from the surrounding slave South. As a young democrat from the

South where poverty was familiar in 1913 and democracy was never town-meeting neat, I was surprised and impressed by the palaces beside the hovels on the still gap-toothed avenues.

Slavery struck Adams in the face, though he admitted or professed an addiction to the Southern atmosphere, heavier than the smell of the catalpas, from which he never escaped. I faced suddenly the Plutocracy about which my father and Bryan talked. I did not understand then, what Frederick Lewis Allen explained so well later, that since American millionaires wanted to live like princes, they required exact replicas of the houses of princes; but I could look up at the châteaux from the sidewalks. They were the last monuments of the Gilded Age which the Democrats were rudely terminating with the income tax. Young Adams did not share with his elders his fascination for the looseness and swagger of nature and man which he found in Washington. It was not my purpose as young provincial to admit that I was unduly impressed by the mansions of the millionaires. I think it finally took the gold place-plates that Mrs. Perry Belmont used at a luncheon one day to break the blasé mask of my brother Frank. In North Carolina he had been hearing Negro hymns about the golden plates and the golden spoons all his infancy. Apparently this was *it;* but I remember that when he looked down on the apocalypse, he giggled.

Mr. Adams was already completely educated before we got to town. He was pointed out to us as a leaf-frail old man in a victoria, drawn by one horse which looked as if it had made the whole trip with him from his boyhood. It was difficult to think that Mr. Adams had ever been a boy, ready to walk across the town in which the government offices looked like Greek temples in the abandoned gravel pits of a deserted Syrian city, to the half-finished Washington Monument. Knowledge of his trip to the monument would have been a tie between Mr. Adams and ourselves and our centuries. We climbed the completed shaft without puffing. We also assumed a proprietary attitude toward the State, War and Navy Building which, in those days in Washington, quite adequately housed all the aides and agents of diplomacy and the armed services. We examined repeatedly and in detail the models of impressive battleships in their glass cases, not disturbed as Father was that the price of our largest battleships had gone up in ten years from $5,382,000 to $14,044,000. Beside such power, Mr. Adams as a philosopher seemed insignificant. We, of course, did not know that Mr. Adams, not long before, had concluded his *Education,* as we began ours, with a feeling that "for the first time in fifteen hundred years a true Roman pax was in sight . . . and even Russia seemed about to be dragged into a combine of intelligent equilibrium." Mr. Adams hedged like a philosopher, if not like the companion of politicians, with the possibility of "continent against continent in arms." His generation, he said, need not repine at missing catastrophe.

Mine, of course, is the generation which did not miss it, and my part in the story is that of a fortunately placed bystander. Even then I was not always an actual witness. The measles kept me from Wilson's inaugural parade. But I did see the crowds of indignant gentlemen, intent upon preserving the best traditions of American womanhood, pushing the suffragettes around on Pennsylvania Avenue when they undertook to parade the day before. It took me longer to understand those gentlemen as the symbols of a tough, elegant, cohesive defense of the things which are—or were. The derbies of that day have disappeared but the heads beneath them are the same.

I was placed where I could see the lean and acid Senator Henry Cabot Lodge, and beside him the admirals and Senators, dowagers and debutantes. I am glad I saw the ladies as well as the statesmen—the two startlingly different Mrs. Wilsons and sensitive Eleanor Roosevelt when she was young. I am still shaken by the roar of the fourteen-inch guns of a steaming fleet which did not seem entirely harmless before new and deadlier weapons were devised. Most of all I am glad that I had a chance as a juvenile to know at first hand, in Washington and even in the Navy Department, my father's faith as a democrat, spelled with both a big and a little "d." He took it from Thomas Jefferson almost with the feeling that Jefferson had personally handed it to him. He never forgot it. Neither, I think, safely can any of us. Here it is:

> "Men by their constitutions, are naturally divided into two parties: 1. Those who fear and distrust the people, and wish to draw all power into the hands of the higher classes. 2. Those who identify themselves with the people, have confidence in them, cherish and consider them as the most honest and safe, although not the most wise, depository of the public interests. . . . In every country these two parties exist. . . . The appellation of Aristocrats and Democrats is the true one, expressing the essence of all."

I cannot honestly say I was as concerned about democracy as my father was in those days. My concerns were with Connecticut Avenue, not Pennsylvania. What happens between the White House and the Capitol on the avenue of triumphal processions did not greatly interest me then. I was more aware of places and people, birds and trees, on and beside Connecticut. That avenue ran its full-shaded residential way from the White House to the Chevy Chase Club to which Franklin Roosevelt so often carried his golf clubs on the trolley. It crossed Rock Creek. It passed the old red brick British Embassy which Roosevelt loved so well, also it passed Rauscher's where debutantes were presented in perennial re-enactment of Henry Adams' observation that society was founded on the law that all young people were rich if they could waltz.

On Connecticut Avenue, too, where Florida Avenue crosses it was Ridgeway's Drug Store. It is not much mentioned in history, but it was a much frequented meeting place of the sons and daughters of soldiers and statesmen, politicians and even diplomats—and of some of their elders, too. Boy met girl there. Also, I remember an Italian secretary of legation with a stubborn case of hiccups. It seemed very funny from the soda fountain. Ridgeway's was, in the increasingly self-conscious capital of a world power, the same sort of drugstore which served as a community center in thousands of towns. It was just down Florida Avenue from the drugstore that novelist Sinclair Lewis and poetess Elinor Wylie laughed so gaily at so many people while Lewis was writing *Main Street* in Washington. He put in it the finding, hardly noticed by sophisticated city readers, that Washington was only an accumulation of thousands of small towns. There is satisfying sentiment in that dictum. It sounds pretty simple. Nothing, however, better proves the basic continuing contest in American democracy between those who believe in government by an elite or by the people themselves than the differences in some American small towns—between Hyde Park, New York, and Raleigh, North Carolina, for instance, or, as was clearer still when Lewis wrote in the teens of the century, between his own Gopher Prairie and Pride's Crossing, Massachusetts.

I did not realize then that the fashionable village on the Massachusetts North Shore could be an item in the education of a democrat. I doubt that any such idea would have occurred to many of its inhabitants. Henry Adams stayed near by in the last summer of his education on earth. We went there in the summer of 1913 to visit naval stations, as a part of my father's intensive education as Secretary of Mr. Wilson's Navy, on a yacht which was a perquisite of his office. I was not conscious of education of any kind that summer. School was out. I certainly was more interested in swimming over the ship's side than in any sociology of the over-privileged. We anchored off Gloucester near some fish houses, I remember. They stank. But we went ashore. It was a pleasant and ordered land. We

visited the polo field at the Myopia Hunt Club, which legend
says was formed exclusively by rich, near-sighted men. We
drove along the rocky rim of the bay and beside the half-con-
cealed estates behind their field stone walls to Pride's Crossing.
My memory is that Franklin Roosevelt, very much at home,
was there at the same time.

As a handsome young Harvard man, Roosevelt in those days
was almost as indigenous to Pride's Crossing as to Hyde Park.
The same sort of people had estates there as those neighbors
and friends of his in Dutchess County who, during his child-
hood, had required the services of Stanford White and Richard
Morris Hunt in the erection of mansions which, when he was
President, became museums. He and his classmate, Livingston
Davis, who was to be his gay wartime assistant, often played
golf there. His close friend, William Phillips, who was to be
made Assistant Secretary of State on the "insistent recommendation" of Colonel House, had an estate in the neighborhood. So
did the bitter Republican partisan, patriot and polo player,
Congressman Augustus Peabody Gardner, to whom FDR was
to slip confidential information in support of his attacks on the
administration of the Navy. Congressman Gardner's father-in-
law, Senator Lodge, at whose home in Washington the young
Roosevelts were made to "feel really at home," lived just down
the shore. It was peculiarly Alexander Hamilton country, com-
memorating his name in the home town of my father's predecessor as Secretary of the Navy, and Hamilton's ideas about
government by an elite everywhere around it. Even Theodore
Roosevelt's daughter, Alice Longworth, when she visited at the
Longworth summer place there in 1912, found it solidly Old
Guard Republican in its sentiments. Also, it was from Pride's
Crossing that Colonel House wrote many of his letters of advice
on democracy and government, war, peace and appointments
to Woodrow Wilson.

Wilson and House talked about the safety of democracy

there. It was in that aristocratic vicinage that Wilson worked on first drafts of his League of Nations while staying at the estate of Colonel House's neighbor and friend, the rich, conservative T. Jefferson Coolidge, who had lent the Colonel the money with which to build a railroad in Texas. In that house Mr. Coolidge kept the prints, china and other relics of his great-grandfather, Thomas Jefferson. Also, he kept there the view, which he had not inherited from Jefferson but had written himself, that he believed himself "to belong to a superior class, and that the principle that the ignorant and the poor should have the same right to make laws and govern as the educated and refined was an absurdity."

The President was not uncomfortable on that estate. Indeed, if Colonel House can be believed, as he sometimes must be, it was while Wilson was driving with the Colonel near Pride's Crossing that Wilson described himself as "a democrat like Jefferson, with aristocratic tastes." That was unfortunate, the President said in self-analysis, because his mind led him where his taste rebelled. It was only afterward that he discovered that his taste took him where his faith was betrayed.

At Pride's Crossing and afterward, too, Franklin Roosevelt had no such difficulty. He was the complete aristocrat to the end of his days, but his life, his luck, his dangers and his requirements led him straight to democracy. At the last, nobody better understood than Roosevelt those countrymen of his who kept Jefferson's relics and cherished Hamilton's philosophy. Roosevelt never betrayed his class; often even at the last he loved it too well. His story was not one of betrayal but of escape. Sometimes in the Pride's Crossing years his passages between aristocratic position and democratic politics were precarious. But he was an aristocrat who clung to no cherry orchards—or any other impeding paraphernalia. Like so many other things in his life, he made a parable about that, unconsciously perhaps—you never could be sure—but with a point as clear as that made for Russia and for aristocrats beyond Russia by Anton Chekhov.

Roosevelt was never quite content to think of himself even at the last as a democrat and visionary. He felt uncomfortable in his reputation as idealist. I was present when he came back to the White House after the conference at Teheran and described Stalin: "I would call him something like me—he is a realist." He did not wait until he spoke it in wartime sometimes to follow quite literally the "nice old proverb of the Balkans," as he called it, which ran: "My children, you are permitted in time of great danger to walk with the devil until you have crossed the bridge." He did not think of himself in terms of any common denominator for the common man. When as President he spoke of Thomas Jefferson and implicitly of himself as well, he said quite truly that Jefferson was "a great gentleman. He was a great commoner. The two are not incompatible." What he represented best was the understanding of the inevitability of the democratic process even when it was opposed by gentlemen or tough men—by strong people urging a new reaction or by charming people with a passionate preference for the past or even for a decorative present. He never showed that more clearly than when he confronted as President an almost comic collision between a memorial in emphasis of Jefferson's meaning in America and some hysterical defenders of the cherry trees on the Washington Mall.

Oddly enough, Roosevelt had just been talking about refugees from old regimes when he was confronted with some determined Washington ladies who had announced their purpose to chain themselves to cherry trees on the site of the proposed Jefferson Memorial to prevent the trees from being cut down. He noted that there had always been opposition, open or evasive, to any memorial in the capital of the nation to the man who had written the declaration of its democracy. He pointed out that the monument had been authorized and its site chosen by clear democratic processes. He talked about cherry trees as expert.

"I don't suppose there is anybody in the world who loves trees quite as much as I do," he said, "but I recognize that a cherry tree does not live forever."

The important thing he recognized was that the democracy which Jefferson proclaimed did live forever, and that neither hysterical ladies nor self-confident young men could disregard it. He had had to learn that loyalty is essential not only to democracy, but within it also. He had had to discover that keeping faith with men is the essence of fidelity to democracy. That education was the basis of the lasting friendship of my father and Franklin Roosevelt which seemed strongest in the years when neither of them had anything to give the other. That was in the time after Roosevelt had been stricken with paralysis—and democracy seemed almost similarly stricken. Whenever my father came to New York, where I was studying law at Columbia in the early 1920's, he always took me to the Roosevelt house in the East Sixties. Roosevelt had not become reconciled to immobility. Mrs. Roosevelt was bringing all sorts of people to the house and to him. I remember that she asked me to bring the young men with whom I lived on the third floor of an old brownstone on Thirtieth Street up to Sunday supper. I delivered the invitation. One had a date with his girl. But the other, who later became a wealthy broker in New York, stated his regrets in more cavalier fashion. He was a realist. I remember once that when he tipped a taxi driver a nickel and the disgusted driver threw it in the gutter, my friend stooped and picked it up. I suspect he has that nickel now. At any rate, I remember that at the time he told me he thought it was very nice for me to go to see my father's old associate. But as for himself, he was young, he had his way to make. A rich world was before him. He did not have any time to spend with a has-been. I went alone.

I never regretted it. I know my father never regretted his first and last affection for Franklin Roosevelt. The simple fact at the last was that with his withered legs below him, he stood tall and joyous before the fulfillment of great hopes for which my father as one of millions of determined Americans, not always wise or always strong, had been fighting all his life. There seemed almost a miracle about Roosevelt's magnificence. There was. Also there was in my father's devotion to Roosevelt some of the sentiment and pride of the story of the prodigal son. But for most of us, the Roosevelt story was more like the re-enactment on a universal scale of Max Beerbohm's fable of *The Happy Hypocrite*. That, of course, is the story of the rich rake who put on an immaculate mask over his dissipated features in order the more effectively to woo a sweet young girl. And when in love, ashamed of subterfuge, he took the mask of innocence off, he found that the face beneath it had become innocent, too. There was not anything evil about Franklin Roosevelt. His fault as a young man was only that of one so self-confident that it did not seem necessary for him to be troubled by fidelity to anybody or anything but himself. That, of course, is the first fault of a man or a nation in democracy. And in Roosevelt's case escape from it is the evidence of democracy's miraculous power.

At Length, the Yeomen

WHEN MR. BRYAN AND MY FATHER DESCENDED, BROADLY SMILING, from the same Pullman car of the cindery Seaboard on the morning before Wilson's inauguration, in March 1913, they did not look like radicals. They seemed instead genial and innocent gentlemen, a little old-fashioned in faith and outmoded in clothes. They were no longer the fresh-faced young men who had brought into the Democratic Party so much of the bushy-bearded protest out of Populism which gave the first impetus to the sweeping American reforms later to become undisputed parts of the American system.

Their innocence did not fool the reporters. They knew that, without ever holding office except briefly as a Congressman, Bryan had at that time done more to change the pattern of government in America than any man in it. He had been the first man in a generation, William Allen White of Kansas said, who was big enough to lead a national party and who "boldly and unashamedly made his cause that of the poor and the oppressed." My father had helped make Bryan that leader and helped him make that cause. No other man was so consistently close to Bryan or to the liberal forces in the Democratic Party over so long a period of time. Both were Sunday School teachers, but that was not all they were. They had faced the Robber Barons and called them that. They had not been surprised at the invective directed against themselves, and my father at least was often amused by the ridicule.

Both were elated and strong as they got off the train. Bryan's wide smile did not conceal his great jaw. Daniels, as one of Wilson's daughters said of him at the time, was "twinkling" but no one who knew him well ever missed the protrusion of his lower lip even when he grinned. They descended cheerfully into the mass of welcomers, well-wishers and reporters. And the reporters wanted Bryan to confirm the unofficially well-known facts that under Woodrow Wilson he was to preside over American diplomacy and Daniels over the Navy. Bryan spoke for himself. The reporters asked him about his friend Daniels.

"Ask him," said Bryan. "He's of age."

That seemed a good, mild Bryanesque joke on the station platform at the time. Josephus Daniels was of age. Though he was only fifty he had been a newspaper editor for a third of a century. He had come into journalism as an amateur but had begun writing Democratic editorials as a professional when he was seventeen, graduating as such from a post as assistant to his mother, who was postmistress in the little town of Wilson, North Carolina. In that work Daniels acquired one of his prejudices. He never wanted to lick a stamp again. Also, reading everybody's newspapers as they came in, he acquired the convictions which later, in his own editorials, helped his mother lose her precious job as postmistress under the Republicans. She had only got it because no white man in Wilson could take an oath that he had not given aid and comfort to the Confederacy, and all ex-Confederates were for her. Also, it was a nice informal way to provide a living for a well-loved widow with three small boys, all useful in licking stamps for the patrons of the postoffice. She taught them more than that. She did not worry about their morals. She fed them onions, she said, and never troubled about the girls. She was more concerned about liquor which provided release for roistering whites and Negroes in a bitterly poor South. Clientless young lawyers were much in their cups. There were fortunate farmers whose horses, unguided, knew their way home on Saturday nights.

Also, the Widow Daniels hated war, in which her husband had been killed when the boys were babies. Her husband had hated war, too, and had been a protesting non-combatant in the divided Union. He did not believe in slavery. As a skilled ship's carpenter, he said there was no place in the slave South for a man who worked with his hands. He had gone briefly to Rhode Island to work, but he came back to marry the girl he had left behind. He helped build the *Merrimac*. He had been wounded when some irregular soldiers fired on a passenger boat. He died because he would not let the doctors take off the arm which served his skill. Not one of his boys ever learned to drive a nail. But none of them ever forgot that their father was one of the Americans who worked with his hands and was not always as fortunate as those who did not.

During the not entirely gay Nineties, when times were hard for all Southerners including editors, Daniels served as chief clerk of the Interior Department under Cleveland. That is when he met Bryan. It was his reluctant duty to carry out Cleveland's orders that the young radical Congressman was to get no patronage while he fought Cleveland's conservative currency policies. They joined forces in 1896, when Daniels, only thirty-four, acted as first lieutenant of the thirty-six-year-old Bryan in the explosive Democratic National Convention. The young Southern editor, as *The Washington Post* reported at the time, was publicly sure (and alone in his conviction) that Bryan was going to be nominated, even before the Nebraskan stampeded the delegates with his Cross of Gold speech. In expressive fantasy, Editor White of Emporia called Daniels "the Secretary of War in the first Bryan administration." He undoubtedly would have held some such post but, since there was no such administration, Daniels received only a succession of handwritten notes of Bryan's thanks in the sad Novembers of Bryan's defeats. They grew older, but as Bryan wrote, too: "Our cause must win ultimately and we can afford to wait." In 1913, they had waited seventeen years.

Daniels was of age. Indeed, as he and Bryan arrived, there was a conscious effort to describe them as old countrymen come to town. As less familiar, Daniels was depicted as less frayed. It would have shocked him to suggest that he was the well-tailored man. Actually, his slightly archaic dark clothes and his white summer linens both required special tailoring. His pleated linen shirts and black string ties had to be specially ordered. He left such details to my mother. But he had the gift of remaining immaculate after a cindery train journey or on the hot floors of political conventions. The description would not have particularly pleased him but even a social commentator who afterward did not care for Daniels' democratic ideas reported that March that "far from being the countryman he has been pictured, he is a broadminded man of the world." However, his seven Republican predecessors were all New York or New England men or graduates of Harvard or Yale. Daniels was pictured as almost the backcountry itself—an inland, small-town editor who could hardly be expected, some suggested, to know a barge from a buoy, or even a barn from a battleship.

The picture did not trouble him much. To those who suddenly suggested that the qualifications of a Secretary of the Navy should include a technical knowledge of the operation of ships, he replied that he had been running a newspaper for some years though he could not operate a linotype machine. Far from undertaking to prove himself citified he seemed glad to contribute to the caricature of those who emphasized and derided his ruralness. The truth was that it did not disturb him that some thought, with much of the same distaste which greeted the arrival of Jackson's men nearly a century before, that the yokels had come to town. Josephus Daniels came with

the romantic feeling that the independent yeomen, in whom
Thomas Jefferson had placed his chief faith, had somehow after
long travail triumphed in 1912. Though he had never tilled
an acre, he liked to regard himself from his shining square-toed
shoes to his round black hat as one of those yeomen in the service of Jefferson's radicalism still.

It was an odd idea for such a time. In a nation concerned
about the concentration of economic power in the cities, but
also more confidently citified than ever before, Washington had
a strong sense of its social sophistication. Its established occupants definitely did not think of it as a small town, but as a
new world capital. It did not seem small and simple to its new
invaders either. To the Democrats, it was Babylon which
needed to be cleansed and chastened. Its palaces paraded Plutocracy and Privilege. I remember myself that I half expected
their occupants to emerge in suits checked with dollar marks
with which Democratic cartoonists had clothed the crude and
careless rich during the campaigns. They did not look crude,
but some were chagrined. The chatelaine of one of the largest
mansions left to history her impression that "the impossible had
happened." Along Connecticut and Massachusetts Avenues the
change and the collision seemed most clearly marked by Wilson's brusque announcement that there would be no inaugural
ball. That, said *The Clubfellow and Washington Mirror,* as
the resentful voice of the socially entrenched, created "a decided
distaste for the President-elect," though the writer added dis-
dainfully that, as everybody knew, an inaugural ball was only
"a stranger's revel, partaking of the nature of a stampede."

It was hardly possible to see the city for the stampede. The
arriving Democrats made such vast and happy crowds as Washington had never seen before. Also, before I went down with
the measles on inauguration day, my fever seemed part of
a national febrile exhilaration. In the crowding I had, certainly, unequalled opportunities for contagion. I was not the

only one who failed to see the whole show. Actually much of the meaning of the celebration for those present was lost in crowd and tumult, fireworks and parade. The real meaning was still in the places from which the crowds came. And certainly as good a place as any other in which to see that was the small town from which Bryan and Daniels had traveled together to Washington. They had seen crowds before. Metropolis did not intimidate them. Bigness was what they had chiefly assailed. Their targets had been such city giants as Tammany and the trusts. They remained insistently small-town men, armed with a purpose to return the rural virtues to a misguided and often misappropriated land. On the train platform they were victors at last but to many they seemed innocents still as they arrived from the inconsiderable, inland town of Raleigh, North Carolina.

That place with a population of 19,000 did not consider itself small town. Even those in it who did not most admire Josephus Daniels resented the effort to deride him as a small-town editor. Raleigh, as a state capital, regarded itself as the center of the society of an old commonwealth. It was, but it was better described at the turn of the century as a center of an agricultural people growing five-cent cotton with which to buy ten-cent meat. Pride and grace as well as poverty walked under its old oaks, nevertheless, and sometimes sat together on the deep porches behind wide lawns. Some limited prosperity had given it a number of new houses much adorned with scrolls, warts, knobs and balustrades. If their occupants could not quite afford Stanford White, they could put scroll saws to work.

One of Bryan's biographers, J. C. Long, who observed that Daniels "always seemed to be opportunely present at the crises in Mr. Bryan's life," also noted how much Bryan loved to visit in Daniels' town. He felt at home there. Indeed, in terms of the town itself, Bryan's feeling about it has been romanticized by some of those biographers who held romantic notions about small towns everywhere. In Raleigh, according to their interpretation, he found neither the sophisticated polish of the East, nor the smartly worded opinions of the intelligentsia, nor the bitter opposition of those who disliked him. Raleigh, they reported, was a part of the country where Evangelical Christianity was the order of the day and where every respectable citizen was a Democrat. Actually no small town in the South, or in the rest of America, was ever that simple.

Undoubtedly, however, Bryan found a reasonable facsimile of the almost bucolic peace attributed to the small town at the Daniels house. It was a comfortable, rambling two-story house of the color of green, much more common in the South then than the gleaming white of columned mansions. There were magnolia trees and a big oak before it but the view, across the rose garden and the lawn, was of slum on one side and of the eroded campus of a small Negro college on the other. It was a house of Southern respectability—even of aristocracy when lady relatives spoke of it in soft voices which claimed lineage all the way from the Confederacy to Charlemagne. My mother, who had been Miss Addie Bagley, belonged to that company always found in capitals, of citizens, descended from politicians who came to take office and remained to take possession. Her grandfather had been Governor and her father clerk of the State Supreme Court. It had not been entirely clear that she was bettering herself when she married the radical young editor who seemed to have a pretty high opinion of his own views, and something less than complete deference for the old Confederates or the new capitalists. She was an organized daughter of both the Revolution and the Confederacy, a Colonial Dame and a Mayflower Descendant. She had an aunt who, as a present, joined her to a new patriotic society every Christmas, which only meant that my mother had to keep up the dues all the rest of her life. Father declined to belong to any organization everybody else could not belong to, which left him quite ontentedly limited to the Democratic Party and the Methodist Church. He missed few of the meetings of either of them.

If the green house which Addie Daniels' father built was no manor house, she had the manor manner. She made its back-door a combination of soup kitchen and clinic for such colored neighbors as were not regularly on her payroll. Also, she seemed always staffed for the sudden serving of plates of home-made ice cream to the politicians in the parlor whose buggies were so often lined up before the curb. During its sessions every member of the legislature came to her house for dinner. She was no more perturbed when a Smoky Mountain statesman drank from his finger bowl than she had been on her fifteenth wedding anniversary when that bowl was new and the cow had somehow got in from the backyard to the parlor where the presents were arrayed. Not even the cow in the crystal could disturb a lady who, as a combative editor's wife, sometimes put on her hat and walked up town to see who was still speaking to her. She held to the view that the way to a politician's vote might be through his stomach. It often was. With her husband, in those days when small-town hotels were hazards and horrors for travelers, she enjoyed maintaining a sort of hostel for celebrities. Mr. Bryan, of whose oratory my brothers and I were less in awe than of his appetite, was not the only one who liked to come to the hospitable house. Woodrow Wilson had been there, Ambassador James Bryce, a good cross-section of the newspapermen, politicians, authors and actors who composed itinerant America. Most of them found their way back when they were in that part of America again. They were welcome.

The house was something more important still. Like similar residences in other Southern and Western small towns, it was a house of revolution. Men from even smaller towns, embattled farmers from the five-cent cotton fields, intense young lawyers, earnest schoolteachers, some angry old men, gathered in that house as they did in so many others to speak something more

than restlessness about the country and the corporations, corn
and cotton prices, high tariffs and economic heartbreak. Some
of them joined the Populists in casting their million futile,
angry votes in 1892. There had been millions more of them
behind Bryan when he ran in 1896. What the muckrakers
began to discover and disclose after 1900, small men in such
little towns had been shouting for all to hear for ten, twelve,
twenty years before. Even Thorstein Veblen's *The Theory of
the Leisure Class*, which received such startled attention in
1899, sounded like the collected protests of the farmers and
small-town people among whom he had lived, men to whom
leisure remained theoretical and to whom class meant the divisions of men on the basis of rank injustice. Long before effective reform lifted its beneficent head in the cities, men, of what
the sociologists and the snobbish called the small-town middle
class (in houses like the plain, green house in Raleigh), were
waging what their enemies called, with high emotion and un-
intended accuracy, revolution in the United States.

That revolution was not simple. The green house was not
the town. And the town reflected no prim, white, town-meeting
version of decorous democracy. Democracy in the Fourth Ward
in Raleigh was unpainted but exciting. It was located—or exercised—two blocks from the Daniels house in a small nondescript,
two-story, plank building on East Cabarrus Street. Although in
addition to the Daniels house there were some other old comfortable houses in it, the Fourth Ward was always poor and
occasionally violent. Most of the residents were Negroes and
poor white people. The plank building was a good example of
its non-residential architecture. It could have been built to
house one of those infinitesimal groceries with a limited supply
of fly-specked merchandise, which abounded before the chain
stores came. It might have been built as a lodge hall for a weak,
non-affluent burial fraternity. Food supply and burial costs
were immediate problems in the Fourth Ward. Generally, be-

tween election days, the little building stood empty and pad-
locked (everything had to be locked up in the Fourth Ward).
It sat off the ground on crumbly brick legs. The weeds grew
all around it. Cats and dogs crept through the weeds to contest for the shade beneath it. A lucky cat might leave behind
the slick, clean skeleton of a stolen fish.

The building was open and alive on election days. Then it
was surrounded by citizens and electors who indicated by their
excessive smiling or determined scowling their immediate concerns for the destinies of democracy—or maybe just for the
chance of a dollar and a drink. Not all of that gathered cit-
izenry were devoted to Daniels, though he had plenty of friends
in the Fourth Ward. He was not only a Democrat like Mr.
Bryan. He was a prohibitionist like Mr. Bryan, too, and in a
time when the prohibitionists, though that may be hard for us
to understand now, were not sissies but the determined opponents of tough liquor men in the tough politics of the time.
Even a child could see on election day that not all the electors
were teetotalers. It was my father's custom as each of his four
sons grew beyond toddling to take one of them to put his ballot
in the box for him. It was an educational procedure which he
thought could not be begun too young. It provided a subject
for amiable pleasantries at the polls. Not even his worst enemies ever challenged the procedure. It became in time not
only an educational custom of Daniels but a part of the regular
and expected ceremonials of the Fourth Ward. It remains for
me a more important part of my education as a democrat than
anything I learned in the civics books or political science sem-
inars.

Neither Daniels' house nor his ward was the town. The poor
and the protesting made only a part of a well-understood strati-
fication. Those who presume a fixed ratio between population
and diversity misunderstand both population and diversity, city
and town. In the newer, more elegant section of Raleigh, near

the new Governor's Mansion, in a big, much-ornamented house with a cupola, Colonel Alexander Boyd Andrews occupied a local position roughly corresponding to that of J. Pierpont Morgan the Elder in the United States. As North Carolina vice-president of the Southern Railroad, which was a part of the Morgan system, Colonel Andrews handled the politics for the Southern and in the process set up at least two newspapers to try to run Daniels out of business. Those papers hit Daniels almost as hard as he was hitting the railroad. He thrived on their attention.

"Toot! Toot! There goes the old railroad organ," Daniels' paper emphasized, and in the race with it he built the circulation of his own *News and Observer* to double that of any other daily in the state, though Raleigh was by no means the largest town. The paper remained The Nuisance and Disturber to a good many of its readers—or just Joedaniels' paper in a state where, in affection and irritation, his two names became one word. In Colonel Andrews' case the word was a snort.

The Colonel was not only a Southern aristocrat and the pro-consul of Northern plutocracy which even in Reconstruction always had its respectable Southern assistants. Also, Colonel Andrews had gained the girth which made him the replica of the cartoons of the Wall Streeters whom he served by such epicurean practices as feeding his tethered turkeys only grain which had been soaked in brandy. It was hard to tell what that did to the turkeys, but it was easy to see what it did to the Colonel. Daniels' comments on the Southern's rates, services, tax privileges and politics seemed to the Colonel first an impertinence and then a menace. His feelings were increasingly shared by the Dukes, twenty-five miles away in Durham, who had established the American Tobacco Company in the midst of the tobacco fields. Daniels did not describe the trust as a mere corporate and financial device. It was to him and his readers a deliberate and brutal conspiracy to starve the farmers and put small manufacturers out of business. It was something of a shock to the Dukes to find their most pestiferous critic in such a close neighbor and active fellow Methodist as Daniels. Their collision nearly broke up the Methodist Church in North Carolina before the courts undertook to break up the American Tobacco Company in America.

It was one of the Dukes who made an unconscious contribution, long before the novelists, to the deflation of solemn nonsense about small-town simplicity. Small-town men enjoyed it. This Duke, named Brodie, had considerable trouble with his money and his marriages. *The News and Observer,* which was sharply critical of divorce, never missed a detail about any of Brodie's divorces or his sometimes equally sensational marriages. On one occasion his appalled friends intervened to prevent his marriage to an entirely too well-known local Durham girl. But Brodie was obdurate.

"Why can't I marry her?" he demanded.

He had asked for it and his friends told him.

"Practically every man in Durham—" they said.

Brodie contemplated their report. "Well," he said, "Durham ain't such a big town."

That marraige was forestalled, but life was not entirely simple in the small towns. Wall Street was not merely a dragon in the distance. It was found and had to be fought where it did its work and not merely where it counted its money. And if Big Business was not an imaginary bogey, neither were political bosses. (Lord Bryce, who was making the final revision of his *American Commonwealth* just as that commonwealth was undergoing major revision, saw the evil of the city machines; his American magnifying glass was not quite strong enough to let him see as clearly the courthouse rings and the state capital rings which combined them.) Like other men in the West and South, Josephus Daniels had an instinctive distrust of the big city political machines symbolized by Tammany. It was not necessary for him to go to New York, however (though as a national politician he often did), to understand the co-operation of the traction manipulators and the Tammany politicians. Only the most innocent in America regarded the political machine as a metropolitan phenomenon. In the Yarborough Hotel and in the rotunda of the State Capitol in Raleigh, men operated with a skill and ruthlessness which they did not have to ask Tammany to teach them—they were only concerned lest *The News and Observer* catch them. In North Carolina the enormous Colonel Andrews could count upon the co-operation of diminutive and agile Senator Furnifold M. Simmons as that head of the state machine could count on the Colonel for contributions. Senator Simmons (Democrat of New Bern, North Carolina, 1913 population: 9,961) was an admirer of Boise Penrose (Republican of Philadelphia, Pennsylvania, 1913 population: 1,549,008), but he did not have to ask him to tell him any tricks. Senator Simmons himself never missed a trick until he was overcome by sudden moral scruples, in his old age, against Al Smith, who was not only a wet, city Catholic, but a critic of power companies in which the Dukes had invested money which endowed Methodists. Neither did Colonel Andrews have to ask itemized instructions from J. P. Morgan himself.

Fortunately, for their purposes in the United States, neither did Daniels have to wait for Bryan or anybody else to visit his house on South Street in Raleigh to give instructions. Indeed, men like Josephus Daniels in small towns and some cities, too, across the West and South were not so much Bryan men as they had made Bryan their man and the voice of their determinations. Many others shared their determinations without ever sharing their faith in Bryan. That altered some American elections but not ultimate American directions. Bryan believed that Theodore Roosevelt stole his thunder but not his willingness to loose the lightning. TR was sure that Wilson appropri-

ated from him the progressive cause which should have given
him the victory at Armageddon, which was his evangelical name
for the election of 1912. The truth, of course, was that the protest and the purpose which pushed them all were no man's
private property. The leaders took their places in a movement
which was no straggling Coxey's Army but the ever-growing
inaugural parade of a new America.

Undoubtedly, in that movement the crossroads folks and the
small-town people did come forward with some strange determinations, as well as with most of the now accepted major
American reforms. The effort of the metropolitan press and
politicians to transform the American radicals from anarchists
to addlepates had other targets than Bryan. Editor White of
Emporia in his famous editorial, "What's the Matter with Kansas," had arrayed a catalogue of derisive terms for rural radicals:
"mossback," "jay," "clodhopper," "shabby, wild-eyed, rattle-
brained fanatic," "old human hoop-skirt." However, White
himself was made to seem one of a company of hypocrites, med-
dlers and male old maids because he was a convinced and prac-
ticing prohibitionist, along with Daniels. I doubt that any later
generation will quite be able to understand the prohibitionists.
I do not. I do know that my father, like White, brought to the
prohibition movement hope and sincerity. He could also be
humorous about it even at his own expense. There was never
a bigot's beam in his eyes.

There were, of course, some strange characters in the company. Not all their proposals made sense then or entered into
law later. Even some country crackpots, however, got to the
diagnosis if not to the cure of the sickness in the American system before there was much sign of consciousness of trouble in
the city clubs or even the college classrooms. Both the fears and
the hopes which roared up around that almost mystical phrase,
"Free Silver," in the Nineties seemed strange afterward. Daniels considered the phrase even then not so much the name of

a currency plan as a label for a crusade. The gold standard seemed less significant than the big signs on the factories, threatening men with the loss of their jobs if they voted for Bryan, which young Daniels saw when he rode with young Bryan through New England. The exciting thing was that that fight over that issue brought together men as diverse as Bryan and Governor John P. Altgeld, Eugene V. Debs, Henry George, Clarence Darrow, who all believed then, as rich, radical Mayor Tom Johnson of Cleveland said, that what they were fighting for was not free silver but free men.

It took a good many people some time to discover that. Their delay was dramatized in the green house behind the magnolias in Raleigh, too, in February 1912, when Woodrow Wilson was energetically seeking the Democratic nomination for the Presidency. Bryan was visiting at Daniels' house. The two men had, as always, much to talk about, and it was while Daniels, already a leader in the Wilson cause, was talking persuasively to Bryan about him that a correspondent for the stalwartly Republican *New York Sun* arrived at the door with a question for Mr. Bryan. *The Sun* wanted a comment from Mr. Bryan on a letter it was publishing in which, in 1907, Wilson had expressed the wish that something could be done "at once dignified and effective, to knock Mr. Bryan once and for all into a cocked hat!"

Mr. Bryan's big jaw set automatically. Behind him, no one could have missed Daniels' protruding lower lip. He knew that Bryan's opposition could put an end to Wilson's hopes. Wilson knew that too, and so did the conservative Democrat who had released the old personal letter. So did *The Sun*. By that time, when the effort had grown to transform Bryan from Murat to mountebank, he had been asked many questions by many reporters. He answered this one.

"You may wire *The Sun*," he said, "that you have seen Mr. Bryan and he says that if Mr. Wilson wants to knock him into a cocked hat, Wilson and *The Sun* are on the same platform.

That's what *The Sun* has been trying to do to him since 1896."

Daniels' mouth relaxed into a smile. It would have pleased Wilson and the Wilson men who were frantically trying to get in touch with Daniels to get him to "interpret" the letter to Bryan if they could have seen that smile. Neither he nor Bryan was under any misconception about Wilson's former attitude toward Bryan. It was Wilson's current performance as Governor of New Jersey and his earlier fight as president of Princeton which had interested Daniels in him and which Daniels hoped would interest Bryan. Daniels undertook no "interpretation" of a fact. Later he told a very nervous Wilson what he had said to Bryan at the time:

"Bryan, we must give these college professors time to catch up with us."

That was no mere joke. A good many Americans were catching up. In my father's view, Wilson had discovered the power of money against democratic purposes in education in the small community of Princeton. Some other wise men learned late. It was not as a law student but as a successful corporation lawyer that Louis D. Brandeis discovered that the great bulk of the leaders of the bar ranged themselves on the side of the corporations and that so did most of the editors and orthodox professors of economics and politics. "As an incident to their professional standing," the best brains seemed always tied up with the most money. That had been noted by lesser men far from Boston and Princeton in the years before. The important thing was that as a result of an educational process that was long, often loud, more intuitive than erudite, the combined electoral vote behind the competitive progressiveness of Theodore Roosevelt and Wilson, in 1912, amounted to ninety-eight per cent of the whole. Old-fashioned conservatism carried Utah and Vermont. Mr. Taft was not entirely alone, but he was momentarily lonely in his opinion that "the day of the demagogue, the liar and the silly is on."

It did not seem so in Raleigh. On the night of February 28,

1913, small town and proud state held a banquet for its Democratic leaders. There were too many people to be accommodated at the Yarborough House. The banquet was served next door in the biggest auditorium in the state. Everybody knew that Josephus Daniels, who had come to Raleigh from an even smaller town thirty years before to constitute himself a public conscience and to operate often as a public scold, was going to be Secretary of the Navy in Wilson's Cabinet, though none of the Cabinet appointments had been officially announced. Months before, Wilson had written to a mutual friend, "Anybody who speaks in behalf of Josephus Daniels speaks to my heart as well as my head." Later it was known that Daniels was one of the first three men Wilson decided upon for his Cabinet.

Certainly when Daniels spoke at the banquet as chosen Cabinet officer that night, he did picture himself with very heavy strokes as a plain, old-fashioned, small-town man. He had been persuaded by his boys to swap advertising in his paper for a high-riding, brass-trimmed Buick, but as a special feature for inauguration day in 1913 he ordered front page space in his paper for Jefferson's inaugural address in 1801. It did not seem antiquated material to him. Mr. Jefferson's "wide and fruitful" America still seemed "kindly separated by nature and a wide ocean from the exterminating havoc of one-quarter of the globe." There was still need for emphasis on "the supremacy of the civil over the military authority." It seemed to Daniels pertinent and imperative in 1913 that neither government nor those operating within the governed land should take from "the mouth of labor the bread it has earned." He knew then, of course, that there were men calling themselves Jeffersonian Democrats who appropriated for the plutocrats of one period the phrases which had been designed by Jefferson for all the people of another. Quite otherwise, and perhaps romantically, too, Daniels felt in terms of Jefferson's faith that, in 1913, triumph belonged again and at last to those independent yeomen in whom Mr. Jefferson had placed his basic hope. He drew a character of himself as such a man, which to the sophisticated may very well have seemed a caricature. Indeed, in the years afterward, when metropolitan America was still too new and unsure of itself to think in nostalgia of rural beginnings, what he said in description of himself and his state at the banquet seemed almost the design for the derision directed at him.

"I love to think of North Carolina," Daniels said in a farewell description of both his state and himself, "as standing apart from the richer and more showy commonwealths, setting an example of frugality and simplicity in an age of luxury and display. I love to think of its people keeping the faith of the fathers, untarnished by the gilt and glitter of fashion, unseduced by the restless ambition of place hunters and by the vices of pleasure seekers; and untouched by the skepticism and irreligion which endanger the strength and permanence of home and government."

The banquet was a tremendous success and Bryan arrived two days later. It was not only the week of the income tax and the Wilson inauguration. Also, it was the week chosen by the North Carolina Peace Society for its annual meeting. That organization, like other similar societies in other states then, was composed of no small group of professional pacifists. If, as Franklin Roosevelt told me in his last years, some of the peace societies which were supporting his United Nations did not carry a vote, that was not true then. Indeed, the Society was one of many flourishing items in the spontaneous movement which Theodore Roosevelt was later to describe as "the iniquitous peace propaganda of the last fifteen years." In North Carolina under the honorary presidency of the Governor, its officers were leading citizens of the state. Its members came by hundreds to its sessions. In the mild March weather its members, their guests, and the masses of school children who had been invited to listen to its speakers, too, filled the streets of Raleigh and the same big auditorium where the banquet had been held. *The News and Observer* reported proudly that the auditorium, which its editor had helped build, was big enough to accommodate the whole population of the town.

It was needed when Bryan came that last Sunday as private citizen to repeat his famous lecture, "The Prince of Peace." Listening to Bryan was one of the major adventures of Americans in such places in that time. If in the cities he seemed already slightly dilapidated after three failures to reach the Presidency, he never failed to fill both with people and with his voice the biggest halls and even the public squares in the towns. He was not quite fifty-three that afternoon in Raleigh —younger than either Wilson or Theodore Roosevelt and at the height of his powers as a speaker. That afternoon the lute was in his voice, as Daniels liked to say. But what he said and how he said it were less important than what Bryan had suddenly and a little strangely become. Everybody in the audience knew that the famous Nebraskan was on his way to Washington to become Secretary of State, just as his friend and their neighbor was to be Secretary of the Navy. It was significant that one said in the applauding presence of the other that it was "the imperative duty of the United States . . . to set a shining example of disarmament." Even more important was what Bryan said to Daniels after the speech.

"There will be no war while I am Secretary of State," he promised. That did not seem a strange promise to make—or a hard one to keep.

THREE

Dutchess County Hayseed

"IF ONLY THERE WERE A DEMOCRATIC PARTY," LOUIS BRANDEIS OF
Boston had written to his brother just three years before the inaugural stampede in 1913, "what havoc could be wrought!"

Neither Bryan nor Daniels when they arrived in Washington
would have used that word "havoc." Their purposes like their
appearances were benign. Their Democratic Party, however,
was not as simple as its celebrating mood. There were men in
the party who persuaded Wilson that he could not afford to
name so radical a man as Brandeis as Secretary of Commerce.
There were many who felt with Mr. Dooley that it made sense
to have Bryan in the Cabinet only because Mr. Wilson would
be safer having him in his bosom than on his back. Colonel
House felt that way. He had never been for Bryan, though he
proudly thought that he had used Bryan to help Wilson. The
Colonel declined Wilson's invitation to go to the Capitol with
him for the inaugural ceremonies. He went instead to the
Metropolitan Club and loafed around with a wealthy banker
friend who had resigned from the Democratic National Committee after Bryan was nominated in 1896.

"Functions of this sort do not appeal to me and I never go,"
the Colonel carefully noted in his diary. He was a small man
with strange cat-like eyes, a broad forehead and a thin face. He
spoke in a particularly low voice, one observer said, almost as
one might speak to another in a cathedral. Bryan and Daniels

50

enjoyed the ceremony. Indeed, one of Daniels' new colleagues, Colonel House's friend David Houston, who had come into politics only when he received political office, regarded Daniels' elation as almost unseemly.

Even in the elation of victory, Daniels shared Brandeis' feeling about the need for a real Democratic Party. He would not have emphasized the sentiments attributed to Andrew Jackson about victors and spoils, but he did believe that, after a decade and a half of Republican administrations putting Republicans in office, there were "deserving Democrats." Also, he felt that there was great need of them. (It was a view which did not seem strange even to the followers of President Eisenhower in 1953.) The phrase "deserving Democrats," which later was extracted from one of Bryan's letters by the always attentive *New York Sun,* did not disturb Father as it did some other Democrats. Colonel House told President Wilson that Bryan was a "spoilsman." The Colonel was trying to help Wilson get the best men regardless of party and in the process had already arranged for his own son-in-law, Gordon Auchincloss (Groton, Harvard and two years out of law school), to be Assistant U.S. District Attorney in New York.

My father remembered—and was much reminded of—old fighting friends who had risked respectability to be Democrats. Even more he was aware of the necessity for vigorous and resolute Democrats ready to fight for the principles of the party in the future. It was of such a vigilant young Democrat that he was thinking when he wrote in his diary that the moment he received Wilson's letter saying, "I cannot spare you from my council table," he himself "immediately thought of Franklin Roosevelt of New York as Assistant Secretary of the Navy."

Roosevelt was not the most "deserving Democrat." There were many who had been deserving longer. While Daniels would have deplored Roosevelt's lack of party regularity, he could have understood the younger man's first vote, in 1904, for a Republican when that Republican was his lively cousin, TR, and the Democrat was the dull and conservative Alton B. Parker. The presumption in history is—and certainly was in Daniels' mind—that FDR voted for Bryan in 1908. It is possible that he did; he undoubtedly gave Bryan the impression that he did. Franklin was not only a Democrat but a Democratic candidate in 1910. In 1912, he was a Wilson Democrat, which in 1913 was more important than having ever been a Bryan one. He was out of the country on a pleasure trip to Panama a good part of the spring of 1912, however, when Wilson's pre-convention campaign was in progress. He helped raise money for the Wilson cause, but he had been unable to get himself elected as a delegate to help nominate him. He was at the convention as a spectator only, though, as Daniels knew when he gave him tickets, he was a vociferous Wilson gallery man. Typhoid fever kept him from taking part in the general election campaign in which Wilson was elected President and he himself was re-elected to the State Senate, though he received fewer votes than in 1910 and won over his Republican and Progressive opponents by a majority of only seventy-three ballots.

Certainly Franklin Roosevelt was not the only young man among the hopeful or deserving Democrats in Washington for the inauguration. Woodrow Wilson himself arrived on a special train full of young Princetonians. Much more prominent in forecasts and the festivities were William F. McCombs (Princeton '98), the thirty-six-year-old National Chairman of the Democratic Party, and his rich young friend, John L. DeSaulles (Yale '01), who had helped run the Young Men's Division in the Wilson campaign. McCombs, whose petulance and desire to dictate all appointments, including his own, had already cooled the President toward him, told Daniels at the inauguration that he would "not be banished" by being made Ambassador to France. DeSaulles, who gave the biggest dinner party for the most important personages at the inauguration, still hoped to become

Ambassador to Chile where he had found his rich, lovely young wife. It was not to be young arrogance which stopped his career but, not long afterward, a bullet from his wife's pistol after they had been divorced because of his attentions to other ladies. Young men full of hopes faced hazards, too, in the Wilson years.

The well-loved American delusion that rich and well-born young men did not go into politics was threadbare long before 1913. Theodore Roosevelt had gone eagerly to the legislature as the candidate of a not very savory local boss in the year in which Franklin Roosevelt was born. Henry Cabot Lodge had already reached the Massachusetts assembly before TR took the political plunge. A third Harvard man, Senator Boise Penrose of the distinguished Philadelphia family, had begun, in 1884, the process of becoming the obese boss of Old Guard Republicanism. Political careers seemed not only worth the pains but the price to those best able to pay. Lodge's son-in-law, Augustus Peabody ("Gussie") Gardner, FDR's friend and Daniels' enemy in the Wilson years, was elected to Congress before FDR was out of Harvard. At least two of Franklin's classmates, one at Harvard and one in the Columbia Law School, were to run as he did for the governorship of New York. Also, his own classmate and four-year roommate at Harvard, wealthy Lathrop Brown, came to Washington for the inauguration in 1913, not seeking a job but already elected as a Democratic member of Congress. With rich, young Harvard men that year—and Yale and Princeton men, too—politics was almost as popular as the boat races.

In such a crowding of young men, including many poor as well as some rich, Josephus Daniels and Franklin Roosevelt came into their long association. It is not quite clear whether Roosevelt first asked for the job or Daniels first offered it. It is clear that Roosevelt wanted the Navy job more than a post which William Gibbs McAdoo of New York, as Secretary of the Treasury, would have given him—and which would have been more useful to him afterward, in his eager efforts to line up political jobs for an up-state, anti-Tammany Democratic organization. The only record he left about the matter was a statement he made long afterward to his Presidential secretary, William D. Hassett, in discussing his long friendship with Daniels.

"When I first knew him," he told Hassett, "he was the funniest looking hillbilly I had ever seen."

Apparently he kept that impression well concealed. Daniels wrote in his diary at the time that Roosevelt told him on the night before the inauguration that "if he served in any place in the administration he preferred to be in the Navy Department." However, in his memoirs, published in his old age and at the end of long affection, Daniels wrote that on the morning of inauguration day as he entered the Willard Hotel he ran into Roosevelt for the first time since the election. Roosevelt was "bubbling over with enthusiasm" and Daniels, in a like frame of mind, there and then offered him the position.

"How would you like to come to Washington as Assistant Secretary of the Navy?"

"It would please me better than anything else in the world."

Roosevelt had hurried to Washington to make sure of getting what Daniels was happy to give him. They did not know each other well. If, as Daniels said later, his first meeting with Roosevelt at the Baltimore Convention in 1912 was a case of love at first sight, they saw very little of each other there or in the campaign. The phrase was not an empty one, however. As the father of four sons, Daniels had a strong predilection for all young men. That was the basis of much of his concern for young enlisted men. And Roosevelt, in 1912, was handsome, tall, clean-cut, energetic, almost the image of the Gibson man who was as much an accepted symbol of the time as the Gibson girl.

There is no difficulty about explaining Roosevelt's eagerness. To his love of boats and water and his increasing fascination with politics he added an energetic emulation of his distant cousin. Daniels' appointment of FDR has been variously, elaborately and still inadequately explained. John Gunther, who knew both men, wrote that the reasons for the choice were (1) that Daniels liked Roosevelt, (2) that "it probably flattered him to have a Roosevelt working for him" and (3) that "he was sure he would do a good job." None of those reasons needs to be questioned, though up to that time Roosevelt had had no administrative experience. He had never had more staff to boss than servants and a stenographer. Daniels certainly was conscious of the Roosevelt name. In his diary he wrote: "His distinguished cousin TR went from that place to the Presidency. May history repeat itself." The habit of historians seems to be to pass over a consideration which was important to Daniels as a seasoned national politician, that since he was from the South the assistant "should come from another section, preferably New York or New England." (When Roosevelt resigned, Daniels named another man from that region though not the one FDR suggested.) However, the principal reason, and the one most overlooked, was that Roosevelt, despite his cousin, his class, his college and his clothes, symbolized exactly the kind of young Democrat the older Democrats of the long push and protest thought should staff a Democratic administration.

FDR had adequate title to his place among the Democrats. Though his father did not vote for Bryan, he had been a longtime member of the party. Furthermore, it had been essential to Franklin's political debut that he was a Democrat. In the strongly Republican district from which he entered politics, in 1910, as a candidate for the State Senate, Republican nominations were not given to unknown young men even if they would finance the campaign, as FDR had agreed to do. As a Democrat, Roosevelt got the nomination because it did not seem to have much value to older, more experienced Democrats. Indeed, his nomination, in the opinion of his first full-length biographer,

Dr. Frank Freidel, was part of an old pattern by which the Democratic powers in that Republican neighborhood "made cynical use of gentlemen politicians for half-hearted sorties." If that procedure won few campaigns, it turned loose some wealthy candidates' cash among Dutchess County politicians. Nobody sought the nomination in opposition to Roosevelt, but there was "a considerable pause" at the convention, as reported by *The Daily Eagle* of Poughkeepsie, before his nomination was seconded.

The delay may have reflected his improbability as a candidate, a feeling of sympathy for the naïve young man or the doubt raised in the campaign as to whether or not he was an actual resident of the district. He had been born there in the house which his father had bought in 1867 in the midst of what *The Eagle* called "the millionaire colony" at Hyde Park. The Roosevelts were never such mere estate visitors as their neighbors and friends the staunchly Republican Mortons, Ogdens, Astors, and Vanderbilts. Like his father, however, Franklin made his living in New York City. When he entered politics he was living and receiving his mail just off Fifth Avenue on Sixty-fifth Street, though Hyde Park was home. He set out to prove his neighborliness from door to door in a red Maxwell automobile. Apparently it did not scare the farmers' horses, but his election was not a personal triumph. It was an item in a general swing in the nation and in New York State, too. That swing gave the New York Democrats their first chance to elect a United States Senator since 1892.

Young Roosevelt arrived in Albany to take his seat in a style which was unusual even in the Empire State at a time when rich young men in politics were no longer strange. In those days a member of the State Senate in New York received $1,500 a year. It could not have lasted long in Franklin's case. He took a three-story house on State Street, suitable not only for entertaining other legislators on a cheese-and-beer basis, but for a formal reception to all his friends and constituents. He arrived accompanied not only by Eleanor and three children but also by his mother, who was then a very active fifty-seven years old and not so scornful of politics and politicians as she was reported to be later. There were also two nurses, a wet nurse and three other servants. Furthermore, for the reception which FDR gave for his "constituents" on the first day of his first session, a body of caterers was called in. Obviously, he made an entrance into American state politics in the grand manner. He must have seemed a strange Democrat as he began.

The first business of the legislature was the election of a successor to Chauncey M. Depew, who with so much wit and humor had been representing both the State of New York and the New York Central Railroad in the United States Senate. Customarily, in those days before primary nomination and popular election of United States Senators, the Democrats (like the Republicans) chose the candidate of the party by majority vote in the assembly. Tammany and its friends held a majority of the Democratic votes. Out of 200 votes, the Democrats had 114. That meant that with a bare majority of the Democrats, 58 votes in the party caucus, Boss Charles F. Murphy could name the United States Senator. A legislator who took part in the caucus was bound by the party decision in the legislature's vote for Senator, but there was no rule requiring a man to attend the party caucus of his party. Roosevelt and enough others stayed out to keep the Democrats from having a majority in the assembly. This resistance to boss rule meant, however, that Roosevelt and his friends with only eighteen votes—less than a fifth of his party's vote—could prevent the election of any Democratic nominee for Senator. In retrospect the angry fight then provides an interesting commentary on Roosevelt's insistence on majority rule in Democratic National Conventions, where he thought the two-thirds rule undemocratic, and on his statements about the "essentials of a party form of government" when, in 1938, he proposed the "purge" of Senators and Congressmen who represented a small minority of interest and people. The atmosphere was undoubtedly different in 1911. The important thing then was that as the captain of a minority his action gave him credit for defeating "Blue-eyed Billy" Sheehan.

That gentleman's name was William Francis Sheehan. His nickname may have described both his personality and his appearance, but it has helped create a false impression in politics and history. It has caused some reporters and historians (with some help from Roosevelt) to assume that Sheehan was just a useful, bright-eyed, ordinary Irish politician whom Boss Murphy of Tammany in perverse power had decided to promote. Indeed, M. R. Werner in his *Tammany Hall* gave Sheehan's name as "John C. Sheehan," mixing him up with the assistant to Boss Richard Croker, Murphy's predecessor. John Gunther, in his *Roosevelt in Retrospect*, refers to the real Sheehan as "a Buffalo boss and Tammany subchieftain." Such a description is fantastically inadequate. Sheehan had been the boss of Buffalo, big enough as a young man of thirty-three in 1892 to demand, if he did not get, pre-election promises from Grover Cleveland, but he had moved to New York City sixteen years before his candidacy for the Senate. He was no saloon-keeper in a checked suit heeling the wards. Franklin Roosevelt found him "delightful personally." His wife was acceptable as a Roosevelt luncheon guest. His house in New York was at 16 East Fifty-sixth Street, an impeccable address. He and his wife were listed in the *New York Social Register*. And Sheehan belonged to the Metropolitan, Manhattan, Lotus, Down Town and other clubs.

He was rich, and had paved the way for his candidacy with large contributions to the Democratic candidates in 1910. He had even offered to send the Democratic *New York World* during his campaign to any Republican or doubtful voters that young Roosevelt might list in his district. Such a procedure was standard for a rich man, Democratic or Republican, who hoped to be a member of a Senate still referred to as the Rich Man's Club. Sheehan apparently had the qualifications for entry. Indeed, much of his appeal to the Democratic leaders of New York State was the same as Franklin's appeal to the smaller Democratic bosses of Dutchess County. Sheehan was a director of important railroad and utility companies, including the Kings County Electric Light and Power Company, an antecedent of Brooklyn Edison. As such he was undoubtedly, as Roosevelt said, close to the "traction trust."

Oddly enough, however, FDR in the fight against Sheehan was taking counsel from attorneys who themselves were not particularly adverse to trusts. One of them was Francis Lynde Stetson, who was known in Wall Street as "Morgan's Attorney General" because he had put together the U.S. Steel Corporation, the Northern Securities Company and other of J. P. Morgan's greatest trusts. Another was Austen G. Fox, who was to be chief counsel of the opponents of the confirmation of Brandeis as Justice of the Supreme Court. Fox even went so far as to suggest that FDR and his bolting friends use their balance of power to block New York ratification of the income tax amendment to the Constitution. Roosevelt silently backed away from that. Clearly, however, he was active not only in a split among Democrats but among plutocrats, too. Sheehan has not only seemed a vulgar politician in history. At the time also he seemed not quite elegant as a businessman to the self-confident men around the magnificent J. P. Morgan. In his highly profitable law practice, however, one of Sheehan's partners was that Alton B. Parker for whom anti-Bryan Democrats had won the Democratic Presidential nomination in 1904. Parker was not only a president of the American Bar Association. He—and with him Sheehan—was the long-standing symbol of conservative opposition to Bryan and all that the people behind Bryan stood for in the Democratic Party.

It was to Sheehan that Parker, after his nomination, sent a

telegram announcing that as candidate he rejected the Bryan currency policies which Bryan had succeeded in reiterating in the Democratic platform that year. In the election which followed, Parker got fewer votes than Bryan ever received in any of his three tries for the Presidency. (In nine Presidential elections, between 1892 and 1932, no Democratic candidate, except Wilson in 1916, ever got so high a proportion of the popular vote as Bryan did every time he ran.)

Contrary to the legend which grew as Roosevelt did, he and his associates in insurgency did not win in the Senate fight in the New York legislature. Their bolt disintegrated. Tammany and its Boss Murphy won the fight. It was true that Tammany did not get Sheehan. There is some evidence that it was not eager for him. Sheehan had lined up its support before Tammany or any other Democrats expected the party to control the legislature. In his place Tammany got in James Aloysius O'Gorman, a former Sachem of Tammany Hall itself, a Senator who seemed more one of their own than Sheehan. The regular Democrats in the legislature celebrated their victory by laughing and catcalling at Franklin when his speech in agreement on O'Gorman was recognized as both a capitulation and a joke. The fact that the Senator was not Sheehan, however, helped the impression away from Albany, which Franklin fostered until he believed it himself, that he and his associates forced the "surrender" of Tammany Hall. He was helped by the fact that the Democratic National Convention in Baltimore, in 1912, almost re-enacted the story.

Tammany and its friends on the Democratic National Committee chose Parker as temporary chairman and keynote speaker of the Democratic Convention which had to nominate a candidate against Theodore Roosevelt and William Howard Taft, and looked forward to almost certain Democratic victory. Daniels as a Wilson and Bryan man on the National Committee had opposed the plan. He was outvoted. But he phoned the news to Bryan who was in Chicago as a newspaper correspondent at the Republican National Convention. What Daniels expected happened. Bryan headed for Baltimore with his jaw set. There he proposed, as a compromise in place of Parker, the same O'Gorman whom Roosevelt and his friends had "accepted" in the legislature. Parker won, but this precipitated Bryan's attack on any Democrats in the convention representing "the privilege-hunting and favor-seeking class," an attack which, Daniels always felt, was instrumental in assuring the nomination of Wilson. Sheehan was in that convention as a delegate along with August Belmont and Thomas Fortune Ryan, the bigger plutocrats at whom Bryan specifically aimed his fire. There was no doubt about who won that fight. Years later in the same big Baltimore Armory Franklin could say modestly and accurately that he "had some small part" in what happened there. It was small: he was not even a delegate. What happened there had a larger part in what happened to him.

After that fight it was not strange, considering the similar cast of characters—Sheehan and his law partner Parker, O'Gorman and Tammany—that Daniels, in 1913, should think of Roosevelt's bolt in the New York legislature in terms of Bryan's thunder in the convention. It seemed clear that Franklin in New York had acted like Bryan against the same forces and the same men. That was the kind of man Daniels wanted in 1913, and he was not shaken in his judgment by some criticism.

Daniels certainly did not notice it when Colonel William D'Alton Mann, who, as editor of *Town Topics—The Journal of Society,* fancied himself as spokesman for both the Four Hundred and Tammany Hall, exploded as perhaps the inventor of the charge that Roosevelt betrayed his own. Undoubtedly *Town Topics* did pay more editorial attention than the daily press to the class to which Roosevelt belonged and which he later was said to have betrayed. Its columns accurately reported prejudices if they were sometimes a little careless of the facts.

The late Alva Johnston wrote that Colonel Mann regarded his publication as "a Heralds' College that gave and took away aristocracy at will" even if, as Johnston added, his American peerage "consisted chiefly of people who lent him money and never tried to get it back." Colonel Mann wrote in indignation among his social items of a report that Franklin, soon after he entered the Navy Department, had conferred with the President on political offices to be filled in up-state New York. Wilson, the Colonel's journal declared, "should have planted his starboard foot on what is nautically called the stern of the Assistant Secretary, and expelled him through the doorway. Surely the President must have troubles enough without encumbering himself with another Bull Moose."

To Daniels, who never looked at a copy of *Town Topics* in his life, that was irrelevant opposition. The new Secretary was more than a little surprised, however, when Senator O'Gorman, whose election had been interpreted as the triumph of the insurgents, expressed agreement but not enthusiasm about Roosevelt's appointment. He spoke well of young Roosevelt, but only said that his appointment would be "acceptable."

"He had not been gone long," Daniels wrote in his diary, "before a New York gentleman came and warned me against having R as assistant secretary, saying that every person named Roosevelt wished to run everything and would try to be the Secretary. I listened and replied that any man who was afraid his assistant would supplant him thereby confessed that he did not think he was big enough for the job. I related this conversation to the President who expressed about the same opinion I had entertained."

That was Daniels' opinion then and afterward, but he recalled later with perhaps more understanding the "queer look" on the long face of this New York gentleman whom he identified in his memoirs as Senator Elihu Root.

"You know the Roosevelts, don't you?" Root asked.

The question was, of course, rhetorical. Also, the use of their common name like a common noun was a considerable assumption then as later. The two Roosevelts were much less closely related than the Adamses or the Harrisons. Indeed, in the consideration of fifth cousins, it deserves note that at the time of TR's and FDR's common great-great-great-great grandfather, Theodore and Franklin each had 128 ancestors, only two of whom presumably were the same. The chance of the common characteristic was one in sixty-four. Undoubtedly, Franklin's marriage to Theodore's niece brought him psychologically closer to "Uncle Ted." In 1913, however, and in the years immediately before and after, Eleanor was more inclined to retirement than to riding at the head of any political parades. Undoubtedly, TR's prominence pointed out possibilities when Franklin was looking to a career. The name served him afterward. There was emulation of the older man by the younger one, early and late, in matters that extended from bird-watching to unconditional surrender. TR, however, had finished being President at an age younger than that at which FDR began. At the age at which FDR embarked upon his great Presidency, TR had become, as he once himself feared he would, an "old cannon loose on the deck in a storm." Those were the years in which Franklin knew him best and copied him most. Daniels, of course, did not know "the Roosevelts." Root only knew Theodore well, though, undoubtedly, afterward his description seemed to serve well for both.

"Whenever a Roosevelt rides," he said, "he wishes to ride in front."

Root who, as Taft's manager had been the object of Rooseveltian derision at the Republican Convention the year before, regarded the whole Roosevelt story in 1913 with astringent realism. He knew the laborious wire-pulling that had been required before McKinley could be persuaded by Henry Cabot Lodge to offer Theodore the post of Assistant Secretary of the

Navy. He also knew how Cabot and Theodore had worked together in their feeling of the imperial necessity for war with Spain. He recalled clearly how one afternoon when Secretary of the Navy John D. Long was out of town, Roosevelt, as Acting Secretary, cabled Admiral Dewey belligerent instructions two months before war was declared. It turned out to have been a lucky insubordination, but Root, particularly in the light of Theodore's unwillingness even to be subordinate to the decision of his party in 1912, remembered it as insubordination all the same. However, that was another day: this was a different Roosevelt.

"I know this young man very slightly," he told Daniels. That was chiefly as a friend of his niece, the daughter of Commodore Edward H. Wales of Hyde Park. "But all I know about him is creditable. And, of course, being a Republican I have no right to make any suggestions. I appreciate your courtesy in consulting me."

This was the Democrats' Roosevelt, with whom Root need not be concerned. And Daniels saw no reason to be much concerned with Root's feeling at that moment about Roosevelts, any or all of them. On the first Sunday after the inauguration he made a note about the long conversation he had with young "Mr. Roosevelt" in the Secretary's big office in the Navy Department across a narrow street from the White House. He liked the young man better and better: "He will make a fine coworker. I look forward with pleasure to the great work we planned for the public good." He was the kind of Democrat Daniels wanted and the country deserved.

In his office that afternoon Daniels snapped open his thick hunting-case watch and noted the time. Also, in a significant way he dated the occasion. He took Roosevelt with him to the New National Theatre facing Pennsylvania Avenue, the wide avenue of American political procession. There Editor McDonald of Toronto, "a big Scotchman . . . made a fine speech" to a Y.M.C.A. meeting. The important thing, however, was that at the laymen's meeting Bryan made his first speech as Secretary of State emphasizing peace in the "friendly feeling existing between this country and Canada." Afterward, Daniels led his tall, new, young, smiling assistant up to speak to Bryan. Franklin had met Bryan before. He said years later that it was his "privilege to know William Jennings Bryan when I was a very young man" and that in the Wilson administration he learned "to know him and to love him." Bryan was loving everybody and almost everything that Sunday afternoon. So was Roosevelt.

After the meeting Daniels left his new young assistant to have dinner with his own four sons whom he had hardly seen since he arrived in the capital. Roosevelt was not left lonely. The town was full of old friends of his, though many of them were among the departing, not the arriving. Some were uncertain as to whether they would keep their jobs or not. A week later, when he came to take over his job he dined in the evening with his Harvard classmate, Ned Bell ("rich and with plenty of brains") who had entered the diplomatic service as a vice-consul in Cairo as a deserving young Republican under Taft. His problem was the same as that already pressed upon FDR in behalf of his Groton and Harvard friend, Joseph Clark Grew, a relative of J. P. Morgan, Jr., who had got his first job as a clerk in Cairo as a deserving Republican under TR. The next day Roosevelt went to luncheon with Colonel Charles L. McCawley and his wife. Colonel McCawley had spent almost his entire career as a marine in Washington and hoped to spend the rest of it there.

That evening he dined with Alice and Nick Longworth, who were going back to Cincinnati because Nick's Congressional career had been interrupted by the Republican split and the Wilson sweep. In Washington, Mrs. Longworth as the "Princess Alice" of the royal Rooseveltian years was almost as famous as her father, TR. Those glittering years were over. A society gossip, with a tongue as sharp as her own, said that her bangs, which were as famous as Mamie Eisenhower's became later, were thinning and her forehead retreating "possibly through long and sympathetic regard for Nick's pate." It was suggested that she wore false ones. *The Clubfellow and Washington Mirror* added the report that as the change of administrations had approached Alice was "pouty and aloof." Alice herself, though she had had "a tiresome time" while the Tafts were in the White House, described the incoming Democrats with only a half-hearted sneer as "odd beings."

At the time, of course, that opinion did not apply to Franklin. After dinner the Longworths took him to see a play by Pierre Loti, then came home and cooked eggs. Midnight eggs at the Longworths' house constituted a social ceremonial which was probably most triumphantly celebrated in November 1919, when, after the Senate had defeated the treaty Wilson brought from Paris, the Republicans came home to the Longworth house and, according to Alice, "Mrs. Harding cooked the eggs." That was six years later. In 1913 Franklin seemed only tall, gay, enthusiastic, purposeful and charming. Alice presumably then shared the feeling of her father who was "very much pleased" that another Roosevelt had been appointed to the Navy post.

"It is interesting," the former President wrote, "that you are in another place which I myself once held. I am sure you will enjoy yourself to the full as Ass't Secty of the Navy and that you will do capital work."

Franklin appreciated such approval from his own elders. He was still young enough, as he always would be so long as his mother lived, for her to send him such counsel as that he should sign his official papers in a big, round, readable hand. (He never failed to do that until the last, when I remember that the weakening signature was the first sign of the failing man.) There was no halting sign about him when, two days after he took office, he first served as Acting Secretary while his chief went home to a banquet given him by union labor in his North Carolina town.

"There's a Roosevelt on the job today," he told reporters. "You remember what happened the last time a Roosevelt occupied a similar position?"

They remembered. It was only fifteen years since the first one had been there under a Secretary described by one of TR's enthusiastic biographers as "a fine old gentleman, formerly president of the Massachusetts Peace Society, and by temperament indisposed to any rapid moves toward war." Nothing significant happened on that day of Franklin's first command, but he wrote home to Eleanor, "Going some!" That was not different in its expression of satisfaction from Daniels' note to his mother that "I am in the same building with Mr. Bryan." So was FDR.

Daniels was pleased to have a Roosevelt working as his assistant, and particularly this Democratic Roosevelt. The name not only carried a sense of drama and of action. Also—and that appealed to Daniels, too—there was a sense of comic and political relief in a man who was a Roosevelt and a Democrat at the same time. Roosevelts had not become commonplace as Assistant Secretaries of the Navy as they did later. Ultimately five of the kinship held the post. TR's swift passage from the Navy Department to the White House was still recent enough then to make the possibility of a repetition by another Roosevelt interesting if improbable. Daniels' *News and Observer* in announcing Franklin's appointment ran over his youthful picture the caption, "He's Following in Teddy's Footsteps."

Something of Daniels' pride in his young assistant was shown in the speed with which he introduced him to his North Carolina neighbors in person, and not merely through his paper. Soon after he took office Roosevelt dutifully accepted an invitation to speak at the Agricultural and Mechanical College in

Raleigh, which in those days was a good deal more agricultural than mechanical. Most of its students came from the small farms around the little towns, and even at the A & M College they were subject to few city dangers. Though the college was in Raleigh, its campus lay far out at the end of a wide street which in parts looked more like a road. It had few buildings. I remember that its campus was cut by red washes which indicated an ignorance about soil conservation even among the agriculturally elect. Its nearest neighbor was the State Fair Grounds, a raw, red area surrounded by a plank fence, to which annually more farmers came for edification and entertainment. Daniels' paper, which boosted the Fair, also regularly deplored some of the side shows in which live young women attracted more attention than the livestock. But the A & M College was a fixed part of his hope and pride. He had had a part in planning for its establishment. Every Sunday when he was in Raleigh he taught a Sunday School class composed of its students. It particularly pleased him to bring together his young man in Washington and the young men at the college in Raleigh.

Eleanor went to Raleigh with Franklin. She wore a big hat and a dress with a high collar. He seemed almost colt-tall in his double-breasted suit under a derby hat. They were warmly welcomed at the college, but not even Daniels' own paper gave the impression that he stirred the students or the citizens. The subject of his talk seemed somewhat less than adventurous. "Stay East Young Man" seemed, indeed, to be less than expansive in its spirit. After many years, however, it is possible to detect a prelude in it to a later, greater drama. What he said about the opportunities to be found in the redevelopment of the abandoned farms of the East suggests some of the ideas with which he seemed so freshly full in the first New Deal years. Daniels sent him in 1938 a clipping of the report of that speech to point out how little he had changed. The speech was described, however, in Daniels' sympathetic newspaper at the time only as "a short businesslike message." Perhaps Roosevelt's most significant statement to the young Carolina students at their cow and cotton college was his self-description. "I am a hayseed myself," he told them, "and proud of it." Those who heard Franklin Roosevelt concluded that Joedaniels had done fairly well in picking his assistant. He was no speaker but he seemed a nice intelligent young man—not exactly a hayseed but not half the dude that he appeared either. It was an impression made then which, grinning as he grew older, Roosevelt never neglected. In a year long after, in which he was leader of what he called "the largest and most powerful democracy in the whole world" and the one to which other democracies look "for leadership that world democracy may survive," he recurred to the phrase.

"I am just a hick from Dutchess County," he said then, "a Democratic hick."

If so, he was also the country boy of Christendom. It was an idea which always appealed to him.

House-Hunting

MOTHER RENTED "A COUNTRY HOUSE," MY FATHER NOTED IN HIS
diary. "A country house" was a city phrase. Also, that description of Single Oak on Woodley Lane was indicative of the expansive but still unexpanded Washington to which we moved.
Actually, the place in the country was only a few blocks beyond
the then new Connecticut Avenue Bridge across Rock Creek,
but its fences ran along the woods where sprawling apartment
buildings were later to rise. It was still a long carriage ride
from the Navy Department. Also, Single Oak seemed a very
long way from the Mount Vernon Place Methodist Church,
South, which on Sundays was almost as important to my father.

The word "South" disappeared from the name of the church
later as a part of reunited Methodism in the United States.
Later, too, the square brick church, commonplace even by
small-town standards, was to emerge in marble, across Ninth
Street where K Street and Massachusetts Avenue come together
in one of those points beloved by Washington builders. In
those days, however, it looked as Southern as five-cent cotton.
Its bare pews, the worn red carpet, the golden brown interior
woodwork seemed, as standard Methodist furnishings, almost
parts of the basic faith of Wesleyans and Southerners who took
their religion and their politics straight and together. Also, my
father thought, they put their religion and their democracy
closer together than the Episcopalians or even the Presbyterians,

who included his wife. He recorded with satisfaction in his diary that "the church is a very plain one, out of the mart of fashionable folk and the people are of the Methodist type. How courteous and cordial they were!" Also, he added: "On the night before Garfields' inauguration I attended a service at that church." He had attended it, too, when he was chief clerk of the Interior Department in Cleveland's second administration. The Washington distances had lengthened since Garfield's time, even Cleveland's. But great as the way seemed from Mount Vernon Place to Single Oak, Father often made it longer going home on Sundays by the Navy Department as he had always in Raleigh gone by *The News and Observer*. He enjoyed the long drives in the carriage with the Negro coachman and footman, Jordan and Willis, so high and erect on the box that their silk hats seemed barely to miss the branches of the Washington shade trees. He seldom stayed long in the big, dark Department building on Sundays and generally he came out smiling for the ride home by Lafayette Square and Connecticut Avenue to Single Oak. But always as we passed the Decatur House on the northwest corner of the square, his smile faded. He shook his head solemnly.

"That was the house I wanted," he would say wistfully. He always said it as if he were mentioning it for the first time. It became almost a ritual as time went by. Jordan learned to slow the horses and then tap them into a trot. Nobody was ever quite certain whether he was admitting a great loss or teasing Mother. Joke or disappointment he was prepared to elaborate it. The fact that the old house had been the residence of Commodore Stephen Decatur gave it a special appeal to a new Secretary of the Navy. Its appeal to my father was not unique. I remember, as a secretary waiting in the hall before his bedroom, that one of the last acts of Roosevelt as President was to agree to a suggestion about the house made by Secretary James Forrestal (who became the last Secretary of the Navy as an independent

Department when he was two years older than my father had been as incoming Secretary). Forrestal wanted Roosevelt to suggest to Mrs. Forrestal that she devote time to raising money with which to buy the house as a naval monument and museum. I never knew exactly why. Perhaps there is always some mystery about men and their wives and houses.

One reason my father wanted it was that he was a Stephen Decatur kind of man in full agreement with the Commodore's hope that his country might always be right but "right or wrong my country." The house's chief virtue as he praised it, however, was that it was only one block from the Navy Department. That preference for proximity was like a similarly solemn proposal which Mother often had to hear in Raleigh, that they erect a residence on the roof of *The News and Observer* so that he could slide down a brass firehouse pole into the news and editorial rooms. Sometimes when the news was breaking he had seemed to his staff to have arrived in approximately that way. Occasionally, also, admirals and young assistants, when they least expected it, were to get that impression in the Navy Department.

My mother in her house-hunting did not stop on Lafayette Square. She had no more desire to live in what might be an annex of the Navy Department than on top of *The News and Observer*. Also she understood intuitively that no neighborhood in Washington better represented old regimes. From the outside, the Decatur House looked as if it might have been available in 1913. One observer at the time said that it looked "like a jail." When it was refurbished in 1916, by its hereditary owners, the Truxtun Beales, neighbors felt that "it really looks well since the missing panes of glass overlooking H Street have been put in place."

The Beales, however, were not looking for tenants. They not only represented old residence in Washington; also Truxtun's sister, Mamie, had married George Bakhmeteff, the last

Ambassador of the czars. They made a parade when they drove by in their carriage with a real Cossack on the box, armed with pistol and silver dagger. Another Beale sister, Emily, had been described by Henry Adams just before the Democrats arrived as Washington's "reigning empress." Adams also said that Emily's husband, rich, gouty John R. McLean who owned among other items both *The Cincinnati Enquirer* and *The Washington Post,* was about the measure of "the Cincinnati regime" which departed with Taft. The longer he lived under it, Adams wrote, "the cheaper and commoner and fatter I find it." It did not seem possible in 1913 to Adams or anybody else that McLean's dissipated son and heir, Edward Beale McLean, might be prominent in the return of another Ohio regime eight years later.

McLean and Beale and Bakhmeteff were easy to see and understand. But the old order to which they belonged also contained the elder McLean's sister, Mildred Dewey, wife of the great and sleepy Admiral George Dewey who in one morning in Manila Bay made America a world power. She looked like some delicate thing the old sailor had brought back from the sea. She kept a figure like a girl's, a house like a museum with a gay Countess as curator, and she handled her ear trumpet as if it were a fan.

The Beales' Decatur House was one house my mother did not consider. Her search seemed interminable even if our old bachelor friend, the fashionable and successful Dr. Sterling Ruffin, with whom Mother and Father were staying in his erect brick house opposite the British Embassy, insisted that they stay there as long as they pleased. It was pleasant for them to be with Sterling. He was not only old-time North Carolina friend, he was also a good part of their old Washington story which now seemed so full of happy endings. Sterling had been a "sundown" doctor in the old Cleveland days. That meant that he could only practice at night because of his need to support himself in another job in the daytime. Father had found him a better government job which had made it possible for him to begin to practice also by day. His position in 1913 was happy and secure. One of his patients then, the pretty Mrs. Norman Galt, was to call him later into consultation when her husband, the President, was stricken in the midst of his fight for the League. Ruffin was, according to reports, "really the master hand" in both the Wilson-Galt romance and that between the President's doctor, Cary Grayson, and Mrs. Galt's young ward and friend, Alice Gertrude Gordon. He was a charming gentleman though he looked as little as possible like cupid.

Even as a fledgling physician in the Cleveland days, however, Sterling had always been the gentleman adequate to any occasion. When young Josephus Daniels had been invited to an important dinner, he was about to decline for lack of a dress suit. Sterling lent him his. And so arrayed, on that night he added to his wisdom about Washington the observation that, while he might feel strange in his clothes, the vest of the famous Senator Blackburn of Kentucky did not reach his pants. That reassuring observation was never afterward restricted to clothes or Kentuckians. Now, in 1913, Sterling did my mother an almost equal favor by producing a gentleman who had something of the air of a weary Robert E. Lee in the real estate business.

He knew the houses he showed her as well as Dr. Ruffin had known the insides of some of their former occupants. He talked about when they were built and by whom and why and how much and whether their owners had moved or died, lost their money or not been re-elected. Also, he waited in courtly patience, dangling more keys, while Mother stood, small, plump, studying and unsatisfied, in house after house and day after day.

There was no pressure or push about the real estate gentleman. But he must have been able at last to tell Mother's decision about each house before she spoke by the way she pursed her lips against her veil. There were fewer and fewer keys in his hands. He seemed less impatient than apologetic. He seemed surprised, however, when she mentioned one other house about which she had heard from Senator Hoke Smith of Georgia who, as Secretary of the Interior, had been Mr. Daniels' boss in the Cleveland years. It was far out—really far out, he thought, "But—"

That house was Single Oak, and my mother made up her mind about it before she saw a single room. It was more place than she had planned but it seemed the place she had always been planning, too. It was perhaps too small to be called an estate, but certainly the acres about it could not be described as a yard. It lay along Woodley Lane just beyond the point where the row houses on Cathedral Avenue came to a sudden and in those days apparently a permanent end. A sluggish stream along Woodley Lane made a green bird-filled margin about the pastures which stretched steep and rurally up to the one big oak and the formal gardens beside the paved terraces around the rambling stucco house. There was a very informal-looking tennis club across the lane. To the south, toward Washington, there were only woods which ran uninterruptedly to Rock Creek half a mile away. There were stables and a hen house. There was a cow in the pasture. It could be home.

The Daniels, of course, would "live at Single Oak during the summer only," a society reporter said. "It would be impossible as a winter home for a Cabinet officer, since it is quite four miles from town." That report as to the Daniels' determinations was wrong. The place was splendid in summer. Also, it was a good house in which to find bright warmth after a long winter carriage ride from the Navy Department. We young Danielses liked it even better in the winter when the unaccustomed snow was on our hill. We grinned and Mother smiled wearily and wryly at the standing joke that Father never passed the Decatur House on Lafayette Square without saying that that was the house he had wanted and had not got.

He was not deprived of all such historical tradition as gave

appeal to the Decatur House. Single Oak was just across a
hedge from Woodley which had been built by Judge Philip
Barton Key and had often been visited by his nephew, Francis
Scott Key. The air of patriotic music which he left about the
place was enhanced by the fact that Woodley had been occupied as summer residence by four Presidents. Also, if Single
Oak seemed far from town, it was never too far for town crowding to the highly nutritive parties my mother loved to give in
the wide rooms, on the big sunny terraces, on the lawns and in
the gardens.

Familiar statesmen, the blue and gold uniforms, and musi-
cians from the Marine Band all helped fulfill her plans and
possibilities. Somehow her parties all had the same easy air of
those days when the buggies were lined up before the house
on the side street in Raleigh. Even after Father had shocked
the social and the convivial in uniform and out of it by his
order abolishing the wine mess in the Navy, his critics admitted
that her parties, which were as dry as he hoped the Navy might
be, "went off with a great flourish." In Washington, as in Raleigh, Mother loved good food and loved to dispense it. She
found no difference in appreciation of it in the state and national capitals. A social commentator not noted for kindly reports practically sang of one of her garden parties: "The day
was heaven sent, the eatables and drinkables delectable, and
the guests were in their best clothes and on their good behavior.
The cake and ice cream, made after Mrs. Daniels' own recipe,
were served by her very good-looking sister, assisted by the Secretary of State, this illustrious Ganymede delivering a bon mot
with each plate. . . . It was a great party."

I remember better a party which the Bryans gave for their
grandson in the big house they had taken which, as an item in
change, had been occupied the year before by a loudly anti-
Bryan Democratic Congressman. The Bryans had quickly made
the house their own. They had brought to Washington the

bronze Korean lions which had guarded their door in Nebraska. A well-loved portrait of Jefferson presided over the huge hall. There were bronze busts of Diogenes, Beatrice and Bryan. All the Bryan things fitted perfectly into the house which had been built long before by a Union general and Republican stalwart who, General William T. Sherman said, was "perfect in combat" but "entertained and expressed a species of contempt for the laborious preparations in logistics that a commander to be successful must carry on." Sometimes Bryan seemed to have similar faults but there was no flaw in Mrs. Bryan's preparation for the birthday party. She not only provided games and refreshments to which I was accustomed. Also, as spectacular addition there was an Indian gentleman, complete with turban, who jumped from a spindle-legged chair to a board full of nails and then to a pile of broken glass without scratching a toe or shedding a drop of blood. That was impressive to a boy who had gone barefooted in the backyards of North Carolina. I would not have understood then if anyone had told me, as many clever people would have been glad to do, that what the fakir did was similar to what Bryan had tried to demonstrate in connection with the currency and also represented his contemporary views about the preservation of peace.

No one, of course, paid much attention to the housing of minor officials. There was a publicized exception when the Franklin Roosevelts took the house from which Theodore Roosevelt had moved to the White House. The selection of that house emphasized also the difference between the housing problems of my mother and the young wife of her husband's assistant. Mrs. Roosevelt did not have to hunt. Neither Mother nor Eleanor Roosevelt had ever had a house of her own free choosing until she came to Washington. And Eleanor Roosevelt did not get one then. Her husband had thought her "quite mad" in New York when she tearfully resented living in a house which her mother-in-law had built and furnished. In Washington, she wrote, "My mother-in-law as usual helped us get settled." Nothing was more natural than that they should move into a Roosevelt house. That was not a strange family coincidence but a normal family condition.

That house on narrow, shaded N Street belonged to Theodore's older sister, Anna, who was in the family variously called Bammie and Auntie Bye. She was not only Eleanor's aunt; she was also the very close friend of Franklin's half brother, James Roosevelt Roosevelt, who had first claim to the nickname Rosy by which Franklin himself was sometimes called in those days. James Roosevelt Roosevelt, who was twenty-eight years older than Franklin, had been "quite a noted whip and always took part in the old coaching parades." He and his first wife, Helen Astor, daughter of *the* Mrs. Astor for whom Ward McAllister invented the Four Hundred, had both been close friends of Bammie. When Helen died while Rosy was First Secretary of the American Embassy in London in 1893, Bammie moved in as his hostess and the foster-mother of his two children—"a warm-hearted gesture which," as FDR's son, Elliott, reported later, "occasioned some lifting of eyebrows." (One of those children, James Roosevelt Roosevelt, Jr., not long after created quite a sensation when he as a minor married a well-known young woman called "Dutch Sadie.") The eyebrows lifted in London in the Nineties, however, relaxed when Bammie, while living in Rosy's house, met and married Lieutenant Commander William Sheffield Cowles, then naval attaché and a bachelor nearly fifty years old. He was probably most vividly presented in history by William Allen White who described him gently snoring after dinner in his parlor while his brother-in-law, Theodore, talked and talked on the night before he moved into the White House in 1901.

Mr. White remembered that the house had "a postage stamp of a lawn" and was, he thought, "typical of the middle class urban residence in America at the turn of the century." The residents of that block on N Street did not regard themselves as "middle class." Most of them were listed in the *Social Register*. The occupants of several of its houses were, like Admiral Cowles, retired and sleepy naval officers. Almost next door lived the retired engineer who had built the State, War and Navy Building—"the ugliest if not the smuggest mass of masonry in Washington"—in which FDR was to spend and to shape so much of his life in the years ahead. Along the block lived a retired director of the census, a one-time Republican Congressman, a general who had served in the Powder River campaign against the Sioux Indians. The block ran into Connecticut Avenue at the point on it of the gawky, red-brick British Embassy where the ailing but amiable Cecil Spring-Rice was in 1913 waiting to welcome the young relatives of his old friend, Theodore. It looked like an embassy Queen Victoria herself might have built. Also, on the block was the home of the dull sportsman husband, an admiral's son, from whom Elinor Wylie, the poetess and daughter of a solid ex-government official, had recklessly eloped with a strange, erudite older man. It was not the general opinion of N Street at the time that she was, as her sister said later, a "winged arrow, bound to be released at some sudden impulse from the bow of the world." Impulses on N Street seemed less important than the proprieties.

The young Roosevelts seemed ideal residents for such a street. Their residential status was indicated by the fact that they rented their house in New York to Thomas W. Lamont, the Morgan partner. They had three children under seven when Franklin was appointed Assistant Secretary. Two more were to arrive in the next three years. It seemed to Eleanor that she was always having babies. I remember that as a boy taken to their house I had the impression that it was full of babies, too, and also that the young Roosevelts had not been taught to blow their noses or just did not care to blow them.

At the outset Eleanor brought down to Washington four

white servants whom she had had for some time in New York, a nurse and a governess. Those servants, she said later, were the basis of an early and shocked memory of her husband's new chief. Daniels had, she recalled, a strong prejudice against white servants and stated it in a way which seemed to her to indicate an almost brutal feeling about the fixed and proper place in inferiority of the Negro. No man was ever more free from brutality, but undoubtedly he did have then a Southern feeling about division of labor along racial lines which must have shocked a gentle young woman from New York long before she stood publicly for the equality of the Negro. They understood each other better by-and-by, and sometimes found themselves together pressing for more liberal measures in a greater hurry than President Franklin Roosevelt thought politically practical or politically wise.

Eleanor was young then, shy, unsure of herself and sometimes overwhelmed. That was more her feeling than her appearance. Pictures of her when she was a young matron, particularly one in a gondola in Venice, show that she was a very good-looking, tall, slim young woman from the hat with the feather on it to the toe peeking from the dark brocaded skirt. She was eager and earnest, too. She tried to get along at first without a secretary, but "found that it took me such endless hours to arrange my calling list, and answer and send invitations, that I finally engaged one for three mornings a week."

Her name was Lucy Page Mercer. She was very pretty, twenty-two years old, aristocratic and very poor. Her mother, Minnie Leigh Tunis, was born in Norfolk where years afterward she left memories of herself as a belle and an heiress. She married Carroll Mercer, who was a lieutenant in the marines and later served in the Army in the Spanish War, retiring as a major in 1901. Mercer was of the family of the Carrolls of Carrollton. At Minnie's request he retired from service and they devoted themselves to society. Mercer was one of the founders of the Chevy Chase Club and a member of many more. Minnie, according to *The Clubfellow and Washington Mirror,* "was easily the most beautiful woman in Washington society for a number of years, and to be invited to one of her dinners was in itself a social distinction that qualified one for admission to any home." Unfortunately, her money began to slip away and with it her friends and at last her marriage. Mrs. Mercer moved to New York where as an interior decorator she had among others such a patron as the banker, Grant Barney Schley. She was able, however, to send Lucy abroad to study with a Countess Henssenstamm in Melk, near Vienna. Minnie and Carroll came back to Washington, but separately, in 1912. Carroll was "a bit grayer, a bit stouter, and much more serious" as one of the managers of the Riding Club of which he had been a leading member before. Minnie was employed "by an art establishment." She had taught Lucy to be self-supporting as "an inside decorator" but she was also suited both by need and knowledge to be a social secretary—a job which included arranging calling lists, sending and answering invitations and, on occasion, cleaning up the Roosevelt N Street house as well. In her status it was an entirely irrelevant comment by a society reporter that she was "old enough to come out."

The Roosevelts were established and it was an easy walk of only six blocks for Franklin down Connecticut Avenue to the Navy Department. He was in expansive mood in those days, he remembered later. Every two weeks, he said, he got his salary in cash and put it in his pocket.

"I don't know where it went," I remember his recalling in 1942. "It just went. I couldn't keep an account with myself. And after about six months of this, certain complaints came from back home about paying the grocery bill.

"And so I began taking my salary by check and putting it in the bank, and taking perhaps five dollars cash for the week and putting it in my pocket—trying to anyway."

He had opportunities to spend money in good company. Conveniently along the way to the office were both the Metropolitan and the Army and Navy Clubs. It cost him nothing to walk as naval enthusiast both by Admiral Farragut's statue and Commodore Decatur's house which his chief insisted was the ideal Washington residence. The walk brought him by the residences of wealthy friends. Franklin, as one with more friends around Lafayette Square, would have been much more at home in the Decatur House than Daniels. Indeed, before he arrived in Washington the William Corcoran Eustises provided on the square a close tie between Washington and Dutchess County, New York, which later seemed an original relationship under the New Deal. The Eustises were old friends. Franklin was to spend frequent evenings with them in those years. Mrs. Eustis had been Edith Morton, daughter of Levi P. Morton ("moneybags," Henry Adams called him), who had been Republican Vice-President under Benjamin Harrison. As a boy Franklin had been a welcome visitor at the Morton estate at Rhinebeck, which long afterward became not a museum, as so many estates did, but a military school for Catholic boys. In their ugly but famous Corcoran House across the street from the Decatur House, Willie and Edith Eustis proved after their fashion that some Democrats could live on the square.

Willie Eustis was an hereditary Democrat though he did not work at the job. Come Democrats or Republicans, he preferred to be with his horses and dogs on his Leesburg, Virginia, place where he was "a typical English country squire." The Morton girls seemed attracted by horse-and-dog men. Edith's sister, Alice, was the first wife of another Roosevelt family friend, Winthrop Rutherfurd, himself the epitome of aristocratic breeding in America and one of America's leading breeders of fox terriers. The Willie Eustises had been "bored to extinction" just before the Wilson administration began, *Town Topics* reported. Willie, however, was prevailed upon to accept the chairmanship of the Washington committee for the inauguration. That not only ended a row as to who would get the job. Also, the society journal gave its flippant opinion that "the sight of Levi Morton's daughter leading the inaugural ball with Woodrow Wilson would be worth the price of admission."

Eustis was not the only Democrat on the square. It might be most important to Franklin and Eleanor that Henry Adams was the close friend of Bammie and "Uncle Ted." Adams still referred to the Democratic Party as "my party" till he died. He made no pretenses about being a democrat. The Franklin Roosevelts did not know him very well but he made, Eleanor said, "a great impression" upon them. Also, Adams made a great but different impression on Daniels who did not know him at all but resented him as a man who had faced all the changing occupants of the White House for forty years with self-confident derision. He would have shared Justice O. W. Holmes' feeling about Adams as an old man (he was seventy-five in 1913) "posing to himself as the old Cardinal and turning everything to dust and ashes." Outside Adams' aristocratic world and the select circle of his friends, Daniels resented the pessimism Adams proclaimed to such young men as gained the prize of his presence.

"Young man," Adams said to Franklin, "I have lived in this house many years and seen the occupants of that White House across the square come and go, and nothing that you minor officials or the occupants of that house can do will affect the history of the world for long."

Daniels could never have been at home in the vicinity of such a faith. He had sought residence in Washington as a part of reform which he believed was not only possible but imperative. He would have been as awkward as Andrew Jackson on his unbalanced bronze charger in the center of the square if he had found a place on its perimeter—certainly as awkward as Jackson and Jackson's men seemed when they arrived in a dignified and dismayed Washington in 1829. The less tightly developed neighborhood on Woodley Lane was better suited to both Daniels' needs and his spirit. Considering all things it was not too far from the Navy Department or the Mount Vernon Place Methodist Church, South. He still managed to look very sad when he passed the Decatur House.

"That was the house I wanted."

And sometimes Mother sniffed and we giggled. But Single Oak was waiting. The butler brought from Carolina, gold-toothed, black Bob Gaines, who was to serve Navy Secretaries through James Forrestal, opened the big door. Sunday dinner was always a special and lively occasion. There were many guests. Often Father brought the preacher home. But no sanctimony was served. Sometimes the guest to whom he gave impromptu invitation might be an admiral or a Senator or merely a lonely boy in town. Some of the preachers or the Senators may have been surprised at the way in which Father welcomed his boys into talk about theology or politics or anything else. He valued our opinions or at least our free voicing of them. We enjoyed his jokes. There was no Sabbath limit on high spirits or loud laughter on old or young. Within a month the Danielses seemed as happily settled at Single Oak as if they had lived there all their lives. The fact that life there was strange and different could be emphasized, however, on Sunday afternoons when the doorbell rang, and there, unexpected and without attendants, might be the President of the United States. Much as he liked jokes and limericks, there was never much gaiety in his smile.

The Wilsonians were settled where their President could find them. Not all had come upon Single Oak. Ellen Axton Wilson, who was relieved by the Republic of the necessity of house-hunting, found the White House in many ways as "big and garish" as she feared it would be. Washington dressmakers and dancers, of course, suspected that she had been the force behind Wilson's decision that there would be no inaugural ball. Daniels knew it. She had asked him about the matter after Wilson's election and though he disclaimed, "as an old-fashioned Methodist who never danced in his life," any competency to advise, he told her about watching the ball from the balcony at Cleveland's second inauguration. (He had been a few months younger that night than FDR was at Wilson's inauguration. He was rejoicing then, he remembered afterward, that the reign of the Robber Barons was ended. Also, he was very much relieved that the next morning, as a deserving Democrat and a very hard-up one, he would have a place on the government payroll. He was not in a position to appreciate Adams' observation in Newport that all the young were rich if they could waltz. He couldn't. He wasn't.) Apparently no romantic memories of the Cleveland ball as seen from the balcony were presented by him as persuasive arguments to Mrs. Wilson. Certainly she was not persuaded.

"I cannot bear to think of Woodrow's inauguration being ushered in by a commercialized ball," she told Father. Also, she was not alone in being disturbed by some of the new dances. Not long afterward the General Federation of Women's Clubs was by resolution to condemn the hesitation and the tango. Even without a ball, Mrs. Wilson found Washington in some ways more appalling than she had expected and not merely so far as she herself was concerned. Her daughter, Eleanor, who was soon to marry Secretary of the Treasury William Gibbs McAdoo, had been astonished even in the excitement of her arrival for the inauguration "to see in some places, little sordid shacks jammed in between majestic buildings." Mrs. Wilson was even more disturbed by the old shacks and slums which were often hidden in the alleys behind the big houses where nobody had to look at them and few did.

Twenty years later the concern of Eleanor Roosevelt, who in 1913 was scarcely aware of such things, about the same slums and others still seemed a little odd to many people. In 1913, Ellen Wilson's concern and the visits she made, on which my mother sometimes joined her, seemed silly to *The Clubfellow and Washington Mirror*. It reported: "If Mrs. Woodrow Wilson intends to spend as much of her time slumming in the alleys of Washington as she has been doing of late, then it will not be very difficult for her to gratify her oft-repeated remark that she will not spend over $1,000 a year for dresses. Just what Mrs. Wilson is to gain by driving through these alleys quite baffles Washington."

She was a little baffled herself. The alley slums were old when she arrived. Despite her efforts they were to remain long after she was gone. They were, nevertheless, disturbing symbols, then and later, and always close at hand, of the difficulties of revolution or reform which even a timid lady could see. She did not look like a reformer. Tiny and shy, she never gave the impression of a President's lady moving with peremptory purposes through the world, or even through Washington. Perhaps she qualified for the remark of Mrs. Oliver Wendell Holmes, which so amused Theodore Roosevelt, that Washington was a city of great men and the women they had married when they were young. Not even children were awed by her position. She seemed to small boys from North Carolina like a good, gentle, small cousin who might have been counted upon to provide cookies in Rome, Georgia. We understood that she was the easy friend of our mother and father. She liked to have parties for the Cabinet children and in long retrospect as one such child I realize that the gay sadness which she showed to children was that of a lady whose world, like her girls, had suddenly grown too big.

But it was not a time of sadness. Triumph and purpose marched together when Wilson went in person to deliver his first message to a joint session of Congress. Some old Jeffersonians even among his supporters shook their heads at his revival of the personal appearance which Jefferson had rejected as a sort of undemocratic speech from the throne. It delighted Josephus Daniels. As a sworn Jeffersonian but not a frozen one, he approved of Wilson's direct beginning of the irresistible year and a half of reform which followed his inauguration. The Congress was young. The country was ready. A disciplined Democratic Party, still waiting for its rewards after sixteen years in the wilderness, moved behind leadership.

It was not quite a simple march. There was not even a simple Democratic Party, even within the households of the administration. Colonel House, who already wrote of himself as the "adviser to the President," did not take a residence in Washington. He kept his apartment on Thirty-fifth Street in New York and liked to have people come to see him, though he complained rather enthusiastically that every office-seeker in the United States followed him there. The President, who found personnel problems distasteful, had put the Colonel in charge of important patronage. In his diary, House said that even Bryan turned to him when he hoped that a friend of his might be appointed as a United States marshal. The Secretary of State apparently did not even ask the Colonel for an ambassadorship. It was in Colonel House's apartment in New York that the Colonel held his conferences with J. P. Morgan, Jr., and other bankers on the proposed Federal Reserve Act in the first month of the administration. Its purpose was to curb the "money trust" against which Bryan and his many followers in Congress had been fighting for two decades.

Colonel House suggested that Mr. Morgan have his bank plan, which the banker had already had printed in final form, typewritten in order not to emphasize the presumption of Morgan power. At the same time the Colonel advised Wilson against Bryan's ideas. It would be over-simplification to say that Colonel House made himself the agent of "Wall Street" in the discussions. He was certainly and frankly the opponent of the "Bryan vagaries." He told Wilson that is was better to face Bryan's disapproval and get no bill at all rather than to get one which the Colonel and his friends did not regard as "sound." The crux of soundness was the issue of Federal Reserve notes by the private banks rather than by the government, and the presence of bankers on the Federal Reserve Board. Bryan opposed such ideas as tending to put the power of the government back of the issues of private bankers. He wanted the government to control the banking power, not the other way around. That was the position by which the Democratic Party had steadily stood. Bryan won. Despite the suggestion implicit in the House diaries, Wilson did not always agree with him. House apparently never agreed with Bryan on anything.

House was fifty-five that year. He had never held any public office. He had always been sufficiently well-to-do as the son of an Englishman who acquired large land holdings in Texas to indulge an interest in politics. He had managed the campaigns of some Texas Governors. He had been brought into the Wilson campaign originally as a possible contributor at about the time when, in his considerable leisure, he had written a book called *Philip Dru: Administrator,* about an American President who took over and redesigned government in the United States. He was fascinated with power but approached it almost with the arts of seduction. He gave the illusion of quiet selflessness to Wilson in the midst of politicians fighting for control in his Presidential campaign. Also he put his relations on a highly personal basis with every politician he could.

During the pressure of that campaign House took Daniels for a long afternoon's automobile ride for "confidential talk" and left Daniels for years afterward under the impression of a "lasting friendship which has ripened with the common purpose which dominated our lives." The Colonel always made it clear that his motives were not those of mere duty but of devotion. He sometimes carried an automatic pistol in his pocket.

He listened while Wilson read aloud Wordsworth's poems. He rejoiced when his friendship with the President and the second Mrs. Wilson was such, as he said, that "there is no subject too intimate to be discussed before me." He was an intimate man even when he was cutting a throat. He did not need a house in Washington. He preferred to discuss the eighteenth century poets and political patronage with Wilson while visiting at the White House. Wilson fulfilled House's need while he got the impression that in self-effacement House fulfilled his.

It seemed a time of almost miraculous fulfillment. At Single Oak the full April blooming of the flowers more than equaled the March promise of the place. There was dark shade under the oak. The terraces about the house were bright and warm with sun. It was cheap at $2,500 a year. That was not all. The Washington correspondent of Daniels' paper sent a special story back to North Carolina. The readers of Joedaniels' *News and Observer* were informed: "The contract for Single Oak provided that Mr. Daniels have the use of Old Moot, a black and white cow, and six chickens, and keep Tabby, an aged brindle cat. The lease was signed and the Danielses moved in. Since then the cow has produced a calf, the cat five kittens and the hens a brood of sixteen biddies and thirty-seven eggs."

That news account failed to mention an old and lean hound named Music, perhaps because he was unproductive. He also seemed by day tired and aloof and unsociable. But in the night there never was such a dog for barking at the moon.

Sailors to the Sea

THE NEW SECRETARY OF THE NAVY HAD BEEN IN OFFICE LITTLE more than a month when orders were issued changing "port and starboard" to "left and right" in commands to helmsmen. *The New York Times* was pained by what seemed to its editors not so much a breach with as an assault upon seagoing traditions. Another publication, able to muster some humor even in outrage, suggested that Josephus Daniels might soon have Navy navigators saying, "Gee and haw," like a countryman's commands in driving a team of mules. The order stood. The new Secretary did not trouble to explain that it had been already drafted when he arrived as the recommendation of the General Board of the Navy headed by Admiral Dewey. The Admiral told the Secretary that so many inland young men were coming into the Navy who did not know the seagoing terms that the simpler ones should be approved. The change gave early opportunity to lampoon the landlubber Secretary. He did not complain about the comic comments at the time, though many years later he was delighted to discover that he himself had not signed the order. The signature under it was that of that lover of naval traditions, of white water and stiff breeze, Franklin D. Roosevelt who, however, did not insist upon full credit for it at the time. Daniels alone, however, got the adverse publicity. That was always part of his job.

Actually it was as a determined traditionalist himself that he took on the first and most trouble. He defended an American tradition, he thought, more important than any naval heritage —"the supremacy of the civil over the military authority." If he had needed any encouragement in that defense he got it before he was sworn in from his predecessor, George von L. Meyer. Meyer was the only one of the half dozen of Daniels' predecessors who had served a full four-year term as Secretary of the Navy. Two had served less than a year. Of them all, Admiral Bradley A. Fiske preferred one who had served only three months. Secretary Meyer had introduced his successor to Fiske and the other admirals who were his principal aides. And after the admirals departed Meyer put both hands flat on the big desk of the Secretary of the Navy. He spoke as if he were telling the new Secretary a significant secret.

"Keep the power here," he said. And Daniels did.

It did not take long to discover what Secretary Meyer meant. The desk sat at one end of a long office in which visitors had to walk a good hardwood distance to reach the side of the Secretary. It was, Daniels always thought, the most beautiful office in Washington, and in later years he liked to present the testimony of Arthur Balfour, once First Lord of the Admiralty, that it was the most beautiful office in the world. Even when the Navy was small and weak, its officers saw to it that, in terms of unchanged traditions of spotless decks and shining brass, the great room was kept gleaming between its inlaid floors and its huge crystal chandeliers. The Navy seemed to take almost too good care of its Secretaries. And some of the admirals were ready and eager to relieve him of onerous duties in the decorative office.

The office was in startling contrast to Bryan's in the same building. The room of the Secretary of State looked neglected then. It still looked a little dilapidated years later when Cordell Hull received the Japanese Ambassador there on the morning of the attack on Pearl Harbor and used language which Bryan would hardly have understood. In 1913, Mrs. Bryan, who could be sharply critical when her husband seemed most sightless in Christian confidence, noticed that the ceiling had been patched and not retinted in one place. Former Secretaries of State were impressive in their portraits, but below them the backs of the chairs had marred the walls. Some of the upholstery was positively shabby. She hoped the room, as Bryan hoped the world, could be put in order during the new regime.

Bryan was not troubled by the shabbiness. Daniels was more disturbed by the grandeur around his position. Some of the perquisites of his office particularly seemed to him to run counter to the frugality which was a part of his democracy. The rise in the price of battleships shocked him. Short of the disarmament of which both he and Bryan dreamed, that could not be avoided. As a private citizen the year before he became Secretary, he had urged his friends in Congress to authorize two new battleships instead of one. He felt personally embarrassed, however, by the fact that "it costs $250,000 a year to maintain the *Mayflower* and the *Sylph* [the President's boats] and the *Dolphin,* the boat of the Secretary of the Navy." His use of the word "boat" instead of "yacht" in his diary indicated less his knowledge of naval nomenclature than his democratic chagrin about having a yacht assigned to him even in an official capacity. He "rather recommended" to the President that they be put into regular service, though the word "rather" was written in his diary as an afterthought above the line. Mr. Wilson took that matter under consideration. He kept it there. He gave Daniels, however, full and hearty approval of his plan to send even those officers, most long-settled in Washington, with the most gold braid and the best connections, to sea.

That order was Dainels' basic policy for the Navy. Throughout his whole service as Secretary, which was longer than that of any other man except that other editor, Lincolns' Gideon Welles, he believed that "the Navy is primarily a thing on the

seas" and that "the business of the naval officer is on the sea."
Under the order all officers who had not had sea duty within
a certain period were detached and sent to sea. It applied not
only to officers Daniels found when he arrived. He made it
apply, too, to those he put in their places. His single term for
bureau chiefs was called by some officers the Single Oak Policy.
Under it even those in whom he placed chief dependence could
expect in their turn to go to sea. In 1913, he did not pretend
to himself that he was not glad the general order sent some
special men to sea and made vacancies in the Department for
others upon whom he could more comfortably depend. He
had not felt safe, he wrote in his diary, with men whom he had
inherited from the previous administration between his purposes and their performance. As Admiral Fiske wrote in his
memoirs of the years before Daniels arrived, "the appointments
of chiefs of bureau had too often been influenced by political
considerations, one reason being that each appointment had to
be confirmed by the Senate." The presence of Theodore Roosevelt in the White House and Senator Henry Cabot Lodge in
the Senate had been important naval facts.

It was not quite true, as the author of Franklin Roosevelt's
first campaign biography was told with humorous exaggeration,
that Daniels entered the Department with "a profound suspicion that whatever an admiral told him was wrong." Daniels
was not, however, prepared to believe that everything an admiral told him was right. Actually, my father entered the Department not only with strong convictions about militarism
but also with a romantic attitude about the Navy. He had
more personal connections with it than Franklin Roosevelt did.
He shared my mother's almost proprietary feeling about it.
Two of her brothers had gone to Annapolis; and her oldest
brother, Worth Bagley, had not only kicked a fabulous field
goal which won an Army-Navy game, he had also been the
"first to fall" in the war with Spain in an action of gunboats

and shore batteries off Cuba which the war-hungry press played up as a major naval engagement. Long afterward beyond world wars, it is hard to understand how much his death meant in those days. The war in which he died was the first since the Civil War, and Worth Bagley from North Carolina was, when he fell, an ensign in the uniform of the United States. He was not only the first casualty but as such (and as a recently popular fullback who had so much trouble with his chemistry that the midshipmen made a cheer about it) the first symbol of a united nation in the time of its adolescent nationalism as a world power. Father wrote young Bagley's biography, which had a quick, wide sale. Also, I remember that I had a feeling long afterward that my grandmother, whose father was removed as Governor of North Carolina by the Yankees, had in some sort of mystic marriage with the Union produced America's sacrificial son. As I grow older I realize where I got that notion. My grandmother, with her gold-headed cane, seemed to have it, too. So did Mother. And Father, while less mystical and only related to the miracle by marriage, took from it an affection for the Navy only surpassed by his devotion to the Democratic Party and the Methodist Church.

He did not, however, have any affection for anything which seemed to him to resemble the martinet or the militarist. He developed a prompt if not a profound suspicion of some of his chief assistants, notably Admiral Fiske, the senior of the four admirals who were his special aides. Fiske was an able officer, inventor and naval writer; also, he was vain, persistent and humorless. With his small size and his moustache with wide curling ends, he seemed often to personify a Navy which was sometimes most belligerent when it was least powerful.

He was obsessed, the new Secretary thought, with plans for a centralized officer control like that of the General Staff of the Imperial German Navy. The diminutive Admiral felt strongly, as he wrote, that his position as chief aide to the Secretary was

—or should be—"exactly like that which is called 'First Sea Lord' in the British Navy and Chief of Staff in other navies and in armies." He believed that as in the case of the German Navy and the Kaiser there should be "no intermediary between the commander-in-chief and the forces which he commanded." Not merely as that intermediary but as a toughly determined believer in civilian control of armed forces, Daniels did not agree with him. His feeling that Fiske favored an hereditary officer caste was, Fiske insisted, unjust. Fiske only said, he wrote later, that in Germany and Japan "every man is in a measure military, as his father and grandfather were before him, and that such nations naturally have a greater military spirit and a greater military ability than nations like ours." Even that amplification did not fit Daniels' ideas about the Navy of a democracy.

Indeed, such ideas, volubly expressed by Admiral Fiske, prompted the new Secretary to look at the records of the chief officers around him in the light of the Single Oak Policy. Some of them had not been to sea—or off the Potomac shore—he discovered, "as much as the good of the service required." That did not apply to Fiske. He had had adequate sea service and was to stay on talkative duty close to the Secretary. It did apply, however, to Captain Templin M. Potts, who as aide for personnel stood between the Secretary and the Bureau of Navigation which made all assignments to duty. A politician as well as an admiral could understand the importance of that post. Daniels noted early that Captain Potts "did not seem to be in accord with my views." Actually the Captain, as naval attaché in Berlin while Theodore Roosevelt was President, had brought back the information upon which Fiske based much of his conviction that the German general staff system should be introduced into the American Navy. A year before Daniels arrived, Potts had been made aide for personnel when his predecessor, Admiral William Parker Potter, resplendent in dress uniform, sword and cocked hat, slipped on the high, ice-covered steps of the Navy Department on the way to Taft's last New Year's reception at the White House. Captain Potts' fall was to seem almost as abrupt. Unexpectedly, however, it was the case of Colonel Charles Laurie McCawley, United States Marine Corps, who was involved almost incidentally in the order to go to sea (or in his case as a decorative marine to a new station far away), which caused the most trouble. As a landlubber at the helm Daniels knew there was a storm in his order; he misjudged the direction from which to expect the strongest wind. And he certainly had no idea of the Gilbert and Sullivan situation which was to follow, in which the stately Senator Lodge was to play a leading role.

The plight of Potts became almost the first order of business at the convention of the Navy League which at the time was holding its first meeting under a Democratic administration. Admiral Fiske conferred with elderly retired admirals about it. He protested in person to the Secretary. Potts went to sea. There was less indignation about Colonel McCawley, but more power behind his complaint. The power came as a surprise to the Secretary. McCawley was not a member of the Navy's high command. He was not a member of the General Board which advised the Secretary and "frequently lamented"—according to the biographers of its chairman, Admiral Dewey—that it was "advisory only" and "could not force its opinions into action." He was far down the line of command from Fiske or even Potts. As chief of the quartermaster department of the marines, McCawley was concerned not with high naval policies but with supplies including the bright blue uniforms with broad red stripes down the sides of the trousers. As such a man he seemed hardly to deserve the vigilant attention even of a new Secretary who rejoiced in his post because it put him on guard against rattling swords, social seamanship and chauvinistic arms suppliers. Colonel McCawley, in March 1913, very carefully did not even talk about such matters. There was a subdued air about him as he drank his favorite white porto at the Metropolitan Club. He had been happily and continuously stationed in Washington under a full half dozen of Daniels' Republican predecessors. It was not his purpose to get in the way of the Democrats. All he hoped was that they would not disturb him in his very pleasant ways. It seemed a good bet that nobody could.

"You'll never get Charlie McCawley out of town," Franklin Roosevelt told his new chief when he heard that the Colonel had been ordered to San Francisco.

"He will go," said Daniels.

"I'll believe it when I see him on the train," said Roosevelt.

Franklin wore then, Daniels remembered, "an impish grin." Also, later the Secretary concluded that Roosevelt "may have known more than he revealed." Not even years afterward, however, was it clear whether Franklin was most amused by McCawley's tenacity or Daniels' temerity. As a part of a class, Franklin was conscious of its power. Daniels seemed almost funny in opposition to it. Sometimes McCawley seemed comic in it. Others too were amused. Indeed, ten years before Daniels became aware of McCawley, Henry Adams put into italics his amusement at the spectacle of McCawley at a White House reception "in his beautiful gold lace and spurs." The last recorded use of his decorative sword had been when "Princess Alice" Roosevelt sliced the tall white wedding cake with it at her White House wedding to Nicholas Longworth in 1906. Mr. Adams was not the only gossip for whose reports the dashing Colonel provided material. His activities were more often reported by the society magazines than by the *Army and Navy Journal*. *The Clubfellow and Washington Mirror* described him in civilian clothes as "trotting around looking as much like a study in pastels as ever . . . the pinkest cheeks, the bluest eyes, the grayest suits and the lavenderest shirts you ever saw. And now that his hair has silvered romantically, Charlie is right to be a stage hero." *Town Topics* added that McCawley was "still in the heyday of middle age, and has a taste for the flesh-pots as well as the ability to dance the turkey trot and grizzly bear in a way that makes his juniors envious."

Franklin Roosevelt had known McCawley long enough to call him Charlie, having first met him probably when he came down as a Harvard junior to Alice Roosevelt's debut party in 1902, the year Adams noticed the spurs. He went to the big McCawley house on New Hampshire Avenue for luncheon the day after he arrived in Washington in 1913. Apparently no note of Charlie's danger was sounded then, though in a Navy which contained then only 3,653 officers, including marines, in the entire world, the gossip could have got around that Secretary Daniels had his aide studying the shore duty records of many popular officers in the capital. Roosevelt himself was excited about arrivals, not possible departures then, though he was always eager to help with the official problems of his social friends. In his letter home he put an exclamation point after his description of the McCawley luncheon, but exclamation points were fairly common with him in those days. He knew the McCawleys well when he laughed about the Colonel's case in his chief's office. Daniels paid more attention, however, when his old friend on the Democratic National Committee, irascible, one-eyed and paralytic Senator Benjamin R. Tillman, chairman of the Naval Affairs Committee, came hurrying to see him about the McCawley case.

"You certainly have raised hell, Josephus," the South Carolinian said. And Pitchfork Ben Tillman knew a hell-raising when he saw one.

Daniels knew Tillman well. Violence sometimes seemed his normal attitude. His tongue was sharp and his nickname came from threatening to apply a pitchfork to President Cleveland's "old fat ribs." On this occasion Daniels understood that he was really disturbed—and disturbed for his friend, Daniels. The Secretary indicated his surprise.

"Why did you dig up so many snakes by ordering McCawley to San Francisco?" Lean in his dark clothes, Tillman looked like a scolding, one-eyed blackbird. "Didn't you know that you would incur the lasting hostility of Senator Lodge if you touched McCawley?"

Daniels said that he did not know that the Senator from Massachusetts had any interest in the case.

Tillman's one eye gleamed: "Well, he has. And he asked me to make an appointment with you so he could talk with you about it. He is deeply stirred. He rarely makes any requests, and I've come to ask you to make the appointment and do what Lodge asks."

The eye roved but focused again with less fire in it.

"In the main," he said, "I think you are right about these officers hanging around Washington all the time, but it is more important to you and to the Navy to have Senator Lodge on your side—" the eye brightened— "than to be so damned consistent in any rules or plans or policies."

Nobody knew better than Daniels from that moment that the McCawley case was no comedy. Indeed, probably more than any other thing, his success as Secretary of the Navy and as official in the Wilson administration was based upon his consistent and continuing understanding of the necessity for clear and good relationships with members of Congress. He knew Lodge's deep interest in the Navy. Not only did Lodge believe that he and Theodore Roosevelt had made the modern Navy; that was almost a generally accepted view. One of Lodge's biographers has said that "ancestrally, connubially, and economically" he was destined to be a navalist and an imperialist. His tradition and his wealth both had come largely from the sea lanes traversed by New England sailing vessels. His wife was the daughter of one admiral and the sister of another. Later FDR was to help with the promotion of her nephew, who was a naval officer, too. Also, Lodge had grown in his Republicanism at a time when the development of heavy industries in the United States had spurred on a naval program which would provide a market for machinery, ordnance and armor plate, steel, nickel, coal—then oil. Daniels to the end of his days thought that Lodge's "devotion to the Navy was apparent."

Lodge came to the Secretary's office, as he had wanted to come, in the late afternoon when there would be no publicity and they would not be disturbed. Daniels knew the legend of Lodge's Boston crustiness, but that afternoon Lodge spoke almost diffidently in his thin Yankee voice. He said that he had hesitated to come, that he rarely made requests as to assignments to duty, and that in general he approved the order but he did not quite see why it should apply to men in the quartermaster's department like McCawley. He said, however, very little about McCawley, but the plush image of that modish marine was almost embarrassingly present in the big quiet room while he talked.

The Colonel was not easily hidden. He had been the dancing beau of generations of debutantes. He belonged to that inner circle of Metropolitan Club members which maintained the even more exclusive Alibi Club a block away on I Street. The Colonel had not only been Theodore Roosevelt's aide but Taft's golf partner. McCawley's "best friend" was Larz Anderson, "the handsome dandy of the diplomatic corps," whose ambassadorships were regarded as in direct relationship to his Republican campaign contributions. Something of their world is suggested by Anderson's statement that as the Republican and Democratic years slipped by his remained "the only house in Washington, except the embassies, which turned out the servants in full dress livery, shorts and stockings, buckled shoes and braided coats." They belonged, Anderson said afterward, to "the old order," but in 1913 it was still a gay order—and a prehensile one, too.

It was not entirely an hereditary society but it was one in which kinships were not disregarded. Colonel McCawley had entered the Marine Corps (or gone on its payroll) at the age of sixteen, in 1881, as a clerk in his father's office when his father was commandant of the corps. (Senator Lodge later tried to get that time counted in terms of his retirement pay as a marine officer.) He officially entered the Marine Corps, however, in 1897 and went off briefly and creditably to the Spanish-American War. He never smelled gunpowder again, but he was useful and charming forever after. He drove Mrs. Roosevelt and Alice to TR's only Washington inauguration. His spurs at receptions apparently did not seem funny to the martial TR, and his sword was certainly useful in cutting Alice's cake. Soon after that wedding cake was cut, McCawley increased his security, if he ended his charming eligibility, by marrying Mrs. Sarah Frelinghuysen Davis, who had been a fixture in Washington society since at least 1882, when her wealthy father, while Secretary of State under Chester A. Arthur, had made her first husband Assistant Secretary of State. McCawley had been only seventeen in 1882. Gossips, however, may have made too much of the differences in the ages of his wife and himself. One at least said that he was thirty-five and she was sixty in 1913. The Colonel was actually forty-seven. True, Mrs. McCawley had been a grandmother since 1902. It may possibly have been true, as one of the social commentators wrote soon after Daniels turned his attention almost incidentally to McCawley's case, that "Charlie is chafing at being an old woman's darling—but then he has been the petted pet of so many generations of debutantes that he ought now to be content to dance to the piper whatever the tune— so long as he does not pay for it." Certainly when Daniels figured it was time for Charlie to be transferred to San Francisco, however, he faced not merely a domestic solidarity but a stubbornly entrenched regime.

"You may not know," Senator Lodge said, "but Colonel McCawley married Mrs. Davis, who came to see me yesterday with tears in her eyes and made such an appeal to me that I could not resist it. My son, who is dead, married Mrs. Davis' daughter."

That son had been George Cabot Lodge, the leonine poet, whom everybody called Bay. He and his wife, Matilda Elizabeth Frelinghuysen Davis, had presented Senator and Mrs. Lodge and Mrs. McCawley with two grandsons: another Henry Cabot who was also to become Senator from Massachusetts, and John Davis Lodge who became Governor of Connecticut. (Continuing from Arthur to Eisenhower, the Davis-Lodge connection was to make a governing continuity of at least seventy-one years.) Four years before Lodge came to see Daniels, Bay Lodge had died suddenly and tragically while he and his father were vacationing on a lonely island off the Massachusetts coast. Now his mother-in-law had come to Senator Lodge with tears in her eyes—at a time when the Senator himself was suffering not only from what his friend Theodore Roosevelt had done to the Republican Party, but from gastric ulcers as well.

Lodge talked with a paternal pathos which went straight to the big streak of sentiment in Josephus Daniels. He said that Mrs. McCawley was a very sick woman, and that it would be a serious matter to remove her from the care of Washington specialists. Therefore, he hoped that Daniels could postpone the transfer of McCawley to San Francisco. All that Lodge said had been verified by less sympathetic reporters. A year before, one had noted that Mrs. McCawley "goes out scarcely at all although she entertained constantly during the season. The weariness of advancing years is creeping upon her, but while eschewing the fashionable world for herself she is most magnanimous toward her young husband and urges him to accept all the invitations that come his way. Charlie does not require very much urging."

Secretary Daniels was touched by Lodge's plea. He felt that the essence of the visit that afternoon was that it showed Lodge had a heart. As a radical, a Southerner and a Democrat, Daniels had doubted that before. When Lodge seemed coldly triumphant over a sick Wilson he doubted it later. That afternoon, however, he would have been prepared on short acquaintance to deny Henry Adams' conclusions on the basis of intimacy that "Cabot's lofty principles compel him to help no member of his family but himself." And that, "when Cabot proclaims his purity, beware the dog! Happy Hooligan is nowhere. . . ." Daniels would have resented such cynicism about noble sentiments. He wanted very much to do what Lodge asked. His heart, as well as Tillman, told him to try to find a way. But finally he concluded that, if his order was to stand, an exception could not be made in the McCawley case. Also, he concluded that there were equally efficient physicians in San Francisco. Regretfully he sent word of his decision to Lodge.

He supposed, he wrote later, that from what Tillman and others had told him the decision would arouse Lodge's resentment and affect his attitude toward him and the Navy. But, he said in charity or misinformation in his memoirs, "it never did." Indeed, he thought to the end of his life that though Lodge occasionally joined hands with his son-in-law, Congressman "Gussie" Gardner, in his later attacks upon the Navy, Lodge remained his counselor and defender. He came "to lean upon" Lodge, he wrote. Lodge sometimes gave the public impression that he could. Privately, however, Lodge bitterly resented him. In 1916 Lodge wrote Theodore Roosevelt that "Daniels has got about him officers who hold their places solely on condition that they are to say what he wants them to say." Daniels would not have put it that way, but he did mean to have a Navy in which the possibility of such conspiratorial insubordination as Lodge and Roosevelt had indulged in behind Secretary Long's back in 1898 was reduced to a minimum. His sensible intent was to have around him officers of his choosing, not yes-men, but men on whose loyalty he could depend. However, even when Lodge wrote about the officers Daniels had about him in Washington, McCawley was still one of them.

"Has Charlie McCawley gone?" Roosevelt asked again after Lodge's visit, grinning even more. Obviously he had been talking about it with others, including undoubtedly McCawley and probably Lodge.

"No, but he will go on the date of the order."

Franklin laughed. "I don't believe you or the President or God will get Charlie McCawley out of Washington."

"He will go," said Daniels, but the question seemed to be attracting attention not merely as a social and naval matter but almost as a sporting event.

On April 24, 1913, *Town Topics* reported with a gossip's satisfaction: "Clever politician though she is, Sallie McCawley has failed to have her husband retained at Marine headquarters in Washington though she has pulled every wire that possibly could avail."

A month later it added: "Sallie McCawley has been checked again." But its secret Washington correspondent hedged: "Mark my words, by hook or crook, she will have Charlie back in Washington."

The Clubfellow beat its New York rival to the great news: "Colonel Frank Lee Denny and Colonel Charles Laurie McCawley are hugging each other, and themselves, at the turn their affairs have taken . . . so much rejoicing at the Metropolitan Club in place of tears."

Where influence had fallen short, ingenuity and some investment in the fortunes of an old friend had triumphed. In the orders sending McCawley to California the officer designated to take his Washington place was Colonel Denny. They were old friends. Denny had even more Washington background than McCawley, as the grandson of a Speaker of the U.S. House of Representatives, the son-in-law of a general and the nephew of an admiral. He had been in the Marine Corps for seventeen years when Charlie entered it. *The Clubfellow* suggested that Denny had been exiled to San Francisco earlier because of a "too free tongue and other like indiscretions." However, he had had six years of sea service and shore duty as far off as Alexandria, Egypt, and Panama. All he needed apparently was money. All Charlie and Sally desperately required was unmolested continuance of Washington residence. Their needs made the basis of a bargain.

The new Secretary did not know it, but under the law old friends McCawley and Denny were the only two officers in the quartermaster department of the Marine Corps at that time whose rank made it possible for them to serve as the chief of the quartermaster department from which Charlie was being relieved. Also, the law required that the chief of that department have his office in Washington. And so, not long after he had told Senator Lodge that he could not revoke Charlie's orders, Daniels signed Colonel Denny's resignation when it crossed his desk. Denny had had thirty-three years' service and was entitled to retire. But that day the two colonels and friends celebrated at the Metropolitan Club and Sallie McCawley followed suit with quiet satisfaction in her house on New Hampshire Avenue. It worked fine for the McCawleys. No further threat to Charlie's Washington residence ever occurred until he retired in 1929. He was active in Washington society until he died in 1935. And his aged and ailing wife survived him by four years, dying in 1939, just twenty-six years after Senator Lodge was so fearful about her delicate condition.

Colonel Denny did not fare quite so well. It seemed splendid to be set up, as he was with Charlie's help when he resigned from the marines as vice-president of the Real Estate Trust Company of Washington. But by October Mrs. Denny had left him: "It is all very sad," said one of the social commentators who had paid close attention to the earlier details of the story. "Only a few years ago the Dennys were on top of the heap socially. Lack of money is at the bottom of it all. Colonel Denny's retired pay is not enough for them to live on, and he has failed to achieve success in the real estate business, which he took up on quitting the corps." A year later, on July 8, 1914, he fell or jumped—Daniels believed he jumped—from a window of his house and was killed.

Daniels had very little time for chagrin about Colonel Mc-Cawley's triumph. While McCawley celebrated, Daniels was suddenly faced with the sort of sword-rattling which he always feared from such general staff control of the armed forces as Admiral Fiske and Captain Potts so much desired. Also, though he could not quite prove it, he had a feeling that he was confronted by a strategic movement in which Admiral Fiske was taking the lead—and one aimed not much more directly at Japan than at the Secretary. There seemed sudden serious danger of war with Japan over the California land tenure laws. The resentment of the Japanese was not new, but this time President Wilson gathered from the extreme perturbation of Viscount Sutemi Chinda (who two years before had presented the cherry trees to Washington as the emblems of peace and friendship) that the war talk behind him at home was serious. Also, in the United States some Army and Navy men were giving belligerent attention to the warnings of Homer Lea, an eccentric or prophetic soldier of fortune, about the dangers of the "yellow peril" including the possibility of a Japanese invasion of the United States. (In World War II Lea seemed certainly a realist though his time schedule was a little off. He was a frail and militant hunchback from California who became a general in the Chinese Army and confidential adviser to Sun Yat-sen in the revolution of 1911-12. He died in 1912 at thirty-six, but not until he had completed his *The Day of the Saxon,* which, he warned, might be at an end.)

Suddenly, while Wilson and Bryan labored for a peaceful solution, *The New York Herald* published under large headlines a provocative "leak" about militant plans of a joint Army and Navy Board which wanted a naval concentration at Manila. The action in the joint board had been instigated by General Leonard Wood, Theodore Roosevelt's dear friend and Rough Rider companion, who, in 1910 under Taft, had · been appointed to a four-year term as Chief of Staff. He had been strongly supported by Admiral Fiske. On the day of the "leak" Daniels jotted in his diary, "Admiral Fiske, Joint Board's Action, Fiske, Joseph K. Ohl, President." It was an almost telegraphic account of what he believed had happened. The repetition of Fiske's name underlined the suspicion Daniels always had that the small, militant Fiske was in some way responsible for the "leak" and that its purpose was "to force the hand of the commander-in-chief." Ohl was the former Far Eastern correspondent and the future editor-in-chief of *The Herald,* the paper of James Gordon Bennett who, though living as an expatriate in Paris, gave lively attention as a Spanish War naval veteran to American naval affairs. *The Herald* sometimes seemed the organ of the admirals. Apparently no suspicion with regard to the "leak" to *The Herald* was directed at FDR's assistant, Louis Howe, who had been a *Herald* reporter for twenty years before he became, at forty-two, Franklin's first assistant in the Navy Department. It would have been a natural suspicion. Howe often used *The Herald* as a paper in which to plant kind words and trial balloons about his ambitious young boss. He looked like the man for such a job. Even small boys got the impression that Howe's interminable leisure in the anteroom of the Secretary of the Navy was a form of eavesdropping.

That room may, of course, have provided his favorite view of the White House across the street. Howe liked to sit there and scowl and talk. He seemed like something that had come from under the dark, damp side of a stone, very dry and dusty all the same. The dusty impression was undoubtedly given by the cigarette ashes which always smeared his slick, dark clothes. He seemed especially designed in the company of Father's secretary, Howard A. Banks, to represent the contrast of the town mouse and the country mouse, realism and innocence, or maybe the ant and the grasshopper whose story Henry Adams loved so well. Though they spent hours together in that anteroom, Howe and the neat, industrious Banks never had anything in common except devotion to their bosses. Howe exceeded Banks in that. Banks left Daniels to become editor of *The Sunday School Times.* Howe died in the White House with Roosevelt. Banks was always headed for Heaven. There was nothing in Heaven Howe wanted so much as pushing the earthly fortunes of FDR.

Undoubtedly in that brief publicized war scare Franklin's sympathies were entirely with the militant generals and admirals. This was, moreover, the first occasion, as one of Fiske's close colleagues, Admiral William F. Fullam, later reported, in which the admirals got the Assistant Secretary to pretend to the Secretary that memoranda prepared by them were suggestions of his own. Fullam had already found that the Secretary did not always embrace his proposals, as when he told the new Secretary he thought it would be better if he addressed new recruits not as "young gentlemen" but as "my lads." Fullam remembered later that Franklin took his memo to the Secretary's office and, in a contortion characteristic at the time, put it on the floor beneath his feet and, through his knees, read it as his own. The Admiral said that "coming from him as a civilian to the Secretary of the Navy, it had some effect." Nothing resulted, however, which might provoke war. The purpose of the Navy was peace.

At a meeting in the White House garden with the President and Secretary of War Lindley M. Garrison, who seemed as sympathetic with his generals as Daniels was supposed to be suspicious of his admirals, Daniels warned that any major movement of American naval forces in the Pacific would be dangerous, provocative and impotent. Wilson and Bryan agreed. The President laid down the law that he wanted no more war planning by a joint Army and Navy Board which could not keep its own councils secret. The tension eased. Indeed, the best thing remembered about that time, until years later when an older Franklin Roosevelt was surprised by the attack on Pearl Harbor, was a statement Bryan made in the midst of the excitement. If he could not make peace, Bryan could make a phrase. In his shabby office he and the Japanese Ambassador reached an impasse in argument. In a state of great agitation, the Ambassador arose.

"I suppose, Mr. Secretary, this position is final?"

And Bryan said, "There is nothing final between friends."

Perhaps Pearl Harbor was only postponed then. Roosevelt himself in the 1920's became one of those most certain that there was no basis for expectation of war between the United States and Japan. Homer Lea's schedule was only delayed. The war danger died. More Japanese cherry trees were planted on the Mall. The whole world seemed as mild as the early summer weather and as secure as Colonel McCawley.

McCawley was promoted to full colonel on the second of June, though *The Clubfellow* noted that he had been "called Colonel for so many years that it was hard to disassociate him from any other rank, but he has been no real colonel until last week." As was customary he went with his wife to establish her at their country place near Bar Harbor, Maine. The same gossips, noticing him in his immaculate flannels at the Chevy Chase

Club, said that in returning to his duties he did not seem in the least to "mind being absent from the gaieties of Bar Harbor and his venerable wife." Colonel Charlie danced wherever he was.

The McCawleys were not the only Navy folk who left the Washington heat for the New England coast. Their patron and the Navy's defender Senator Lodge was always happy to get to his well-loved estate on Cliff Street in Nahant, a high rocky island off Lynn which reminded Henry Adams of a ship just stranded on the rough coast of Cape Ann. Among the diplomats Mrs. Bryan noted that Newport seemed to be the favorite resort. It was the favorite of the Navy, too. Naval officers were almost as welcome as diplomats at the big parties in the palaces along Bellevue Avenue and Ocean Drive. Most important, Narragansett Bay was the base of the fleet for the summer months. The intermarrying Navy brought its daughters to Newport to be near the congregation of young officers. Old admirals often went to Newport as they were later to move to California. As was his perennial custom, Admiral Fiske was in Newport that summer. He spent one evening at the Casino on Bellevue Avenue opposite Stone Villa, where Ambassador Bakhmeteff and his plump wife Mamie Beale lived, and violently objected to the cab line waiting before their residence for such naval or other visitors to the Casino as did not have conveyances of their own.

Fiske watched the dancing with Admiral Charles H. Davis, retired, brother of Mrs. Lodge, who had graduated from the Naval Academy when it was located at Newport during the Civil War.

"A dance was going on," Fiske recalled later, "in which some couples were exercising themselves with the 'turkey trot' which at that time was a most ungainly performance."

Apparently he had not seen it executed by Colonel McCawley in such a way as to make even the young envious. He made some laughing comment about it to Admiral Davis but that old sailor was not amused.

"You know that this is not new," he said, "and is all over Europe?"

Fiske said that he thought that at least the turkey trot was new. (Daniel Frohman, the theatrical producer, is authority for the statement that the turkey trot originated in San Francisco in 1911. The grizzly bear was a popular variation of it.)

Admiral Davis glowered under his brows. "This especial step may be new, but dancing crazes are old, and this is a part of a dancing craze. I am quite sure that it portends evil. . . . There have been several dancing crazes in recorded history. One dancing craze preceded the Crusades, another dancing craze preceded the Reign of Terror. Every dancing craze has been followed in about a year by an awful war."

Admiral Fiske heard the older man with great interest. He stored that pessimistic statement away with some satisfaction in his records. "This suggests," he commented in his memoirs, "the degree of preventability of war by mortals."

Secretary Daniels, who had no such sense of the inevitability of ill fortune, also came to the New England coast that summer on part of a swift inclusive journey which carried him to all the shore stations of the Navy from Key West to San Diego and Seattle. En route he had seen every kind of ship. He had been down in a submarine and, as seemed to many in those days, with special daring he had been up in a hydroplane. Now he and Mrs. Daniels and their boys sailed to the naval stations which seemed particularly numerous along the New England shore on the Secretary's yacht, the antique *Dolphin*. As a yacht the *Dolphin* made no impression of extravagant elegance. She was not only the first steel war vessel built in the United States. Also, in terms of her cost and quality, her building had been a naval scandal. She outlasted many better boats. Daniels sailed happily aboard her.

At Newport he listened to Admiral William S. Sims, who had been Theodore Roosevelt's naval aide, talk of the need of a naval organization like that of the British Admiralty. At Boston he had a friendly talk with TR himself when both spoke at Bunker Hill. Roosevelt told him that he had good reports of him from Franklin. It was a pleasant journey, though Daniels was not pleased with all he saw and did not please everyone who saw him. He marked for abolition a coaling station up beyond Bar Harbor on Frenchman's Bay which had served only the satisfaction of a Republican Senator. An admiral who had retired to become president of the Fore River Shipbuilding Corporation was shocked at his suggestion that the Navy might build its own ships in its own yards and save money.

He was seeing the Navy and the Navy was seeing him. At the Naval War College, Daniels always remembered with amusement, he was taken to the library and "conducted into a room in which a bar was fitted up in a manner that would do credit to any saloon. A bartender with the regulation apron stood behind the counter."

"What will you have, Mr. Secretary?" asked the Admiral in command.

"White Rock," he said.

"And you?" the Commandant asked each of the half-dozen admirals who had accompanied them to the library.

"White Rock," each answered promptly.

Afterward one bluff old seadog, who never failed to have his stiff drink before lunch, but had joined the White Rock parade, explained himself above another and different drink.

"I be damned," that Admiral said, "if I was going to let any one of you other fellows appear more temperate before the Secretary than me."

Anchor and Plowshare

"I LOVED HIS WORDS," FRANKLIN ROOSEVELT SAID LATER OF THE
first time he was present at a meeting of his new chief with a
group of armor-plate suppliers. It was the sort of action, too,
which Roosevelt "loved" all his life. In the Secretary's office he
found the representatives of the Midvale, Carnegie and Bethle-
hem steel companies sitting around the Secretary's desk. Daniels looked both solemn and mild. The steel representatives
were attentive. The price of armor for new battleships, as
Roosevelt recalled it later, had gone up in the bids from $460
a ton to $520, though the cost of production and the wages of
labor had not risen. The Secretary held the bids of the three
companies in his hands. Their bids were identical.

"Gentlemen," he said. He looked at the documents and at
them. "This, I am afraid, is collusive bidding for you, all three,
to arrive at exactly the same figure. I am afraid I have got to
throw the bids out and ask for new bids."

One of the three gentlemen stepped forward, Roosevelt remembered, "with a perfectly solemn face." The faces of the
others were perfectly solemn, too.

"Mr. Secretary, it was pure coincidence."

And Daniels said, "Well, the bids are rejected and we will
open new bids at twelve o'clock tomorrow. Sharpen your pen-
cils, think it over during the night, and don't have another
coincidence."

All made similar bows. They walked out together. And behind them Franklin laughed and the Secretary grinned. They were amused by the obvious distress of the gentlemen at a new type of Secretary of the Navy. They had been accustomed to a Navy depending upon and persuaded by the Navy League which accepted any bids they saw fit to offer. Identical bidding had even been made to seem a patriotic plan by which the three companies were kept in the arms business. The departing gentlemen were not amused. Next day, however, their bids—all three of them—were $520 a ton. It was a unity which they seemed to feel should shake the Secretary. It was an unyielding unity which the unyielding new Secretary regarded as naked monopoly. He was not grinning when he called young Roosevelt in. At his big desk he had a newspaper open in his hand.

"Do you see who has landed?" he asked Franklin.

"Who?"

"Sir John Hatfield."

"Well," said Franklin, "who is Sir John Hatfield?"

The Secretary seemed both a little surprised at Roosevelt's ignorance and happy to inform him. "Why, he is one of the three or four great armor-plate makers in England, and makes a lot of armor plate for the British Navy. Can you take the train right away?"

"What do you want me to do?"

The Secretary was specific: "Go up to New York, see Sir John Hatfield and ask him if he will take this order for this armor at $460 or less."

Franklin went. He saw Hatfield. The Britisher made a firm offer of $460 a ton. Roosevelt brought it back to a delighted Daniels. The identical representatives of the American companies were brought in again. Daniels showed them the offer and, by another coincidence, all agreed to meet the price. The incident did not endear the Secretary to the steel makers. Daniels seemed not only pleased with getting more steel for less money; he seemed to take a positive pleasure in curbing arms profits. The armor dealers were not reassured by the Secretary's prompt support of proposals that the government manufacture its own armor plate. They deplored his suggestion that the Navy build its own ships in its own yards. But they felt as Admiral Fiske did, who said that when he argued with Daniels, he "might as well have tried to scratch a diamond with an iron file."

The ablest of the friends of both the steel companies and the militant admirals, like Colonel Robert Means Thompson, understood that the spring and summer of 1913 were no times for scratching. If frugality sometimes looked like socialism, and peacefulness like pacifism, both were what the country had ordered. Peace was not only popular in 1913; it was fashionable, too. The hope of peace got no more pleasant attention that year than it received from Colonel Thompson. As perennial president of the Navy League, chairman of the board of the International Nickel Company, and expansive host, he enlivened the summer at its beginning with a party for peace itself. His guests included not only a British Empire delegation in Washington planning, a year and a half in advance, the celebration of a century without war between English-speaking peoples as a sort of model for mankind. Also, prominently present was Mr. Bryan, who hoped to negotiate treaties of peace and arbitration between all the nations of the world. Colonel Thompson was in a peaceful mood that spring. It pleased him when Franklin, as his guest at a Navy League banquet, expressed the opinion that "there are as many advocates of arbitration and international peace in the Navy as in any other profession." The implicit presumption was that that was also true among the Navy's organized friends.

That year the word used to describe the Colonel (he secured his title on the staff of a Governor of New Jersey; officially he was a retired ensign) was "debonair." He was a big man, with a large round head, a fleshy nose, a wide moustache which hung like thatched eaves over his mouth, and a large dimple in his chin. At sixty-four he was gay, generous and convivial. He seemed nowhere so much at home as in the Navy Department. Indeed, romantic society chroniclers had noted in February 1913, a time of the year when the Colonel was usually on his big houseboat in Florida, that he was tarrying in Washington in connection with "his desire to be named Secretary of the Navy by President Wilson. To hold the marine portfolio would crown the debonair Colonel's greatest ambition." Such an appointment would have been fantastic politically (Daniels thought that it was when Taft was elected that Thompson was a hopeful) but it would have put neatly together service, social and business ties in the Secretary of the Navy's big, gleaming room.

Colonel Thompson was a Naval Academy graduate who had resigned after three years' service during what he called "the stagnation of promotion that existed between the close of the Civil War and the beginning of the Spanish War," and become rich in mining and banking. The Navy League seemed almost as much his private property as his houseboats, his big houses, his securities or his stables. Indeed, when in 1912, the League had given a banquet to Franklin Roosevelt's predecessor, Assistant Secretary of the Navy Beekman Winthrop, Harvard lawyer and Wall Street banker, it was recorded that all present knew they were the guests of Colonel Thompson and that the League seemed to be the "chosen means of scattering his shekels." Another former Assistant Secretary of the Navy, Herbert Livingston Satterlee, son-in-law of J. Pierpont Morgan, was general counsel of the League. Some, indeed, thought it was significant that the League was proposed in 1901, the year in which Morgan organized U.S. Steel, and that other steel men were prominent in its membership. Some of its leading members were also to be prominent later in the Liberty League where they angrily parted with Roosevelt, who was so popular a member of the Navy League in 1913.

The Navy League was not the Colonel's only means of scattering his shekels. He was, as was later testified by a bronze bust in Mahan Hall at Annapolis, "the Naval Academy's Best Friend." In support of the Academy and particularly its athletics, he was the perfect alumnus among a body of alumni whose cohesion created a uniformed class. Also, as sportsman and patriot he was for years the principal supporter of American Olympic Teams. Once he leased an ocean liner to take a body of friends, including old Navy ones, on a cruise around the world. Furthermore, with less publicity but sometimes with more philanthropy, the Colonel gladly handled the investments of his friends among naval officers through his investment house of S. H. P. Pell & Co. Even more important to some other officers, he enthusiastically supported their proposals for more officer—and less civilian—control of the Navy Department.

It seemed only natural the year before Daniels arrived that when the Colonel went to the Olympic Games he was accompanied by a naval aide. He was not so accoutered when he left again for Europe on the night of his peace party. He was not chairman of the American Olympic Committee that year. The imperial Republican years had come to an end. No alarums kept officials at their desks. The always attentive Republican newspapers gave the impression that Secretary Bryan was leaving on a perpetual round of Chatauqua lectures to unimportant people in hot tents and overspread groves. The Secretary of the Navy went off to see more of the Navy on the West Coast. Left in Washington, Franklin, as young Acting Secretary was finding the Navy Department almost doldrum still. He no longer felt the fresh elation as the young, new Roosevelt which he had had when, soon after his appointment, he and Eleanor had gone to TR's house at Sagamore Hill for the wedding of Ethel Roosevelt to Dr. Richard Derby, another Groton man. That occasion had been a sort of final Roosevelt fling before the ex-President set off for his Brazilian explorations. It was not, however, reported *The Clubfellow,* which then shared conservative irritation with TR for splitting the Republicans, "the holy show at the White House with all its glitter and buncombe" which Alice Longworth's wedding had been. Though a special train was run from Pennsylvania Station and six hundred guests arrived where preparations had been made for half that number, the country as a whole did not seem quite to be watching agape. *The Clubfellow* reported a new and surprising opinion of the Roosevelt clan at that moment: "they are a deadly uninteresting-looking bunch."

Franklin felt "uninteresting" in Washington. It had not taken him long to discover that his specific responsibilities for purchases, shore stations and civilian personnel (all of which interested the Secretary, too) did not give him the continuing exhilaration of seagoing command. Then and later, career officers handled most of the purchases under policies fixed by the Secretary. For the first time Roosevelt dealt with labor but he dealt with it, also, under the Secretary whose pro-labor bias seemed to his critics almost as shocking as his concern for the welfare of enlisted men. As a lawyer, or as a state Senator, he could at least have been off Campobello Island in a cat boat. One of the reasons he gave later for thinking of running for the United States Senate was that as a Senator he could spend the whole summer there with his family. That appealing idea had some reality until he himself became President and kept Congress in session the year round. Wilson was doing something of the same sort that summer. Just across the narrow street from Franklin's office the President was remaining in town as a summer bachelor, too. The White House lawn was hot and yellow. It was no place in such a summer for a pale lady like Mrs. Wilson. Only the alley slums in which she was so interested seemed crowded in July. Some Congressmen and many lobbyists remained, but there were fewer members in the dining rooms and bars of the Metropolitan and Army and Navy clubs. Many charming people had followed Colonel Thompson to Europe. Henry Adams at St. Crepin in Oise observed that "every château in the Verein seems to be occupied by Americans." And as a philosopher, not entirely immune to the prejudices of his class, he added, "Some Jew is of course the swellest." Few of the fashionable were left in Washington. Dry Louis Howe there talked with steady irritability to the round, gentle Banks who seemed sometimes in the Secretary's absence, FDR said, like "a lost soul in Israel."

The quiet did give Franklin the opportunity to work on a matter which always interested him—and Howe—at least as much as the sea. Though as President he looked back on the process as "a rather petty thing which took a good deal of my time," he then greatly enjoyed trying to get postmasterships and other political appointments for his friends and supporters in New York, particularly when he could snatch them away from regular Democratic Congressmen with Tammany Hall affiliations who felt they were entitled to them. He—and Louis Howe—were already watching the shaping contest in which Tammany Hall was to be beaten that fall in New York City itself by a Fusion ticket headed by young John Purroy Mitchel. Mitchel's election might have meaning for another young anti-Tammany man. Also, Franklin happily wrangled an assignment to Mexico for Cousin Warren Delano Robbins, then aged twenty-seven, who had entered the diplomatic service under Taft, and then was shocked to learn that his young relative was not pleased.

"If I were in the Dip. Service," he wrote his mother in indication of both his surprise and his own restlessness, "I would beg for Mexico, as it is the only place just now where there is real action."

It made Franklin feel more than ever that he was in an eddy

when he took some old Harvard friends down the Potomac on the *Sylph* on a weekend cruise. "We covered every subject on the globe!" he said of their talk. His fellow passengers were going to all the interesting points on it: Berlin, London, St. Petersburg. Their trip and their talk was fun but it made a sleepy, peaceful, hot Washington in July 1913, seem more than ordinarily dull. However, he had plenty of time for golf. Also, on the day after he got back from the Potomac cruise he went out to spend the night with his Harvard roommate, Lathrop Brown, who as a new and opulent Democratic Congressman had rented Doughoregan Manor, the magnificent and antique mansion house of Charles Carroll of Carrollton in Maryland. It was pleasant but quiet. The katydids seemed to make more noise than anything else in the world. Just before he went out to Lathrop's manor house, he wrote to the Secretary about "our quiet existence" in the Department. It was quiet. So little was happening that the slow hoofbeats of occasional passing horses sounded loud in his office. He could hear the trolleys on Pennsylvania Avenue and even those on H Street across Lafayette Square.

"Things have been going on from day to day so uneventfully since you left," he told his chief, "that I have not written you before."

There was still not much to report. A Southern Pacific gentleman who had been reported lost in Mexico was safe in Guaymas. The Bureau of Yards and Docks wanted to buy oil from the Standard Oil Company though the bid of the Union Oil Company was a penny less per barrel. He dated the letter July 29, 1913. It was the date of a dull day in a quiet time. Also, it was the beginning of the year before the outbreak of war in Europe. It was not to be a dull year. It was Woodrow Wilson's year of irresistible reform. It was Bryan's year in which with increasing confidence he negotiated his peace treaties. It was certainly not going to be a quiet year around Roosevelt while his chief with toughness and exuberance pushed, through admirals and their friends, to cut costs, to hold back profiteers, set up schools for sailors, open appointments to the Academy to enlisted personnel, cut out wine in the wardrooms, and not only see that officers had sea duty, but that young farmers from Iowa who joined the Navy to see the world really got a chance to see it. That world seemed almost suddenly filled with peaceful good sense.

Sir John Hatfield was not the only Englishman who came talking about armor. Sir William Tyrrell, then senior clerk in the Foreign Office and private secretary to Sir Edward Grey, the British Foreign Minister, came with what his new friend Colonel House described as "almost boyish enthusiasm" to talk among other things about disarmament. Tyrrell was not exactly a boy. He was forty-seven and had been in the Foreign Office for a quarter of a century. He seemed on that visit even more suspicious than Daniels was of what he called the "armament trust." He told House and Wilson that that monstrous thing was "forcing all governments not only to pay excessive prices but was creating war scares." It was Tyrrell, some time before he came to America, who had suggested that House go to Germany on the same disarmament question. He urged that House have the American Ambassador, as the Colonel wrote in his diary, "whisper to the Kaiser that I was 'the power behind the throne' in the United States." House recorded no distaste for the term or Tyrrell's use of it. The Colonel presented the Englishman to Wilson and was pleased that they got on splendidly, talking of new British support for America's Mexican policy and of equality in tolls for British ships in the Panama Canal. Mainly, however, Tyrrell talked "of the necessity of curbing armaments and of the power of the financial world in our politics today." Wilson so met Tyrrell's enthusiasm with his own that the diplomat spoke to House of his delight with the candor of their conversation. It did not seem possible then

that the time would ever come when even such a Britisher as
Harold Laski could describe Tyrrell as "a clever fellow but
something of a Metternich, with his nose in all sorts of dark
corners sniffing for scents which are not there." In 1913 the air
he breathed seemed fresh and clean. Like one joining the "boyish" diplomat's crusade against armaments and financial power,
Wilson said, "It is the greatest fight we all have on today, and
every good citizen should enlist."

Daniels, of course, was already enlisted. He regarded as the
"most important proposal" in his first annual report a suggestion for an international conference called by the United States
to seek an agreement on a permanent policy of limiting the cost
and size of the navies of the world. That suggestion went
beyond a mere naval holiday such as Tyrrell and Winston
Churchill, then First Lord of the Admiralty, were proposing—and
proposing despite German jeers that it was a British plan to
postpone any naval competition by anybody with Britain. Daniels agreed that such a conference as he wanted be deferred, as
his friend Bryan hoped it could be, until Bryan completed the
negotiation of his peace treaties. Meantime Daniels called for
"a golden mean" in American naval construction. That was
just about half of what the General Board of the Navy had
recommended, Daniels said, "not because of opposition to the
progressive plans of that able body of naval statesmen, but because it is deemed wise to suggest a budget that will be within
the resources of our government." (The resources of our government then in terms of the Federal government's total annual
income amounted to less than three-fourths of one billion dollars.)

By December Daniels was completing the reorganization of
the Navy Department in a way which made him feel secure in
command. He had let the Navy as well as the Navy League
know that he felt it was time to "have done once and forever
with silly boasting and stripling, that we are able to lick any

nation on the face of the earth." (That word "stripling" as reported in the press was a queer one. The dictionary defines it as a half-grown boy and that may very well have been what Daniels meant.) There was something about the way he said it that Colonel Thompson and others did not like. The Colonel would have liked it less if he had known that on the occasion of a Navy League banquet Daniels had put the phrases "armor plate" and "Navy League dinner" side by side in his diary. Also, in his first report the Secretary seemed to have a positive addiction for words like "trust," "monopoly," "collusion." However, when Colonel Thompson came to pay his respects to the Secretary on one of his frequent visits to the Navy Department neither of them mentioned nickel-steel upon which Daniels had placed some special emphasis in his report. The Secretary of the Navy and the president of the Navy League were heartily polite to each other, though Daniels must have sometimes seemed a little puzzled when the Colonel with equal fervor opposed the income tax and urged a big Navy.

That December 1913, was the triumphant and untroubled month of the Wilson administration. It was in a very real sense the Christmas time of progressive reform. Before Franklin Roosevelt went off with his family to spend Christmas with his mother, he wrote Daniels that he was sending him a picture of the old U.S.S. *North Carolina* made about 1850. And Daniels wrote Franklin that he had come to Washington anticipating association with him; now he sent Roosevelt his "regard and appreciation of you as a man and as a fellow worker." It was a time of good will and good wishes. Wilson, who had sometimes seemed uneasy in his relationship with Bryan, was ready publicly to express himself about his Secretary of State's tact, capacity, mastery of principles and definiteness and dignity in policy. Not only was Bryan increasingly lining up the nations behind his peace treaties. Also, it was clear that Bryan, despite Colonel House, had helped secure the passage of the Federal

Reserve Act in a form which Wilson felt was an improvement over his own original thinking about it. Though more reforms were to follow, that act was a capstone of the Wilson reforms. Its signing on December 23, 1913, with three golden pens for souvenirs had about it the air of a celebration. "It was a happy group," said *The New York Times*, "but the happiness was most apparent on the face of the President's wife." Nobody then apparently had the least idea that she was dying. She had looked, my mother had thought at the inauguration, "like the embodiment of a golden pheasant"—golden not only in hair and costume but also in the light of her eyes. Her eyes were bright in December and her cheeks were so bright, too, that gossips suggested that the color must have come from a box.

That December, however, the Military Order of the Carabao, composed of militant veterans of the Philippine campaigns, began with a certain inebriate boldness an attack on the Wilsonians which was not soon to cease. At its annual banquet, Daniels noticed that his "anti-imperialistic speech found little response." Actually the military and naval officers, who had by force and arms helped overcome the reluctance of the Filipinos to being taken over by the United States, regarded Wilson's ideas about more self-government and "ultimate independence" for the Philippines as moralistic and brotherly nonsense.

They had a special treat for Secretaries Bryan and Daniels at their speaker's table. Not long before the dinner in one of his speeches Bryan had pictured metaphorical battleships bearing such names as *Friendship* and *Fellowship*. The Carabao gaily brought into the hall models of the U.S.S. *Friendship* and the U.S.S. *Fellowship* and also, as an addition to Bryan's fleet, the U.S.S. *Piffle*. Wilson, who read about the dinner in the newspapers, was not amused. And his letter to the Secretaries of War and Navy, ordering reprimand for the officers involved, indicated that perhaps one reason why Wilson was satirized as a schoolteacher was that he did not hesitate to rebuke men as schoolboys when they seemed to him to act that way. He could quiet the Carabao, but the Carabao banquet really served only as a rather reckless signal for the mounting jibes of those who not only did not like revolution but also were bored—or bothered—by reform.

The jibes did mount. Mrs. Wilson, who had been ridiculed as she arrived for her ideas about clothes budgets and inaugural balls, seemed to some of the same people continuously comic in her concern about the alley slums. *The Clubfellow* wondered for the benefit of its sophisticated readers whether Mrs. Wilson was trying to make herself "ex-officio a member of the engineer department of the District." By early 1914, she was able to do less and less about the work herself. Indeed, in the whole enterprise she was only joining, though joining with a stout, warm heart, Washington women who could and did regard many of *The Clubfellow's* readers as parvenus. Before and after Mrs. Wilson came, their leader was Mrs. Archibald Hopkins. She and her husband lived on Massachusetts Avenue, and had been Washingtonians since the Garfield administration. Few couples ever did so much for the health, the humanity and the beauty of Washington. Hopkins' father had been that almost legendary president of Williams College, Mark Hopkins. He was a member of the Metropolitan and Alibi Clubs at which *The Clubfellow* did not dare sneer. Good works did not seem comic to all nice people, even in those days.

But a small woman who was a President's wife and a Democratic President's wife at that could expect scorn. She got it and not only as fragile reformer but as first lady, too. In January 1914, *Town Topics* reported that "never were the glooms more ably represented than at the President's recent diplomatic reception; never was frugality more perfectly observed, and never were the arrangements for a White House entertainment more abominable." And it added in almost weird substantiation: "The diplomats did not linger long in the dining-room, or anywhere else for that matter. As soon as etiquette permitted they fled, Madame Bakhmeteff leading the rout. I saw her as she approached the private elevator, wonderfully bejeweled, her diadem of enormous aquamarines nodding with every step as she pulled the ambassador along and expressed palpable anger in fluent Russian." Mrs. Wilson almost disappears in history in obviously unequal contrast with Mamie Beale Bakhmeteff.

Even if she had not been already ill, Mrs. Wilson lacked both the gifts and the taste for the glamorous parties in which society editors reveled. Colonel Thompson was the man for that. In a little less pacific mood than he had been the preceding summer, he organized a fencing club at a party which brought together "as smart a company as Washington has seen gathered together under one roof in many a moon." It was noted that the Colonel in his middle sixties could "draw the rapier with the most expert fencers of the continent." It was also noted that at that party, "Lady Spring-Rice was present and danced a few numbers, as did her intime, Madame Dumba. A touch of officialdom was added in the charming persons of Mrs. Henry D. Breckinridge and Mrs. Franklin Roosevelt."

The report of the Colonel's party still symbolized peace in coupling as intimates the ladies of the British and Austrian Embassies. That seemed strange sooner than the coupling of Mrs. Breckinridge and Mrs. Roosevelt. They seemed admirably joined then. FDR had written not long before of the energetic fun he and his opposite number in the War Department, Assistant Secretary Breckinridge, had had when they went together to see the fleet off on a cruise to the Mediterranean: "We climbed, and vaulted, and lifted, and ran, and in every instance there was a tie. He is a bit taller than I am and weighs less. I am three years older, but there we were, in a perfectly even contest every time." Breckinridge was to become a member of the Olympic fencing team in which Colonel Thompson was so much interested. He was to be one of the Colonel's successors as president of the Navy League. The contest was not so even, however, nor were they such admiring friends when, in 1936, Breckinridge as a "constitutional Democrat" set himself up as a candidate against Roosevelt's renomination as President of the United States.

April 1914, was a dramatic and disturbing month for Daniels. It was for Roosevelt a month of both disappointment and good luck. The younger man was off on an inspection trip to the West Coast when the increasingly critical Mexican situation exploded and the peaceful Daniels dispatched the ships and ordered the marines ashore to occupy Vera Cruz. "It is certainly a curious coincidence," Roosevelt wrote almost plaintively on a later, less serious such occasion, "that as soon as I go away we seem to land marines somewhere." He headed east talking steadily. "The war spirit is sweeping the West like wildfire," he told reporters on the way home. "War and we're ready," was his interpretation of the crisis, but when he reached Washington his excitement or at least his interviews ended. Daniels saw to that. Arbitration, not war, ensued.

Also in April—and Franklin was very quiet about that at the time; he was out of town—Daniels announced his wine mess order, which was to have louder reverberations in the Navy than the landing at Vera Cruz. Admiral Fiske not only, as usual, expostulated in person, also he wrote in his diary that "officers think it unwise, and that the effect will be to influence officers to smuggle whiskey and cocaine on board, and to take meals ashore, where they can drink whiskey—instead of wine and beer on board."

No bottle ever found a friend in Daniels. He acted, however, on the basis of a report by the Surgeon-General of the Navy on the bad effects of drink in the fleet particularly among young officers. There was a special situation to deal with in a peacetime Navy in which there was much idleness between four-hour tours of duty. Sometimes at sea the idleness was filled with quiet and sometimes chronic drinking. Even Admiral William S. Sims who was later to be Daniels' bitter enemy said once that it "was the best thing that ever happened to the Navy." He recalled cases of chronic alcoholism incident to unoccupied leisure. Undoubtedly, Daniels' sense of democracy was also offended by the fact that alcoholic beverages had long been denied in the same places to enlisted personnel. He expected some of the indignation he aroused. The Democratic *New York World* said sharply that the order is "not reformatory. It is revolutionary. It is a shameful reflection upon a noble profession. We send our officers to sea chaperoned like schoolgirls." In general, however, the indignant did their lambasting by lampoon. Mr. Dooley, who felt that all Secretaries of the Navy were "seasick ex-officio," wrote a whole column on Daniels and his dry order. Several satirists turned to poetry in parodies of *Pinafore*. One forgotten epigrammatist put the whole Josephus Daniels business together from the "left and right" innovation to the wine mess order in one line when he said, "At one swoop larboard, starboard, and sideboard have been jettisoned."

My father took the ridicule more easily than I did. When Arthur Brisbane, in what seemed to me the final straw, wrote an editorial for the Hearst papers sneering at Father for forbidding sailors to have themselves tattooed, I wrote him that Father had done no such thing. Mr. Brisbane not only apologized. The next time he came to Washington he invited both Father and me to lunch. The incident remains my greatest triumph in public relations. Also, the meal was ordered by Brisbane in an imperial manner calculated to impress the whole dining room and one which certainly impressed me. The Brisbane correction was made to seem like a citation, but the glittering impression he made was of his magnanimity, not his mistake.

With sardonic satisfaction, Howe reported to Roosevelt on the wine mess situation. "You will doubtless be given an opportunity to sustain this program, certainly by private argument with the officers you meet on the Coast and possibly at some formal occasion. I know how greatly you regret not being here at the time to share in some of the glory. As it is, of course, I can tell the newspapermen nothing except that you are away and naturally know nothing about it." Also the order gave Howe, who was always listening for one, an opportunity to spread among the disgruntled the impression that the real he-man in the Navy, who understood the ancient association of grog and glory among hairy-chested seadogs, was FDR. (Oddly enough as President when Roosevelt expansively remembered that Daniels had said he wanted him to be Acting Secretary "even if I have only stepped out to the washroom," he told Hassett that it was he, not Daniels, who was responsible for the wine mess order. FDR told him: "The Chief took the blame, but he didn't formulate the order at all. I did it." Not even Howe suspected that at the time and Roosevelt certainly kept it a secret. Actually FDR had nothing to do with it.)

The wine mess order completed a caricature of Daniels with which Roosevelt did not interfere. He became, indeed, so fond of Daniels jokes and imitations that his friend, Secretary Franklin K. Lane, who did not always agree with Daniels, rebuked him. As President Roosevelt told Hassett, Lane said, "You should be ashamed of yourself. Mr. Daniels is your superior and you should show him loyalty or you should resign your office." Roosevelt remembered the lecture later if he did not profit by it then. Other critics of Daniels found him amusing. Also, though FDR was actually growing fond of his chief, he understood the feeling of some officers, not always humorously expressed, that Daniels had it in for the officers and was trying to curry favor with the bluejackets.

This feeling erupted violently when Daniels' educational

program for sailors was announced. Schools at sea, indeed! It was in fact a revolutionary procedure. Daniels' foresight in an increasingly technical Navy was that a revolution was required. The much romanticized old-time sailor—in his place which was the forecastle only—was often illiterate and sometimes disreputable at sea and ashore. Daniels envisaged the educational program for both the Navy and the men. There was a disciplinary advantage in using the men's spare time in training which would let them leave the Navy with knowledge and skills. The opportunity at training would attract better men and the Secretary understood apparently almost alone that Navy enlisted personnel would more and more have to be a group of trained technicians using intricate equipment and requiring education and knowledge. Elmer Ambrose Sperry, the inventor, was in process of electrifying the Navy. His gyroscopic compasses had recently been introduced. His gyroscopic stabilizers for ships appeared in 1913. Tying knots was no longer enough for a sailor to learn. In the face of such change Daniels' educational program was not only essential then; it was also the precursor of the elaborate training courses which became so important a part of the work of the armed services in World War II.

Some felt that the most shocking thing Daniels did was opening the Naval Academy at Annapolis to enlisted men. Destructive as that was said to be to class distinctions which were essential to Navy discipline, however, one officer wrote an anonymous letter to the papers minimizing its effect: There was little reason to worry because very few in the forecastles could pass the examinations. It did not turn out that way. Forty years after Daniels secured a first few appointments for men from the ranks, 160 appointments for enlisted men were available each year. Furthermore a preparatory school to help them pass the examinations had been established at Bainbridge, Maryland, with a student body of seven hundred. Many subsequently distinguished officers went to the Academy that way, and there seemed no blot on their escutcheons because they got their places by competition rather than through Congressmen. The Secretary was made to seem by old-line officers and their civilian sympathizers to be almost brusquely careless of service distinctions. When he found there was not enough money to build two barracks for marines in Philadelphia he ordered one built to be occupied, under the same roof, by officers and men. He even modified the time-honored custom of sailors washing their own clothes by ordering laundries installed on new battleships. He made no secret of his lack of awe for fuss and feathers, ceremony and gold braid. He was delighted when later he could write in his diary: "Signed order ending cocked hat and full dress. Long-tailed coat not tabooed yet, but—"

Young Roosevelt was ceremonial by nature. His favorite naval joke, directed at all politicians but himself, was based upon landsmen's lapses in connection with naval customs. He was accustomed to certain ceremonials among his neighbors which seemed a little silly to some plain and impudent Americans. Late in May 1914, he came back to Washington from a wedding at one of the great estates near Hyde Park at which "the picturesque custom" was continued of "having all the little village maidens, in their Sunday best and squeaky shoes" present as a sort of baronial background for the gentry. A society reporter noticed that he "came with his sensible little wife, who is a Roosevelt by birth." Eleanor was six months pregnant at the time. Franklin went back to Washington alone —to the empty house on N Street. He arrived safely, he wrote Eleanor, and got Albert, his chauffeur and handyman, to telephone "Miss Mercer who later came and cleaned up."

Another summer was just beginning in Washington but it advanced with increasing heat, steadily, slowly, and so far as the Navy was concerned, almost as dully as the summer before. Franklin made arrangements for the Navy's transport homeward of the body of a Venezuelan Ambassador. A House committee wanted the Navy's proof that Admiral Peary not Dr. Cook discovered the North Pole. June was hot and peaceful and apparently Roosevelt like the rest of the world paid scant attention to the assassination late that month of an archduke in Bosnia. In July, Wilson sent to the Senate twenty more of the Bryan peace treaties. In the end they were to be signed by every important nation except Germany and Japan. The world seemed on the way toward that "age of settled peace and good will" which the President had prophesied.

But on July 23, Mrs. Wilson's condition was such that the President's Navy physician, Cary Grayson, moved to the White House to occupy a room next to hers. She had not been well for months but on March 1, she slipped and fell in her room. It was thought to have been an accident; actually it was the beginning of the final phase of her illness. She was able to take her part showing, one newspaper account said, little sign of her "recent illness" at the quiet marriage of her daughter Eleanor to Secretary McAdoo on May 7. Her last public appearance was when she went to hear her husband address Congress on the acute Mexican situation on April 20.

Dr. Grayson was an old hand in the White House. He was only thirty-four at the time but he had already served as friend and physician to both Presidents Roosevelt and Taft. He was a charming and handsome Virginian whose name had been romantically coupled with that of every young lady of the White House, notably that of Helen Taft, but as was noted when the Wilsons arrived, he was "due for service in the fleet" and "his influence died with the late administration."

It was about that time that the peaceful Mr. Bryan acquired some old sabers. Not everything was peaceful. Roosevelt had got back to town from Campobello in July just in time that time not to miss handling some of the details in connection with the dispatch of marines to the naval base at Guantánamo, Cuba, where they would be available in connection with "an interesting situation in Haiti and Santo Domingo." That was the occasion on which he based one of his favorite anecdotes about the ignorance of Bryan, who with Daniels made the decision in the matter, of the difference between a battleship and a gunboat. Roosevelt enjoyed the business at the time though he was not as happy as Bryan or Wilson or Daniels about the apparent solution of the Mexican problem.

"We drift from day to day," he wrote Eleanor. "The time has come for a concrete program."

His own program seemed less than concrete. He spoke of "next year *if* I am still Assistant Secretary." On Saturday, July 19, he played forty-five holes of golf and by the middle of the next week he was off again to Campobello. He attended the ceremonial opening of the Cape Cod Canal on July 29, and was apparently surprised that Livy Davis could not go with him because of the effect the war news was having on the stock market. The news had caused an immediate crisis in American financial circles. Two days later, on the motion of J. P. Morgan, the Stock Exchange was closed.

On that same last day of July Franklin went at the Secretary's direction to the German-settled town of Reading, Pennsylvania, on an Assistant Secretary's typical task: to defend the authenticity of an anchor from the battleship *Maine,* the sinking of which in Havana Harbor in 1898 pulled the nation together and to war as the attack at Pearl Harbor was to do forty years later. The *Maine* was still the emblem of patriotism and Daniels had let a Congressman, up for renomination and re-election, have an anchor, which had been dredged up, as a memento for Reading, the principal city of his district. That seemed good patriotism which was good politics. His opponent for the nomination, however, charged that the anchor was a "fraud" and had never been a part of the *Maine.* Thus not only the authenticity of the anchor but the honor of the Navy

Department was at stake. FDR wrote a speech and took the train. He traced the record of the anchor from its removal from the Cuban mud to its arrival in Norfolk, to the Navy Yard in Washington and on to Reading. Then he talked about the superiority of the government in Washington to the kind of government provided in such state capitals as Harrisburg and Albany. He did not say a word about the war news from Europe, which was suddenly filling the American papers. The occasion was a great success, he wrote Eleanor, "fine parade, lots of bands—ending with an impassioned oration by hubby to 5,000 people in the park!" The anchor was there to stay in the company of monuments to Columbus, McKinley, Reading's Volunteer Fire Department, the Ringgold Light Artillery, and a deceased local brewer. Roosevelt had accomplished his mission. On the train back from Reading, however, he wrote Eleanor also about the war and Daniels.

"A complete smash up is inevitable," he said, "and there are a great many problems for us to consider. Mr. D. totally fails to grasp the situation and I am to see the President Monday a.m. to go over our own situation."

It is not clear whether "our own situation" meant the Navy and the war, or Roosevelt's own political plans, specifically his candidacy for the Democratic nomination for the United States Senate. Apparently he did not see Wilson on Monday about any situation. (Incidentally FDR is not mentioned in the volume of the official Wilson biography dealing with the months from the inauguration to the European war.)

Though Wilson seemed not to have understood it or to have admitted it to himself until the very last, Mrs. Wilson was dying in the White House. As late as Sunday, August 2, he believed that Mrs. Wilson was "struggling through the deep waters of nervous prostration." Apparently he did not see—or would not see—the simple physical facts. Dr. Grayson said afterward, that with Bright's disease and tuberculosis of the kidneys, her case was hopeless from the beginning. In those early August days Wilson was only reluctantly absent from her bedside, even for the Cabinet meeting which discussed the European crisis. It was by her bedside that he wrote out in shorthand notes the message tendering his good offices as President of the United States, if they should be desired, "in the interest of European peace"—a mesaage which Bryan had urged and House opposed. It was not a time when he would go over "our situation" with an Assistant Secretary.

That was a strange time for Mr. Bryan to have his old sabers melted down. The Secretary of State, however, was never more concerned for peace than he was then. Some of the most important of the treaties he negotiated were signed in his shabby office by the Ambassadors of Great Britain, France, Spain and China after the hope of averting the war had passed. The signing was regarded as an important occasion, nevertheless. Bryan had Mrs. Bryan sit at the end of his desk. Behind him stood practically all his colleagues of the Cabinet. The militant Secretary of War Garrison stood almost directly behind him. Daniels, looking very young and serious, was at the other end of the line.

Bryan made much ceremony over such signings. The representatives of more than thirty nations put their signatures to his plan. And to each of them he gave one of the nickel-steel paperweights he had had made from the sabers. They were beautifully designed. A sense of movement was given in the keen blades of the miniature plowshares into which the sword metal had been molded. On the blades a verse from Isaiah was engraved: "They shall beat their swords into plowshares." Above, on the beams were phrases from Bryan: "Nothing is final between friends" and "Diplomacy is the art of keeping cool." They went to many countries. Someone many years later gave one to Harry Truman which he kept on his desk at the White House during the cold war with Russia.

Bryan gave a few to old friends at home. The one he gave to Josephus Daniels, which now belongs to me, bears the date, August 13, 1914. That was the same day Franklin Roosevelt announced his candidacy for the Democratic nomination for the United States Senate.

The symbols of the anchor and the plowshares were not soon to be forgotten. Bryan's plowshare was already being sneered at loudly by gentlemen like Colonel Thompson who understood the beauty of a saber blade and the economics of nickel-steel. Theodore Roosevelt, back from Brazil with a fever, knew that "no country would observe the treaty should its interests be involved." Franklin Roosevelt shared their views about the paperweights. But to Eleanor Roosevelt waiting for her baby on Campobello Island the plowshares "were not in the least ridiculous." She had an instinctive belief in Bryan's stand on peace, as did millions of other Americans. Only long afterward did pacifism become anathema and almost subversive-seeming in America. It was then an age of faith and hope for a decent world achieved through good and Christian feeling among men and nations. That did not seem silly.

Ellen Wilson never knew the peace was broken. She also had faith in Bryan, to whom she had turned in the good, last peace for help in her work in the alley slums. It was of them she was thinking in her last days. She expressed the hope that she could know before her death that Congress had passed the bill providing better housing conditions for the alley dwellers. The Senate acted quickly and she was told, before she died late in the afternoon of August 6, 1914, that the House would take similar action. (The bill prohibited the use of alley dwellings after 1918. No serious attempt was made to enforce the law in a Washington then crowding with big government for big war, and a District Court decision finally ruled the act unconstitutional.) Even on that last day Wilson found time to send a suggestion to Daniels and to Garrison regarding strict neutrality among officers of the military and naval services. On the next day he wrote to a friend: "God has stricken me almost beyond what I can bear." Like the war, indeed very like the war, her death seemed "incredible catastrophe." On the day of her funeral he went to the Executive offices for a short time to confer with a very gentle and regretful Bryan about matters which could not wait. Young Franklin Roosevelt, who had learned that Mrs. Wilson was dying on Wednesday, probably from a very grim Daniels who was losing not only a first lady but also a fast friend, feared that Wilson would have a breakdown. He did not know, he wrote Eleanor, whether Assistant Secretaries would be expected to go to the funeral or not. They were not expected. And only the family went South for the burial, but they remembered the train and the people. There was, a Georgia newspaperman on the funeral train wrote, no "token of the train's approach save the tolling of the bell, yet even sweeping through the unpeopled hills and valleys of north Georgia, those on the train saw old men with hats off in front of their cabin doors."

Perhaps her death was a better symbol of the year which ran to war than either the anchor or the plowshare. She lived long enough to know that the legislation about the alley slums would pass. She died carefully protected from knowledge of the war. Long afterward when Eleanor Roosevelt (who was herself to ride a funeral train through Georgia seeing the people, people, people before their doors) came as a President's wife to Washington, the alley slums were still there, more crowded and more filthy still. Ellen Wilson was a little woman in life. She has a small place in history. But somehow in her dying, reform confronted death in a big dark room late on an August afternoon.

SEVEN

The Crazy War

ROOSEVELT HAD SEEMED ALTOGETHER TOO CASUAL ONE DAY IN midsummer 1914 when he had come into the Secretary's office for one of the late afternoon talks both he and Daniels liked very much. Franklin always had the gossip of the clubs and Daniels kept in close touch with the talk in Congressional cloakrooms. That afternoon the Secretary realized quickly that his Assistant had something very special on his mind. There was time for talk. The summer somnolence was still on the Navy Department. Roosevelt stretched his long legs out on the polished floor before him. He was never more beautiful than he was that summer—or, Daniels realized, more restless. Franklin did not mention it, but he had been Assistant Secretary then longer than Theodore Roosevelt had been when he left the post as an already-used steppingstone. Almost incidentally Franklin told Daniels that "they" wanted him to run as an anti-Tammany man for the Democratic nomination for the Senate in New York. And what did Mr. Daniels think?

Daniels was not surprised. He had been noticing the trial balloons in the New York papers, some of which he suspected had been launched from Howe's office in the Navy Department. His advice was ready. "Don't yield to temptation. I have a hunch that you can't win in the primary, and even if you do the indications are that the Republicans will carry the state."

As editor and politician, my father then had been evaluating such matters for thirty years. He did not want to see Franklin hurt and he seemed almost pathetically young and innocent that afternoon. It was odd that it was going to be such a short time before Daniels appeared antiquated and innocent to Roosevelt.

Franklin went undecided to Campobello, where Eleanor was waiting for the baby. Two of his English friends, Martin Archer-Shee (who had married a Dutchess County girl) and his younger brother sailed with him in the *Half Moon* on the high tides and swift currents of the Bay of Fundy that summer. There was some wind and fog but bright weather, too. Then, even on Campobello, the neglected news about the assassination of an archduke in Bosnia swelled like a Fundy tide into the inescapable news of war. The Archer-Shees left to join their regiments, the younger brother to die in action a month later. Eleanor wrote later that a wire recalled Franklin to the Navy Department on July 29. Back from holiday, he stopped in Washington for an afternoon and a day between the ceremonial opening of the Cape Cod Canal and his defense of the anchor in Reading. He wrote Eleanor of his dismay at the innocence he found.

"These dear people like W.J.B. and J.D.," he wrote, "have as much conception of what a general European war means as Elliott has of higher mathematics." Elliott was a frail four years old. He was often sick. They were to be worrying about his fever at Christmas that year. He was so bowlegged that he had to wear braces. Also, the summer before at Campobello he got too close to a bonfire and burned his little hands very badly. He was an adequate figure for a metaphor about innocence.

(Colonel House a little later after a talk with Bryan wrote in his diary, "He talked as innocently as my little grandchild, Jane Tucker. He spoke with great feeling and I fear he may give trouble. . . .")

"To my astonishment," Franklin continued in his letter to Eleanor, "on reaching the Department nobody seemed the least bit excited about the European crisis—Mr. Daniels feeling chiefly very sad that his faith in human nature and civilization and similar idealistic nonsense was receiving such a rude shock."

Daniels was indeed shocked. So was Bryan, who called his assistant secretaries back from vacation and kept them at hand. By the bedside of Mrs. Wilson, the President regarded the situation beyond it as incredible.

"So I started in alone," Franklin went on, "to get things ready and prepare plans for what *ought* to be done by the Navy end of things."

Though that seems always to have been the general impression he gave Eleanor and others on such occasions, he did not start in completely alone. Daniels assigned him to work on a board dealing with problems of neutrality, including Wilson's direction that all officers, whether active or retired, refrain from public comments of any kind upon the world war. That, of course, included him. Roosevelt worked in arranging for the swift departure of the *Tennessee* to the war zone to aid stranded American nationals in Europe—an operation at which he had scoffed when Daniels first announced it: "tourists (female etc.) couldn't sleep in hammocks." Roosevelt's scoffing did not delay Daniels' dispatch of the battleship. It was suggested, Roosevelt wrote, that he go to the war zone when the *Tennessee* sailed with over $5,000,000 in gold aboard, shipped by American banking houses for the relief of their patrons abroad. He declined in favor of his equally militant friend Assistant Secretary of War Breckinridge. Even in "the greatest war in history," as he already called it, Roosevelt had other matters on his mind. Undoubtedly, however, those first two weeks in August 1914, were among the most melodramatic of his life.

August 5 (he wrote Eleanor): "Alive and well and keen about

everything. I am running the real work, although Josephus is here. He is bewildered by it all, very sweet but very sad!"

August 7 (he reported to Eleanor again): "Gee! But these are strenuous days! I'm going home to bed after three nights at the various Departments up till nearly 3 a.m. . . . Most of the reports of foreign cruisers off the coast have really been of *my* destroyers."

And his admiring clerk, a young man named Charles H. McCarthy, wrote the absent Louis Howe, on August 8: "The Boss has been the whole cheese in this European business and is going along great."

Five days later, however, Franklin suddenly announced for the Senate. And that same week he left for Campobello again to be there until September 2, and away from Washington until September 7. The baby came a little early; the labor was a little long. The elaborate preparations they had made for the delivery at that remote resort did not quite work out. Dr. Albert Ely, described in the *Personal Letters* as "the Roosevelts' family physician from New York" but actually one of the leading gynecologists of the country, failed to arrive. Eleanor was delivered by Dr. E. H. Bennett of the little town of Lubec, across the Narrows, whose obstetrical practice had been limited to the wives of fishermen and the women workers in the sardine canneries.

"Why, she is just like one of us," he said with a little surprise when he was done.

Roosevelt sailed across the Narrows and sent a wire to the Secretary: "Future admiral arrived last night." Daniels replied recognizing two important matters at once: "Congratulations to the young Senator and his mother." He did not call Roosevelt back. He did ask him if he had ever written a report on an inspection Franklin had made of the New Orleans Navy Yard as they were planning to reopen it. They could not find any papers about it in his office. Roosevelt hastily sent one from

Campobello and with it his hope that the Secretary might "get off even for a few days." No Acting Secretary was to be available, however. Roosevelt was going to be very busy indeed, and away from the Department. He had just returned to Washington when Tammany announced its candidate against him. He was James W. Gerard, a Tammany man but also Wilson's Ambassador to Germany. Herbert Hoover, who began his European relief activities that fall, said later that he had expected to find Gerard "a typical Tammany lawyer, whose appointment had been imposed upon an unwilling President by a crooked political machine." Hoover was surprised: "Instead of a callous ogre I found a man of polished attainments, of fine intellectual insight, helpful, courageous, who at once inspired confidence in his fine integrity." Something of the same impression was getting into newspaper headlines at home. Franklin was as surprised by the Gerard candidacy as Hoover had been by Gerard's character.

"I am not yet willing to believe," Franklin commented in a rude shock of his own, "that [Boss Murphy] can drag an Ambassador away from important duties to make him a respectable figurehead for a bad ticket."

He was not willing to leave such a shocking possibility to chance, however. Secretary Bryan might be, as Franklin had written Eleanor a few days before, infantile in a world of crisis, but Franklin hurried to him in this Roosevelt crisis. Roosevelt had been attentive to the Secretary of State. He and Eleanor had given a dinner party for the Bryans that year. To Bryan, he always talked Bryan's language. Indeed, as late as 1923, he was writing to Bryan about the "reactionary forces" in the party and about "hopeful idiots who think the Democratic platform will advocate a repeal of the 18th Amendment." Bryan liked the young man very much in 1914 and later. Also, in 1914, he had little more affection than Roosevelt for Tammany Hall.

They had fought the same forces and the same men. Glad to help the young candidate, W.J.B. sent a note to the President:

Asst. Sec. Roosevelt is as you know a candidate & has, as I understand, the endorsement of Secs. McAdoo & Redfield. I have also felt that Roosevelt would be the best man. Gerard could not, of course, leave Berlin in the near future. What do you wish said to Gerard? He will do as you wish.

Wilson did not wish to say anything to Gerard. Two weeks before, twenty regular Democratic New York Congressmen had protested to him that persons professing to be spokesmen for the administration were picturing them as "crooks and grafters and political buccaneers." The President made it clear that no such spokesman spoke for him. Tammany men regarded Roosevelt as one of those making such charges. He was to them, as one who professed to be their spokesman said, "renegade, meddler and bootlicker." He had been very successful in getting postmasterships and other jobs for his anti-Tammany friends. His correspondence about postmasterships at the time filled thirteen large filing cases. The administration, however, needed the votes of Democratic Congressmen if it was to enact the party's legislative program. Wilson had learned that he could depend on the regulars.

"They will at least stand by the party and the administration," he said about that time. "I can rely upon them better than I can on some of my own crowd."

Years later that Presidential pronouncement seemed less like a slap-down than a civics lesson to FDR. He spoke of it as such when he was talking persuasively to runaway liberals in California in 1935.

"Years ago," he said then, "President Wilson told me a story. He said that the greatest problem that the head of a progressive democracy had to face was not the criticism of reactionaries or the attacks of those who would set up some other form of government, but rather to reconcile and unite progressive liberals themselves."

Certainly in politics, in 1914, Franklin started in very much alone. He ended very much alone, too. He spent, his son Elliott as the editor of his *Personal Letters* reported, "six weeks campaigning." Though he thought he had had a successful trip, the returns showed, his son said, that he received "less than half of the total votes." Actually he got less than a fourth of the total vote and Gerard, who never came home from his job in Germany, beat him 210,765 to 76,888. (An inconsequential candidate named McDonough got 23,977 votes.) Roosevelt carried only twenty-two of the sixty-one counties of the state. Tammany not only won four to one in its metropolitan stronghold but two to one in Roosevelt's upstate country, too. The result, says Dr. Freidel, was "as thorough a chastisement . . . as Murphy could have wished."

Less objective observers in New York at the time, however, were not merely content with his defeat for the Senate nomination. One contemptuous organization Democrat in New York wrote demanding, "What naval duties has the Ass. Secretary of the Navy ever performed? Is there any naval necessity for the existence of such an Ass. in the Navy Department? If he is kept to do the dirtiest political work of the Administration, why is he allowed to deprive some good naval officer of the position . . . ?"

Eleanor Roosevelt remembered that time later: "I do not think my husband ever had any idea that he was going to win out and I have often heard him say that he did not think himself suited to serve in the United States Senate; and, therefore, it was probably a great relief to find himself back at his desk in the Navy Department."

"It hurt Roosevelt," said Daniels who was there when Franklin came quietly back to Washington and the empty house on N Street. The war was two months old but, though he had immediately recognized it as the greatest war in history, he had been able to give it his undivided attention for less than two weeks. He walked, very tall with his head high, down Connecticut Avenue by the Metropolitan Club to the Navy Department. It was not long before he could write a friend, who should have known better and perhaps did, that the campaign was worth while "as I carried a majority of the counties of the State and was beaten only through the solid lineup of New York City." He was able "cheerily" to say, "Never mind: we paved the way." The way then, however, was not nearly so clear as it seemed afterward.

Other people were also slowly coming back to Washington. Admiral Fiske had left Washington for his regular summer month at Newport at the end of July when Franklin, passing through, had been astonished at the lack of excitement in the Department. The Admiral sent back some recommendations by mail from Newport, but he did not return to the Navy Department where his regular duties were until a month later. Then, back from the shore, he was shocked, too. He expected to find, he said, "an atmosphere of tension and excitement. I found perfect calm. No one seemed to think that anything in particular had happened or was going to happen. . . . Some of the higher officers, however, were distinctly uneasy." Admiral Fiske was even more uneasy a few days later when he recorded in his diary that Daniels, "made an out & out peace speech! Gosh. This foreshadows his attitude. . . ." There were only four men, Fiske said, who "came out plainly before the public and advocated preparedness" for war. They were Theodore Roosevelt, Representative Gardner, General Leonard Wood and "my humble self."

There was also the only momentarily subdued FDR. Within two weeks he was engaged in a greater campaign, and before the more sympathetic electorate of his friends in Washington. There he was only one of many who could think of the war in

Europe as almost a personal matter in terms of "Coz. Susie and Henry and Aunt Jennie and Laura and Sara" who at the war's beginning had been caught in the war zone, or of his elderly half brother, Rosy, who had been at sea with a new bride on the German liner, *Kronprinzessin Cecilie*. Daniels still stubbornly hoped America could be, as Mr. Jefferson had described it, "kindly separated by nature and a wide ocean" from European catastrophe. Also, he knew the meaning of cotton, cut off from world markets, selling for five cents. That ocean, however, never seemed to him "the pond" which some of Roosevelt's friends had called it and made it. Livy Davis had made nine trips to Europe before entering Harvard. Franklin had made twenty crossings before he became Assistant Secretary. The Atlantic had seemed suddenly very wide when many of their friends had wanted desperately and quickly to get back home to America that August.

The residents of the Lafayette Square neighborhood seemed to be caught in Europe almost in a body. Henry Adams on the Avenue du Trocadéro rather liked the experience at first: "to me the crumbling of worlds is always fun." By the time he got to England, however, he described his escape as one that "verged on hell, and no slouch of a bad one." His Washington neighbors, the Willie Eustises, who had been living on an estate in England since soon after Wilson's inauguration, realized reluctantly that they would have to come back to Washington even if they had been "bored to extinction" there. Willie helped mightily with the "American refugees" who were clamoring for ship space in the lobby of the United States Embassy in London. So did Franklin's other friend, Congressman Gussie Gardner. Gardner's in-laws, Senator and Mrs. Lodge, were abroad, too, and not "strictly happy," as Adams put it. The war even persuaded their daughter-in-law, Bay Lodge's widow, to come home to America, but she managed to bring "some stunning frocks." The report of her return also mentioned that the health of her mother, Mrs. McCawley, was not good—"she goes out scarcely at all and receives rarely"—but that Colonel McCawley was "seen everywhere and is as gay as in the days of his bachelorhood." It was already possible to perceive change, however. When Adams got back to his philosopher's gossip station on Lafayette Square, he wrote: "The social tide seems violently set one way, and we are all allies. Even those who at first talked German have shut up." Neutrality was unfashionable long before it was unpopular.

I can remember that the majority opinion in the world of Washington juveniles was largely pro-Ally, too. I recall taking particular pleasure in the act of a French aviator who flew his plane straight into the belly of a zeppelin. Furthermore, if my father seemed pacifistic to Admiral Fiske, his place at Single Oak took on early the aspect of a small training camp. General Wood, of course, was ahead of my brother Frank and me. He started his civilian training camps in 1913, a year before there was any European War. We were not far behind. We slept in the summer in a Marine Corps tent Father had bought for us. And we had, as part-time instructors, Sergeant Robert Finucane and Corporal Milton Ober, who had been on duty as orderlies in the office of the Secretary of the Navy for twenty years. No go-to-sea order applied to them; they had been on duty in Washington longer than Colonel McCawley. Finucane was tall and silent. Ober was round and voluble. Both recalled Secretaries as far back as Cleveland's time. Finucane said little about them. But Ober was both a gossip and a bugler. He claimed to have had the duty of rubbing the smell of whisky on the lip of the glass when Assistant Secretary Theodore Roosevelt's doctor wanted him to get a milk shake while believing it was a milk toddy. I doubted then and afterward that TR could be so easily fooled. From him by our tent and under our flag at Single Oak we learned not only the foibles of our father's predecessors but how to blow the bugle in such a way that if we did not make the neighborhood melodious we were at least prepared to spread alarums among the lethargic.

Congressman Gardner needed no bugle. He came home marching. He was no longer "scared blue" about his re-election that fall as he had seemed to Henry Adams in 1912. He had a strong natural feeling, however, shared by his father-in-law, by Theodore Roosevelt, Leonard Wood, Admiral Fiske and others that this was no time to trust the Democrats, particularly a Democratic administration which contained such outspoken peace men as Bryan and Daniels. There was no question about Gardner's patriotism or his Republicanism; he regarded them as synonymous. Both undoubtedly contributed to his blasts at the Navy which began two weeks before the Congressional elections. Daniels and Roosevelt spoke for Democrats in that campaign. But in Washington, Roosevelt's ideas, ambitions and old friendships put him in the company of some of those whose aggressive patriotism often seemed like aggressive partisanship or vice versa. Some of those who were most militant with regard to the war in Europe had also been most antagonistic to reform in the United States. Wilson noticed that. Early in the war he mentioned it to Daniels.

"Every reform we have won will be lost if we go into this war," he said. "We have been making a fight on special privilege. We have got new tariff and currency and trust legislation. We don't know yet how they will work. They are not thoroughly set."

That did not seem so apparent to Franklin then. Long afterward I remember hearing him say in North Carolina, just a year before another European war began, that it was "one of our great national tragedies that just when Woodrow Wilson was beginning to accomplish definite improvements in the living standards of America, the World War not only interrupted his course, but laid the foundations for twelve years of retrogression." He was not directly concerned with those domestic reforms in the fall of 1914. Also, he was lonely. Not even the servants were there when he first came home after the disastrous primary. He went out much. He spent an evening with John George Milburn, partner in the firm of Morgan lawyers, Carter, Ledyard & Milburn, where he had worked as a clerk just a few years before. He went to "a most interesting dinner" with a group of Uncle Ted's friends which included General Wood. The group almost constituted belligerency unlimited.

Walter Millis, who wrote *Road to War* in 1935 when many Americans including FDR insisted they did not want to take that road again, said that General Wood "had devoted himself, long before the outbreak of the European War, to the upbuilding of an American militarism." Wood had begun as a medical officer, served as the Colonel of TR's Rough Riders in Cuba, and in 1901 had been jumped from captain in the medical corps to brigadier general in the regular Army by McKinley, whose family physician he had been. TR made him a major general two years later. He had been appointed Chief of Staff by Taft. When Franklin dined with him, the General was on duty at Governor's Island in the harbor of New York and was in Washington working to get himself sent to Europe as an "observer" so that he could come back and make speeches about the war.

Apparently Franklin was not helpful in Wood's hope to go to France at that time. He was very helpful, however, in Gussie Gardner's efforts, which began in the Congressional election campaign, to convince the country that the armed services in general and the Navy in particular were suffering from serious deficiencies. On October 16—about the same time as Franklin's dinner with General Wood—Representative Gardner rose in the House and began an angry attack on the current condition of the Army and Navy. (He was to be joined soon by Senator Lodge, who told TR that he did not let himself go about Daniels, "as I would like to do" because that "would have been called partisan and I think might have lowered its effect." The Senator, however, cited startling instances of supposed incompetency, none of which went back of the Wilson administration.)

Though Gardner was twenty years older, he and Franklin had long-standing ties. Both were Harvard men; also a Groton man could regard as almost equal a graduate of St. Paul's, and vice versa. Not only had Gardner married Constance, daughter of Senator Lodge at whose house the young Roosevelts were made to feel so much at home. Also, he had paid flattering attentions to Franklin soon after the latter arrived in Washington. He shared his secretary's opinion, Gardner wrote Roosevelt after the younger man had been Assistant Secretary only two months, that "you are the promptest and most efficient Assistant Secretary in any Department with whom we have dealt in our eleven years of service here."

They got along splendidly. Both were lawyers, though as Gardner said, he "never practiced, devoting himself to the management of his estate." Both were gentlemen in politics. Both were country gentlemen, too, with landed inclinations. Gardner was a cattle breeder and polo enthusiast. He had been born in Boston but his home and political address was Hamilton, in Essex County, seat of the famous Myopia Club. His estate was in Pride's Crossing. Also, as a natural member of the hard-riding Northern colony he had a place at Aiken, South Carolina, which after his death was purchased by Winthrop Rutherfurd.

Gardner did not begin his political career until after he married Lodge's daughter, following service in the Spanish War. Then he served one term in the Massachusetts State Senate and moved on to Congress to fill the vacancy caused when William H. Moody became TR's first choice as Secretary of the Navy. Henry Adams reported after Gardner ran for Congress that "Hay tells me that Gussy's seat is the most expensive ever bought in the House." Colonel Archie Butt, who was a White House aide under both the Roosevelts and the Tafts, thought that the Lodges were more responsible than anyone else for the bitterness which grew between the two Presidential families. Clearly, however, Constance Gardner did not have to arouse her close friend, Alice Longworth. Like her father, she was ready to resent anybody else being in the White House.

It is not in the record when—or if—Roosevelt and Gardner talked about the latter's proposal for the creation of a "National Security Commission" to investigate national defense. However, at approximately the same date as his dinner with General Wood and friends, and two days after Gardner began his attack, Roosevelt, as Acting Secretary of the Navy, was in a mood to assist him. Woodrow Wilson laughed at Gardner's charges but Franklin gave a statement to the press which, in the guise of supporting Wilson, actually served Gardner. It contained the statement that the Navy needed 18,000 more men and for lack of them could not keep thirteen of its second-line battleships in commission. If he was fooling Wilson, he was not fooling himself. He realized that he was shooting at his superiors in the midst of an election campaign on a subject about which Republicans hoped the war in Europe had made American voters sensitive.

"The enclosed is the truth," he wrote Eleanor, "and even if it gets me into trouble I am perfectly ready to stand by it. The country needs the truth about the Army and Navy instead of a lot of the soft mush about everlasting peace which so many statesmen are handing out to a gullible public."

There was no official explosion. A Tammany man, still unsatisfied with Roosevelt's chastisement in the primary, wrote that Daniels had been "taught practically that a renegade who betrays his party will betray his chief." If any such idea occurred to Daniels he did not show it. In November, however,

Roosevelt issued another press statement. It did not attract so much attention. Roosevelt never exultantly referred to it. Equivocally, it denied without repudiating his statement which had helped Gardner in October. Emphasizing the word "recommended" he declared that "I have not recommended 18,000 more men, nor would I consider it within my province to make any recommendations on the matter one way or the other." There was no trouble but the province was clearly and publicly defined.

Daniels was satisfied with the election and more habituated then to the shock of war. Indeed, at that time, after the first battle of the Marne, some called it a "crazy war," foreshadowing the "phony war" phrase used to describe the first fall and winter months of World War II. The Democrats lost seats but kept control of Congress. Also, the second part of Daniels' prediction to Roosevelt was fulfilled when Gerard was defeated by James Wadsworth, Jr., a young man as elegant as FDR (St. Mark's and Yale), who had married the daughter of John Hay. Hay's friend Adams cackled with delight about that and also about his feeling that "our friend Roosevelt [meaning TR] and his following are disposed of. I suspect he is busted and done." He was a little premature.

If the election was over the battle was only begun. Familiar figures began to appear in it. Colonel Thompson, Admiral Fiske said, was "most flattering and kind in his congratulations" to the militants. The National Security League, composed largely of gentlemen with the Colonel's social and financial standing, was established under the patronage and encouragement of General Wood. They organized just in time to hear Wilson in his address to Congress in December lay down the administration line on the subject of preparedness.

"We never have had," he said, "and while we retain our present principles and ideals we never shall have, a large standing Army."

As to the Navy: "A powerful Navy we have always regarded as our natural and proper means of defense. . . . We shall take leave to be strong upon the seas, in the future as in the past; and there will be no thought of offense or of provocation in that. Our ships are our natural bulwarks."

Even with regard to the Navy, however, he did not seem impressed with the professional navalists. And when he said of preparedness in general that "we shall not alter our attitude because some among us are nervous and excited," laughing Democrats looked at Gussie Gardner and some Republicans joined them. Gardner sat "silent and solemn-faced," *The New York Times* said. The applause at the end of Wilson's speech showed that there was little doubt where a majority of the Congress stood—or the people behind the Congress.

Two days later Daniels went to the Capitol and spelled out the administration's naval position: It was almost identical to that of 1913. Once again it included the construction of two new battleships, rather than four as the General Board regularly recommended. It proposed no additional enlisted men until the next session of Congress. It definitely did not seem to Gardner and other big Navy men (including Franklin) a sufficient bid to be strong upon the seas. It was, however, the official position of the administration. In the naval hearings, Gardner complained that "a most alarming case of lockjaw has come upon Army and Navy officers alike since this pestilence of mine started." Admiral Fiske thought the testimony of Admiral Frank M. Fletcher, commander of the Atlantic Fleet, "too rosy." It seemed to him that what Admiral Charles J. Badger, the fleet's former commander, said was too neutral and colorless. It hurt him that other admirals did not share his excitement.

However, before Roosevelt testified on December 15, Fiske noted that "he was in my office two hours yesterday, getting data, etc., etc., etc." Franklin made a fine appearance. He got much newspaper attention. Though he stood with Daniels in the opinion that the Navy was more efficient than in the past, the details of his testimony added up to a much less optimistic report than Daniels had made. His analysis left the Navy certainly no better than third among the navies of the world. He urged a stronger naval reserve and differed with official estimates as to the need for personnel. Franklin presented his facts, however, in a new bland manner after the prudent declaration that "it would not be my place to discuss purely matters of policy." His appearance was coupled with the receipt by the committee of a letter from Theodore Roosevelt which said that he had no testimony to offer. Franklin spoke for the Roosevelt name and Gardner found in what Franklin carefully said facts which he continued to use in his attacks on the Secretary.

Franklin apparently was thinking very prudently about his province without altering his opinions. There was no question in his mind any longer as to whether he wanted to be Assistant Secretary next year. His appearance at the hearings, he wrote his mother, was "really great fun and not so much of a strain." Most important of all, "I was able to get in my own views without particular embarrassment to the Secretary." He made that delicate balance even more clear in a letter to his relative and landlord, Admiral Cowles, who, in retirement and in the new militant spirit of the northeastern states, had been made naval aide to the Republican Governor of Connecticut. On the day Franklin testified he described himself to the Admiral as a moderate in the preparedness business and predicted that he would be "grilled between the 'peace-at-any-price' sophists and the wild-eyed enthusiasts like our friend Hobson." Congressman Richmond Pearson Hobson, a Spanish War naval hero and an almost comic militant, as Roosevelt indicated, was the man to whom in secret sessions Admiral Fiske was taking younger officers in connection with his plans for a Chief of Staff "to have 15 assts!!"

There was room in the middle in that fight. When Gardner

began it the Democrats were already preparing to elect, as both majority leader and chairman of the Ways and Means Commit-ι ?, Claude Kitchin of North Carolina, who in his fight on "jingoes and war traffickers" was sometimes to regard even his neighbor Daniels as entirely too war-like. There was nothing secret about Kitchin's views as agrarian radical and agrarian pacifist. There was nothing silent about millions of people in the country behind him. He was not popular with some prominent people in the metropolitan and militant East. Even before the war began in Europe *The Saturday Evening Post* undertook to write him down as an obstinate, cantankerous nonentity. He came from an even smaller town than Daniels, which practically proved his provincialism to the city press. Actually the Kitchins, who had owned plantations in Alabama as well as North Carolina, regarded themselves as at least as much landed aristocrats as the gentry around Hyde Park. They had a good deal less money but at least as much pride. Indeed, Kitchin pride as expressed in Kitchin tempers was notable in their neighborhood.

Late in 1914, some Eastern papers, including *The New York Times,* hinted that Wilson would oppose the choice of Kitchin as Democratic leader of the House. That was wishing, not reporting. Gussie Gardner did not underestimate Kitchin. The North Carolinian was the youngest majority leader elected by either party in more than a quarter of a century. Gardner who fought him thought that his leadership equaled the standard set by any of his predecessors on either side of the House. Kitchin feared militarism—calling by that name what others called preparedness—and fought it when that meant not only opposing Gardner but Wilson and Daniels as well. There was room in the middle both in the House and the country, but it was not going to be comfortable there—or anywhere else in that debate.

It had already sharpened. If Henry Adams in his secure position could report that the social tide in Washington—and in

Boston and New York, too—had already violently set one way in early November, by December there was already talk about the "cowardly farmers" who must be made to understand what would be the meaning of the "capture of our coasts." *The New York Tribune,* to the surprise of nobody, upheld Gardner in his attack on the Navy and attacked Daniels with a violence unusual even in that Republican newspaper. Daniels was not surprised at *The Tribune's* attacks. He would have been amazed if *The Tribune* ever said a kind word about him or any other progressive Democrat. In that first December of the war he was not merely a peace man but what always stiffened and strengthened him, a man engaged in a fight for it. He hardly had time to notice that Christmas Eve was the hundredth anniversary of the Treaty of Ghent and the end of the century of peace it had been planned to celebrate as an example to the world. Instead, the British, in extending their claim to the right to blockade even vessels from the United States to other neutral nations, were presenting what one historian of the time has called "the threadbare excuse that the cause of Great Britain is always the cause of humanity."

"I am told it is Christmas," old man Adams wrote that year. Franklin had to tell his mother that for the first time the young Roosevelts could not spend Christmas at Hyde Park, not because of the war but because Elliott was just over a fever. Franklin himself seemed less feverish, too. The Danielses, who always made Christmas a festival full-blown out of Dickens wherever they were, celebrated in customary fashion at Single Oak. The tree was high; long logs blazed in the fireplaces. *The New York Tribune* and Gussie Gardner only seemed like the Scrooges necessary to brighten a legend of good cheer.

I remember that that Christmas was also brightened and saddened, too, for us by the remembrance that the President was spending his first Christmas at the White House since Mrs. Wilson's death. There was not much anybody could do about that, but Mother drove down in the brougham and took a cake. It was a very small-town sort of thing to do. There must have been many cakes in the big house that year. But it helped, as the President wrote on his portable typewriter on the day after Christmas, "to keep the cloud from descending on me which threatened me all day." And Mother cried at the other things he said. And so did the Secretary of the Navy.

"You are both," he wrote, "of the sort that makes life and friendship worth while. It is fine to have a colleague whom one absolutely trusts; how much finer to have one whom one can love! And when marriage has united two of the same quality, one can only wonder and be thankful that Providence has made them his friends."

Wilson was undoubtedly emotional that holiday season. Also he could be angry. He showed that not long after Christmas to Mrs. Crawford H. Toy, the "Nancy" of old friendship whose husband had been professor of Oriental languages at Harvard for thirty years. She was one of the friends the President's family were constantly bringing to the White House in an effort to break the hard mass of his loneliness. While she was there someone referred to a current slighting story that Daniels in almost comic neutrality had forbidden the singing of the British war song "Tipperary" in the Navy. Actually some naval commandant had been criticized because he held the song improper as part of an official naval occasion, and Daniels upheld the officer. The story, however, was only one of many like it. Daniels had framed on the wall of his study a cartoon showing him sternly stopping sailors from eating German cooking, using English mustard, petting a Russian wolfhound or casting an eye at an ankle above a French heel. Wilson was not amused. Mrs. Toy wrote that she had never seen him angry before and "I never want to see him angry again."

His fist came down on the table. "Daniels did not give the order that 'Tipperary' not be sung in the Navy," he said. "He is surrounded by a network of conspiracy and lies. His enemies are determined to ruin him. I can't be sure who they are yet, but when I do get them—God help them."

It was not always an angry time. Even the Roosevelts' friend, the always half-sick Ambassador Spring-Rice, who had sometimes seemed almost hysterical that fall when Bryan insisted that Britain could not disregard the rights of American shipping, kept for his intimates a whimsical humor. Spring-Rice, of course, approved of Gussie Gardner's pro-Ally sentiments, but even he made a comic verse about it:

> What does Gussie Gardner say
> In his nest at break of day?
> "Wake up, every mother's son,
> Buy a double-barrelled gun,
> Shoot a Dutchman or a Jap,
> Or some other foreign chap."

Franklin had an easy feeling in the British Embassy. Though he had to be officially careful in other places, he was secretly scornful of Wilson's suggestion that Americans should be neutral "in thought as well as in action." When it came his turn in 1939 to announce that America would "remain a neutral nation," he added, "but I cannot ask that every American remain neutral in thought as well." He did not even have to pretend neutrality in the good association with the Spring-Rices which he and Eleanor had inherited from Uncle Ted. Franklin and Eleanor liked the Embassy set. Indeed, he had numerous British friends. One in particular who matched that period in Franklin's life was Nigel Law.

Law, in his first year as a diplomat, had been one of the British Embassy staff in imperial and waltzing Vienna who were handed their papers when Britain and the old Austro-Hungarian Empire went to war. In the late fall he was one of those sent to Washington to staff the increasingly busy British Embassy. He was only twenty-four, and he was the sort of young

British bachelor who got the immediate attention of society editors. They described him in that December as belonging to "the House of Ellenborough, and, although the present head of that family is childless, there are many standing between it and Nigel." It added in consolation, however, that the young diplomatist's father, Sir Algernon Law, was for years head of the commercial department of the Foreign Office. His maternal grandfather was the late Reverend Charles Walter Bagot, rector of Castle Riding. Later it was discovered that he was also the great-grandnephew of "one of Washington's earliest financiers, Thomas Law, who was associated with Warren Hastings in India." That earlier Law, "a talented but eccentric land speculator," married a daughter of George Washington Parke Custis, who was raised at Mount Vernon by George Washington. Custis' other daughter married an Army officer named Robert E. Lee. Law's connections seemed adequate on both sides of "the pond." Also, his impressions of Franklin Roosevelt in that time and society were enthusiastic.

"I found him the most attractive man whom it was my good fortune to meet during my four years in America," he wrote me years later. "One was first struck by his gaiety and kindliness. He always seemed to be considering the feelings of others and doing all he could to make those in his company happy and cheerful. He was intensely interested in other people, not I think as a mere study in diverse humanity, but because he liked all people. He was intensely patriotic, but next to his own compatriots I think he preferred the English to other nationalities and during the period of American 'neutrality' he never disguised his strong pro-Ally sympathies."

Law summed up the picture of Roosevelt as the young man about Washington:

"He was a fine physical specimen in the days I knew him, delighting in all sorts of outdoor activity. But he was not just a gay athlete, for he had a deep understanding of politics and a sound knowledge of history and foreign affairs, strong convictions and ideals and a deep desire to serve his country with all his powers. In my own mind I gave him the highest praise an Englishman can give to a man, that he was a perfect example of the English Country Gentleman, and by that I mean (a type which is fast passing away) the landowner, whether large or small—with roots in his family estate who nevertheless disinterestedly devotes all his talents to his country, in local affairs, in Parliament, in the Army and if need be as a great Minister of State, Viceroy or Ambassador and who, when the need of his services is past, returns once more to his fields and his library with relief.

"Such Franklin seemed and still seems to me, a man I loved and admired."

They were young then. The eight years' difference in their ages did not separate them. Both were very serious about the war and sometimes during the war very gay, too. Law arrived late in the year but in January he was dining at the Roosevelt house on N Street.

Nigel came over on the *Lusitania* which six months later, when a U-boat sank her, was to take down with her much of the possibility of a neutral America "kindly separated by nature and a wide ocean from the exterminating havoc of one-quarter of the globe." Peace for America seemed to many already only the adherence of the innocents to the impossible.

Thunder in the West

EARLY IN 1915 MY FATHER BROUGHT A VOLUME OF VACHEL LIND-
say's poems to me at the old Naval Hospital where I was con-
fined as a diphtheria carrier. I felt fine but I was isolated until
I ceased to be a menace to others. Mother and Father brought
me many books, but Father brought the Lindsay poems with
the enthusiasm of a man sharing excitement. He did not generally care for "modern" poetry. He was a devoted Tennyson
man. He liked poetry which rhymed neatly and ran smoothly
to the conclusions that progress was graceful and inevitable. He
had found reform quite otherwise, a tough, hard, far-from-in-
evitable business, and Mr. Tennyson's lyrical optimism gave
him sustenance and release. I know now that in 1915 he was
not so much trying to institute reforms as to hold them. He was
not only tenaciously concerned about peace in the world; also
at home he was trying to defend the naval oil reserves, which
had been set aside in California, from the encroachments of
the same kind of diamond watchchain lawyers and spondulix
speculators as those at whom Lindsay directed defiant poetry.

Father told me about the party at which he had heard Lindsay read his poems. Mr. Bryan himself had read a poem by
Theodosia Garrison about peace. But the real poetry of the
occasion was about that "prairie avenger and mountain lion—
Bryan, Bryan, Bryan, Bryan!" It was about the great American
crowds which, when Bryan spoke, came by buggy, buckboard,

carryall, carriage, phaeton, whatever would haul. Vachel Lindsay, who had just been acclaimed by the critics, put drumbeat, cymbalsound, whistles, the people's yells and the people's whispers into his verse. In a real sense Lindsay and Bryan came to the occasion by the same back-country but main-traveled roads. Lindsay had been born across two counties from Salem where Bryan was born in Springfield, Illinois, Lincoln's town ("Abraham Lincoln Walks at Midnight") and where Altgeld the Governor "pardoned the anarchists" ("The Eagle That Is Forgotten"). Before he was recognized in the East he had traveled the country swapping poems for bread and board. He recited from barns and porches, in tents and lodge halls. He not only read poetry in such places, he made it, too. He was in process that night of shaping poetry which Democrats (even such a Tennyson man as Father) liked:

> Where is McKinley, Mark Hanna's McKinley,
> His slave, his echo, his suit of clothes?
> Gone to join the shadows, with the pomps of that time,
> And the flame of that summer's prairie rose.

> . . . . . .

> Where is Hanna, bulldog Hanna,
> Low-browed Hanna, who said: "Stand pat"?
> Gone to his place with old Pierpont Morgan.
> 'Gone somewhere . . . with lean rat Platt.

> Where is Roosevelt, the young dude cowboy,
> Who hated Bryan, then aped his way?
> Gone to join the shadows with mighty Cromwell
> And tall King Saul till Judgment day.

> Where is Altgeld, brave as the truth,
> Whose name the few still say with tears?
> Gone to join the ironies with Old John Brown,
> Whose fame rings loud for a thousand years.

Where is that boy, that Heaven-born Bryan,
That Homer Bryan, who sang from the West?
Gone to join the shadows with Altgeld the Eagle,
Where the kings and the slaves and the troubadours rest.*

They were not the sonnets of Wordsworth, delicate and smooth, which Wilson liked to read aloud and which Colonel House often discussed when he moved sleekly to grave discussions with Lord Grey. And Bryan was no longer Boy Bryan. The black wing of hair which once swung across his forehead when he spoke was thinning. That evening, however, seemed to my father a high time in Bryan's life. It may have been the highest. His publicly known troubles then were familiar. Those who constituted that social tide which Henry Adams said had already set in solidly for the Allies did not appreciate Bryan's stubborn neutrality. Also, though it was no new discovery, a social editor reported at the time that society found "the great William adhering to democratic simplicity with a loyalty which would have made his prototype, the great Jefferson, blush." Despite his neutrality and his grape juice preferences which became parts of one pattern, the party at which Lindsay read his poems indicated that the Secretary of State was not socially neglected.

The occasion crowded with carriages the block on Twenty-first Street about the house of Assistant Secretary of Agriculture and Mrs. Carl Vrooman. They were a young and eager couple who represented an inland America not entirely occupied by provincials. Vrooman had not only been to college in Kansas but at Harvard and Oxford, too. Mrs. Vrooman was a niece of Mrs. Adlai Stevenson, whose husband had been Vice-President under Cleveland and candidate for the Vice-Presidency again when Bryan ran in 1900. Mrs. Vrooman's mother had been president general of the D.A.R. and owned twelve

* From *The Golden Whales of California* by Vachel Lindsay. Copyrighted 1920, 1948 by The Macmillan Company and used with their permission.

thousand acres of rich Illinois and Iowa farm land. Though it seemed irrelevant then, Mrs. Vrooman was the cousin of another Adlai Stevenson who was then just three days short of being fourteen years old. It seems to me a nice detail that that second Adlai, who was to put both toughness and poetry into Presidential campaign oratory in 1952, was then like myself ready for the kind of jubilant word-music Vachel Lindsay brought out of his middle American vitality that night.

Mr. Bryan was not universally regarded as a subject for poetry. He certainly was not always lyrically treated in prose. The latest blast at him, coming from the normal direction of *The New York Sun,* was routine. That paper had just obtained and printed the Bryan letter in which he had asked a new appointee at a Caribbean post: "Now that you have arrived and are acquainting yourself with the situation, can you let me know what situations you have at your disposal with which to reward deserving Democrats?" The letter supported the view of Bryan as "a spoilsman." Among others holding this view was Colonel House, who had just got a promotion in the government service for his young son-in-law, Gordon Auchincloss. Also, at the Colonel's "insistent recommendation," according to the editor of his *Intimate Papers,* William Phillips, House's North Shore neighbor, had been brought in as one of Bryan's Assistant Secretaries.

It was at Phillips' residence in Washington, which the Colonel often used in his diplomatic operations, that House, just two weeks before the Vrooman party, told the British, French and Russian Ambassadors, before he told Bryan, that he had secured from Wilson the right to take from Bryan a job which Bryan wanted more than anything else in the world. All details had been arranged when he informed Bryan with soft-spoken assurance that he was leaving for Europe as the President's emissary for peace.

"He was distinctly disappointed," House wrote blandly in

his diary, "when he heard I was to go to Europe as peace emissary. He said he had planned to do this himself. . . ."

There was no roar from the Mountain Lion. There was no such explosion as took place in the administration of Franklin Roosevelt when Raymond Moley tried unsuccessfully to climb over Cordell Hull as Roosevelt's special emissary to the London Economic Conference in 1933. For all his forensic violence, Bryan was little qualified for personal combat. It would have been alien to both his personality and his vocabulary to tell the Colonel from Texas and the Massachusetts North Shore to go to hell. In diplomatic intrigue Bryan was undoubtedly unequal to the Colonel, who liked a description of himself to the effect that he could walk on dead leaves and make no more noise than a tiger. Also, the Colonel was insistently Bryan's friend. He had urged Wilson to name Bryan as Secretary of State, but in such a way as to stress an onerous necessity. Then, he had suggested as an impossible alternative that, instead of making Bryan Secretary of State, Wilson might say to Bryan that it would be of great service if he would accept the ambassadorship to Russia "at this critical time." Apparently House was not joking about Siberia. Bryan, who had been to Russia—as he had been to more other parts of the world than probably any Secretary of State in his generation—regarded Leo Tolstoy as his saint of peace. Apparently, however, that alternative was not mentioned to Bryan. The Russian post actually seemed so uncritical that Wilson did not fill it for months. Then finally, it was given to a rich Californian, George Thomas Marye, who had inherited a banking business, gone to college at Cambridge and always afterward listed himself in *Who's Who in America* as a member of the Church of England. He was a deserving Democrat but one with protective social coloration.

There were no visible signs of Bryan's disappointment at the Vroomans' party that first week in February 1915. Bryan wanted peace, and peace in the world did not seem more improbable than the crusade out of the country of which Lindsay made his poetry. Both seemed parts of the same procession. It was moving. Certainly the probability of peace for America was indicated by President Wilson's feeling, which Daniels noted in his diary, that the s. fety of the nation was such that military and naval budgets could be cut. Daniels himself, along with Secretary of War Garrison, was reluctant, but he understood the pressure of Congressional leaders on the President and agreed. Even Franklin Roosevelt at that time, when he lunched with Spring-Rice at the Metropolitan Club and suspected that the German Ambassador at the next table was trying to overhear what they were saying, was concerned lest his enlisted sympathies might lead him to unneutral action.

"I just *know*," he wrote Eleanor, "I shall do some awful unneutral thing before I get through."

He did not. Indeed, the confidence in continuing neutrality as an American reason for celebration was almost perfectly demonstrated by Franklin himself. The announcement by Germany on February 4 that its submarine commanders would regard the waters around the British Isles as a war zone did not seem to him or anybody else a reason why he and his friend, Assistant Secretary of State Phillips, should not leave Washington on a long, pleasant trip. As officials who could be spared for decorative duty, they went in March as representatives of the national government to the Panama-Pacific Exposition in San Francisco. That was not quite the world's fair it had been expected to be. Some nations were preoccupied with war. Herbert Hoover had turned from his job as the fair's European representative to war relief. In the continent the young Assistant Secretaries crossed there was much to celebrate all the same.

The Roosevelts and Phillipses set out in holiday mood. Mrs. Phillips had been Eleanor's friend, Caroline Astor Drayton, in their girlhood days in Switzerland. Caroline had lived much abroad. Her divorced mother had married an Englishman. She and Phillips had been married in Rogate, Sussex, when he was First Secretary in the U.S. Embassy in London under Taft. Phillips, who was a little ahead of Franklin at Harvard, had entered foreign service as private secretary to Ambassador Joseph H. Choate, whose diplomatic service crowned a legal career notable among other things for his arguments which helped postpone the income tax in America for nearly two decades. Within five years Phillips had become an Assistant Secretary of State under Theodore Roosevelt when he was younger than FDR was when he became Assistant Secretary of the Navy. He had withdrawn from the foreign service to be secretary of the Corporation of Harvard University, when Colonel House brought him back to Bryan's Department. On the trip west, Phillips and Roosevelt served as decorative aides to Vice-President Thomas R. Marshall, chief governmental emissary to the fair. Marshall, headed westward behind his eternal cigars, shocked Eleanor by his declaration that he "never did like scenery," and, on a visit to the fleet in San Francisco, vastly amused Franklin by his inland awkwardness in Navy ceremonials.

"Much to our joy," Eleanor Roosevelt remembered, though it could not have been much to their surprise, Secretary and Mrs. Lane also accompanied them to the coast. Lane, as the California Cabinet member, had undoubtedly arranged for his two younger friends to be the government commissioners to the fair. They had known about it for a year. The Lanes, the Phillipses and the Roosevelts were close friends in Washington. Their alternating Sunday night suppers had already become a fixed custom of the companionship which was to continue across the Wilson years. The Lanes, Eleanor said, were "a charming couple who appealed to young and old."

As a plump, well-fed and well-groomed man with a large white face and bald head, Lane reminded me immediately of Humpty-Dumpty. He had a jolly look and loved to go to parties. Some of his Cabinet colleagues thought he impaired his strength and usefulness by too much social life, but all agreed on his charm. He and Mrs. Lane had enjoyed society in Washington since Theodore Roosevelt had brought him there as a member of the Interstate Commerce Commission in 1905. He was the personal choice of Colonel House for the Cabinet. House had known him first as a law school classmate of his brother-in-law. Wilson had never seen him until Lane introduced himself to the President as his Secretary of Interior at the inauguration. Some thought that Mrs. Lane was just a little fastidious in the selection of her friends. She had her phone placed on the private list which seemed to some not exactly symbolic of the democratic simplicity expected of the new administration. She set up, it was said, "a code of calling which exceeded in exclusiveness anything ever attempted at the White House." Obviously, such remarks were unsympathetic if not unjust. Lane himself was a man very easily loved, and who loved life very much. He could write beautifully of the conservation of natural resources but he often had difficulties with his own. In the circles in which he moved, he reported, almost as a chronic state, that "financially we are up to our eyebrows." He was an idealist who could not spare the fleshpots.

Like Roosevelt and Phillips, in the early spring of 1915, Lane was free and gay. He had great boxes of flowers brought on the train to welcome his friends to California. Also, he arranged a "memorable day," which Eleanor described, at Senator James D. Phelan's beautiful ranch overlooking the Santa Clara Valley south of San Francisco. The Senator's place was worth remembering. Even native Californians recalled that the last flare of open-house hospitality in the California tradition took place in his great tile-roofed two-story Villa Montalvo. When such hospitality in the grand manner had faltered in the depression, Roosevelt's WPA guide writers added that Phelan had "entertained legislators, opera stars, and the literary elite with luncheons on the terrace, open-air banquets at barbecue pits, and dinners in the patio where screaming macaws vied with a string orchestra in the balcony." Phelan was also to have a house adequate to his entertaining in Washington.

The Senator had everything that the gay Lane often bitterly lacked. They were good friends and were to be collaborators later when Phelan in the Senate worked for what he insisted were the oil rights of Californians. Lane and Phelan took a more charitable—or more Californian—view of those "rights" than Daniels sometimes did. The Secretary of the Navy believed that many of the claims of oil companies, that they had established rights in the oil reserves before they were turned over to the Navy, were fraudulent. Lane and Phelan and many other Californians felt that the Secretary of the Navy took too rigid a view about the development of the California oil industry. Such differences were not soon to be solved. Almost identical differences were involved in the controversy between oil men in the states and the Federal government over so-called tideland oil areas forty years later. It was a coincidence, that it was almost exactly at the time of the Roosevelts' "memorable day" at Phelan's ranch that President Wilson, following President Taft's example, and with Lane's approval, added Teapot Dome (not in California but Wyoming) to the naval oil reserves. Lane apparently hoped that the addition of new reserves in Wyoming might make Daniels a little less stubborn about leases in California. Perhaps he did not foresee that when the oil men got their way they would take both reserves.

The Roosevelts did not hurry home. They stopped for a visit with old friends in New Mexico. From there, however, Franklin wired Daniels that he had some ideas about filling the new post of Chief of Naval Operations which Congress had just created. The position, as created by Congress with Daniels' agreement, carried the label of Admiral Fiske's chief of staff plan but left the power with regard to it in Daniels' hands.

Daniels wired Roosevelt that he would wait to hear his ideas before he named the chief. There is no record of the ideas which Franklin presented except Fiske's statement about himself in his diary: "Roosevelt and I agree that opinion of all is that Fiske ought to be Ch.Nav.Op." There was at least one dissenter—Daniels—he turned for his man to the younger captains and named Captain William S. Benson, then commandant of the Philadelphia Navy Yard, of whom Fiske did not approve and who Roosevelt always regarded as too rigid and deliberate. There was, it is true, nothing dashing about his appearance. However, even Colonel House, who had a very sensitive ear for British preferences, noted in wartime that "the British thought Admiral Sims a first-rate man until Benson appeared upon the scene." The Admiral was a pious Catholic who could work well and loyally with the Methodist Secretary. Daniels never regretted the choice. Benson never had any interest in playing a double game with the Secretary through the Assistant Secretary like that in which Admiral Fiske and friends engaged.

In the month of Benson's appointment, which completed Daniels' organization of the Navy, both sea danger and sea power were dramatically demonstrated. The *Lusitania* was torpedoed on May 7, and the American fleet moved in review before the President off New York. It was a time of high satisfaction for Daniels. Admiral Dewey celebrated the occasion in a letter declaring that the Navy was "not excelled, except in size, by the fleets of any nation in the world," and that, as president of the General Board of the Navy during the preceding fifteen years, he could testify that its efficiency had "never been so high as it is today." Even more important, Daniels was never more certain of the President's affection and support.

"Before I speak of the Navy of the United States," Wilson said at a banquet in New York on May 17, which was the eve of Daniels' fifty-third birthday, "I want to take advantage of the first public opportunity I have had to speak of the Secretary

of the Navy, to express my confidence and my admiration, and
to say that he has my unqualified support."

He paused for applause and went on:

"For I have counseled with him in intimate fashion; I know
how sincerely he has it at heart that everything that the Navy
does and handles should be done and handled as the people of
the United States wish it handled. Efficiency is something more
than organization. Efficiency runs to the extent of lifting the
ideals of a service above every personal interest. So when I
speak my support of the Secretary of the Navy I am merely
speaking my support of what I know every true lover of the
Navy to desire and to purpose; for the Navy of the United States
is, as I have said, a body specially entrusted with the ideals of
America."

That made my father feel very good. The President himself
was in high spirits that evening. Among those applauding was
Mrs. Norman Galt. I had seen her, I remember, for the first
time that day. In my memory she is dressed in purple with
purple flowers at her ample bosom. I watched from a hidden
place among the deck houses when she came from the President's barge up the sea ladder of the *Dolphin*, anchored in the
Hudson, where my mother was entertaining her and the wives
of the chief officers of the fleet at luncheon. She was a decorative
lady, I concluded. She was forty-three then and had been eight
years a widow. The President, who was fifty-nine, had proposed
to her just before she came to the fleet review as his and his
daughters' guest. Mrs. Galt was then still to reporters who
covered the social aspects of the occasion just "a cousin of the
President, an intimate of his daughters." Mother and Father
knew better. They were a couple who always liked to feel that
there was romance in the world.

Apparently, however, not everything was pleasing on that
New York visit. When Franklin Roosevelt got back to Washington he reported to Eleanor that he was surprised to have

been invited to dinner with the Danielses "who were cordial (!) but no reference was made to the New York episodes." Those "episodes" may have involved Roosevelt's and Daniels' slightly contradictory speeches at a special Navy League meeting at the time of the review, to which invitations were issued by Colonel Thompson, J. P. Morgan, former Assistant Secretary Winthrop and General Horace Porter, soldier diplomatist and vice-president of the Pullman Palace Car Company. All of them were gentlemen who shared the new mood of impatience following the sinking of the *Lusitania*. Daniels spoke for a powerful Navy but warned against "the depressing pessimists, who are resolved not to see anything but the hole in the doughnut." His use of a favorite metaphor of FDR's may have been directed both at some of the Navy League men and at FDR. Daniels praised "the forward-looking Sixty-third Congress" which had recently passed into history after enacting the Wilson reforms, but without matching the militant mood of the Navy Leaguers. Franklin was less polite to Congress and less complimentary to the people who elect it.

"Most of our citizens," he said, "don't know what national defense means. Our extraordinary good fortune in our early wars has blinded us to facts. Let us learn to trust to the judgment of the real experts, the naval officers. Let us insist that Congress shall carry out their recommendations."

(That was not a view he always held. He was certainly sometimes impatient with Congress as President, but as President in wartime also he came to the view, which I remember hearing him express in 1943, that "you can't leave things to the military, otherwise nothing gets done.")

While Daniels had a different attitude toward Congress and naval officers in 1915, he had heard the whole business about leaving the Navy to the naval officers many times before. The remarks did not constitute an episode which would have prevented cordiality. It is just possible that Roosevelt's conscience made him expect a lack of cordiality. Within the week in which he dined with the Danielses, although he himself had proposed "an official reporter or censor" to make public information about the war games of the fleet, he telephoned to Congressman Gardner confidential information about certain weaknesses shown in the maneuvers. Gardner could and did use it in the increasingly acrimonious attacks which he and the National Security League and other impatient patriots were making on the administration in general and Daniels and Bryan in particular.

Such critics were suddenly and unexpectedly elated that June. Though Bryan's resistance to every step which might lead to war had been clear to his enemies as well as his friends, his resignation on June 8 surprised both. In the debate in the Cabinet following the sinking of the *Lusitania* Bryan felt that while the administration should protest vigorously the German submarine action which caused the loss of American lives, it should press with equal force against Allied disregard of American rights by the British naval blockade. The *Lusitania,* he said, carried munitions which seemed to him like "putting women and children in front of an army." He wanted Americans warned to stay off British ships. He felt that the note which Wilson dispatched to Germany might lead to crisis and war. Franklin Roosevelt was jubilant about Wilson's choice of the more militant course.

"What d' y' think of W. Jay B.?" Franklin crowed in a letter to Eleanor. "It is all too long to write about, but I can only say I'm disgusted clear through."

And he added: "J.D. will *not* resign."

One of the odd little items in history is that on the day Bryan resigned and two days before Franklin wrote this note, his office records listed among FDR's callers, Mr. William Jennings Bryan. It seems probable that Bryan dropped by the young man's office as he did others in the big building to say good-by. Only the day before his resignation was announced he had sent word to Daniels that he would like to drive out to Single Oak with him as Mrs. Bryan was there at a tea. It was such an ordinary request that Daniels invited a lawyer who was working on the protection of the naval oil reserves in California to ride with them. He realized during the silent drive that that was a mistake. There was no opportunity for him and Bryan to talk at Single Oak. Bryan asked Daniels to come to his house for breakfast in the morning. The whole matter was already decided then. Bryan showed him his resignation and Wilson's acceptance. Daniels, as anxious to prevent war as Bryan, thought his old friend had made a mistake. He did not share Bryan's view that Wilson's position would lead to war.

"I don't think," he said, "in view of our long friendship you ought to have taken this course without talking to me about it."

"I feared it might embarrass you," Bryan told him. "You must stay in the Cabinet. The President will need you."

Daniels remained, as Franklin had predicted. Franklin was the witness of his mood at the time. The younger man prepared a long, cold and unsympathetic memorandum about a talk they had had as they walked slowly one June day soon afterward to luncheon at the Shoreham. Daniels, Roosevelt wrote, was "worried & bewildered." Apparently he talked straight out of his heart to his young assistant. He was disturbed by what seemed to be an incontrollable hastening toward war. Clearly he did not contemplate the ocean-crossing war ahead. He was not sure what could be done. The people were not ready to raise a great Army. He himself felt that to introduce universal military training would be to end the kind of government America had possessed.

"I hope I shall never see the day—"

Roosevelt did not indicate any arguments of his own in which he tried to reassure his chief or alter his opinions. In his memorandum he did show that he had been talking about Daniels and his attitude with other more militant people, particularly Secretary of War Garrison. Undoubtedly he talked about it also to his friend, Garrison's Assistant Secretary of War Breckinridge. Suddenly, however, Franklin was out of both the open and the undercover debate. At six o'clock in the morning one week after he talked with Daniels in the square, he was stricken with acute appendicitis. From the first of July until the end of September, he was on duty only a little over two weeks.

Daniels sent a sweetly paternal note to the hospital: "The doctor has just telephoned me that your temperature is normal . . ." Daniels wrote him, "You can, therefore, make your arrangements to go to Maine as soon as the doctor will let you travel, feeling perfectly free, and it will be a pleasure to me to remain on deck. You need the salt air and bracing climate after your stay in the hospital. For the present, you need to rest and sleep, with your mother near you. Your friends will look for your early getting out and ready for play."

The letter must have seemed almost too sweet to a confident and belligerent young man. Before he got back he was "tired of making toy boats for children." He was upset at not being in the Department when the marines that summer, at last and for a long stay, landed in Haiti which had reached a final stage of political and fiscal chaos. Later he rather gave the impression that he had handled the Haitian business almost single-handedly. Some of Franklin's impatience at the time was certainly reflected in a comment he made about the Naval Consulting Board set up by Daniels, under the chairmanship of Thomas A. Edison, while Roosevelt was at Campobello. The board was, in effect, the precursor of the Office of Scientific Research and Development which, when Roosevelt set it up as President in June 1941, the editor of his *Public Papers* said: "His foresight in this field was an incalculable contribution to ultimate victory." In 1915 Daniels' foresight in this field received much approving publicity but privately Franklin felt with some naval officers that it was another one of Daniels' impractical ideas.

"Most of these worthies," Franklin commented contemptuously, "are like Henry Ford, who until he saw a chance for publicity free of charge, thought a submarine was something to eat."

Edison was appointed, one of his biographers said, "despite his well-known aversion to war." Possibly that was actually one of the reasons for his choice, though Daniels described him as "the man above all others who can turn dreams into realities." Ford was Edison's friend, as the inventor said, "in the fullest and richest meaning of the term." Edison and Ford were, of course, very plain men. Neither conformed to any pattern of conventionality. In appearance they were more countryfied than Bryan. Ford had thrilled Daniels and shocked some of his fellow employers when he set up a minimum wage of five dollars a day in 1914. In 1915 he was advancing to a position as fool and crank which in the estimation of the eager preparedness people was beyond Bryan's. A month before Franklin sneered at him, he had announced that he had set aside $1,000,-000 to fight "preparedness" in the United States and other countries then at peace. He questioned the patriotism of the bankers, led by J. P. Morgan & Co., who were floating the loans of the Allies. He said that the Navy League and the new National Security League were largely composed of munitions manufacturers. More outrageous still, as it turned out, he was preparing to send his Peace Ship to Europe. It was to be made to seem an idiot's Noah's Ark filled with a menagerie of meddlers. The country, however, felt that such men of peace could be effective in the technology of defense.

It troubled Franklin to be sick and away when the President decided in that July of 1915 to take the leadership for preparedness, which had so long seemed the private possession of his political enemies. He wanted the advice of the naval officers, though he did not share FDR's announced view that it was the business of Congress only to carry out the officers' recommendations. Wilson had Congress very much in mind when he instructed Daniels and Garrison to draw up adequate plans for programs to be submitted to it. Daniels did "not mean to impose any work" on the convalescing Roosevelt but he gave him the relatively minor role of planning for the development and utilization of navy yards.

When Franklin got back to Washington in August still a little ailing but confident he was "going to make things hum," Bryan was important to him only for adverse comparisons. When he dined with the new Secretary of State Robert Lansing at a dinner for a "dusky gentleman and his duskier wife and daughter" from a South American republic, he was much pleased.

"It was a delight," he reported, "to see a Secretary of State who is a gentleman and knows how to treat ambassadors and ministers from other countries."

(Franklin did not always take such a dour view of Bryan. In 1934, when there was much concern about munitions makers and neutrality he wrote Daniels: "Would that W.J.B. had stayed on as Secretary of State—the country would have been better off.")

Roosevelt did not share, in 1915, Daniels' considered view that Lansing was "capable, industrious, meticulous, metallic and mousy." Lansing certainly was not a deserving Democrat. There was some doubt as to whether he was a Democrat at all. Indeed, apparently the person most responsible for his appointment as Counselor of the Department from which he had been promoted to Secretary was Republican Senator Elihu Root, who at the time was actively aiding Wilson in his effort to eliminate discrimination against British shipping in Panama Canal tolls. Lansing fitted neatly into State Department tradition. His father-in-law, John W. Foster, had been Secretary of State for less than a year under Benjamin Harrison, though his term seemed to expand steadily in the recollection of his friends and relatives afterward, perhaps because of his long and profitable private law practice in connection with the Department. Lansing lengthened the family tradition. He soon found jobs for both his young nephews, John Foster Dulles and Allen W. Dulles, in his Department. Also, he provided a still better place for Colonel House's young son-in-law, Gordon Auchincloss. *Town Topics* had noted prophetically when Lansing was appointed that "all ancient families of Washington have large hopes for their sons, nephews and remote cousins . . . but some plain Democratic legislators are threatening to cut down the State Department contingent if these sons of great men are supplied with posts to the detriment of workers for the party." It was a puny threat. Even when "poor Bryan was Secretary of State the Lansings and the Phillipses did all the entertaining and they did not serve grape juice either." Civilization was safe even if democracy had yet to be defended.

Franklin's time to make things hum, arrived, however, though it did not last long. On August 21, while down the river on the *Sylph,* Franklin exchanged felicitations with Daniels going down the river on his belated vacation on the *Dolphin.* On September 2, Franklin wrote Eleanor with an air of elated insubordination that he had announced a plan for the creation and training of a naval reserve.

"Today I sprang an announcement of the National Naval Reserve," he said, "and I trust J.D. will like it! It is of the utmost importance and I have failed for a year to get him to take any action, though he has never objected to it. Now I have gone ahead and pulled the trigger myself. I suppose the bullet may bounce back on me, but it is not revolutionary nor alarmist and is just commonsense."

As a matter of fact Daniels never objected to the naval reserve idea. Indeed, he rather irritated Roosevelt when he showed his interest in it by naming its first operation "the John Paul Jones Cruise." Daniels did not attach as much importance to the reserve as Franklin did. A student of that phase in Franklin's career says that Franklin was preoccupied with "wealthy men's speedboats" and with "luring a number of influential yachtsmen into supporting the Navy." His general idea was a sort of seagoing counterpart to General Wood's Plattsburg program. Daniels tried to put the emphasis on skilled craftsmen. But despite FDR's promise that its appeal would not be directed just at the yacht clubs, the enrollments which slowly came in included a high percentage of well-to-do gentlemen whose patriotism took aquatic directions. That fall, however, after Franklin had sprung his announcement, pulled the trigger and risked the bouncing back of the bullet, he stayed in Washington only two days before he left on September 4, the same day Daniels returned, for a moose hunt in Maine which the doctors at the Naval Hospital said would do him good.

Daniels was concerned about things which seemed to him more important. The Navy program which the President had approved was to Theodore Roosevelt only a "shadow program." Wilson's "half preparedness," the elder Roosevelt thought, was as dangerous as the schemes of Bryan and Henry Ford. The Navy League was not satisfied and some of the League's friends and members were irritated by new complaints which Daniels made about steel prices and steel scarcity as shown by the bids of private companies for new battleships. On the other hand, strong opposition to the Navy program showed itself in the Congress for the opposite reason. Though he remained Daniels' friend, Majority Leader Kitchin thought his program was "stupendous" and would "shock the civilized world." Also, he charged that Daniels had not been quite fair with Congress in pressing his program. He accused him of failure to stand by an appropriation he had accepted in conferences with House leaders when he found he could get a bigger appropriation for the Navy in the Senate. Moreover, though Bryan wrote Daniels that his opposition did not mean "any dimunition of my affection and regard for you," Bryan was active in opposition in the country. He did not lack support. William Allen White, who was troubled by the galloping belligerence of his old friend Theodore Roosevelt, described the troubled Bryan at that time. Bryan showed no sign that he recalled that it was the Kansas editor who had begun the design of his caricature in his famous editorial, "What's the Matter with Kansas?" White was glad to see Bryan. The Commoner was certainly then no longer the Heaven-born boy about whom Vachel Lindsay sang. He was paunchy, baldish and heavy-jowled. "But his voice was fresh and his eyes were keen." They talked about the war and about peace.

"As we sat together," White recalled, "his rhetoric full of Biblical metaphors and similes, his voice lovely to my ear with its modulating cadences, though he was not an oratorical talker, left an impression on my mind and heart that I have carried, even cherished, through all these years. I am ashamed now, and was ashamed then, that two decades earlier I had scorned him."

Between the crossfire of complaints from old friends and old enemies, Daniels was much pleased to receive an entirely unexpected letter from Colonel House about his activities in defense of Daniels and the Navy. He had, the Colonel said, secured an admission from Edward S. Martin, editor of the comic magazine *Life,* that Martin had been unjust to Daniels. *Life* earlier had printed a whole derisive "Josephus Daniels issue." The Colonel said he was working on other editors to put Daniels' administration of the Navy before the country. He felt, he said, that friends of the President could not serve the administration "better now than by working in this direction." Daniels was delighted.

"The best thing in the world," he wrote House, "is a real

friend and I count myself rich to have garnered your friendship."

Daniels wrote that on the day before the President formally announced his engagement to Mrs. Galt. Colonel House had busied himself in that matter, too, and had made up, Mrs. Wilson said later, a story which he hoped would prevent or postpone the marriage. He had told the President that if he announced his engagement to Mrs. Galt she would be subjected to humiliating publicity because another lady and old Wilson friend, Mrs. Mary Hulbert Peck, would "come out against the President" and produce compromising letters he had written her. Mrs. Wilson's *My Memoir* on the subject seems a little overwrought, but Wilson apparently was pretty emotional about the matter. However, if he really suspected that Mrs. Peck might be planning to do what the Colonel said he had information she would do, the President did not indicate it when he wrote Mrs. Peck, telling her in advance of the engagement and sending her "affectionate regards." House's plan did not work. Dr. Grayson, who had brought Mrs. Galt and the President together in the first place, brought them together again.

Colonel House, however, had not been the only person worried about the match. At about the same time, Postmaster General Burleson had come to see Daniels about it. He said that at a conference of "pretty big men in the Democratic Party" it had been unanimously decided that Daniels was the man to go to Wilson and urge him to postpone his marriage until after the 1916 election. Daniels declined "the difficult and, perhaps, dangerous high and exalted position of Minister Plenipotentiary to the Court of Cupid on a mission in which neither my heart nor my head was enlisted and in the performance of which my official head might suffer decapitation." Despite Colonel House's generous help with his public relations, Daniels knew that he had plenty of troubles without adding that personal intrusion to them. Besides, he was in favor of the match.

Other problems required his diplomacy. The militants were loud in the land and the peace men had power in Congress. The Navy was at the center of the concern of both. It was probably at this time more than any other that Daniels' close and carefully attended relationships with the Congress and particularly members of the Naval Affairs Committees proved most effective. His relationships with their chairmen were easy and intimate. That was made the more evident by the contrast with Secretary of War Garrison, who was the favorite of the preparedness forces, but "exhaled a kind of military impatience and authority, highly irritating to the men on the Hill." Garrison was in open feud with the Democratic chairman of the House Military Affairs Committee over the pattern of the expanded Army. He was impatient with the President. Finally he urged, with Assistant Secretary Breckinridge, a policy of compulsory military service which went far beyond the plan they had submitted to the President. Congressmen might disagree with Navy plans, but few even of the most pacifist Congressmen had their backs up against Daniels as a militarist when, in St. Louis early in 1916, Wilson called for "incomparably the greatest Navy in the world."

That was a phrase which after the war was to seem more disturbing to the British than it did to the American peace forces in 1916. It was one of the President's phrases on his preparedness tour, however, which brought a letter from an obviously angry Bryan to Daniels which disturbed him more than any loud attacks of the Navy League.

"I told you I would send you my statement in regard to the President when he announced his candidacy," Bryan wrote with regard to Wilson's second term plans. "I think I had better not embarrass you by doing that, for my statement may not be favorable to him."

Then the words tumbled out in an almost illegible, repetitive and ungrammatical scrawl: "I have been amazed at the slush he has been pouring out upon the West. Is he simply imposing upon the public and trying to scare the voters into accepting his policy? or does he really mean that he is writing notes only because our preparedness prevents a resort to force? If he means the latter then he wants the increase in order to enter into this war and if that is his reason what difference is there between him and [Theodore] Roosevelt? It is distressing to see our party's chances of success destroyed and the country's peace menaced by one in whom we had such great hope."

Bryan put his purpose in simple language to his old friend: "If I find that his purpose is to drag this nation into this war I may feel it my duty to oppose his nomination. I can conceive of no greater calamity than an endorsement by the Democratic Party of such a policy."

Daniels did not agree with Bryan but the situation was not simple. He did not agree—he hardly ever had agreed—with Secretary of War Garrison. He was sorry, however, about Garrison's resignation, which came with greater suddenness than Bryan's, on the morning of February 10, 1916. Daniels was still opposed to the militarization of America which it seemed to him Garrison's plans proposed. But he was going to miss Garrison. Undoubtedly the War Secretary was too rigid in his own opinions—as was Bryan. He talked too much. All the same he was a "delightful gentleman" of "deep convictions," Daniels thought. He felt that night, as he wrote later: "If I could possess what Wilson critically called a 'legalistic mind,' I would wish one as clear and honest as that possessed by my dear friend, Lindley Garrison. If I could be a conservative, which God forbid, I would like to be one like forthright and honest Garrison."

He felt differently about FDR's friend and Colonel Thompson's fencing companion, Assistant Secretary of War Breckinridge. Daniels was friendly to him because Breckinridge's brother had been the roommate of Worth Bagley at the Naval Academy and both had lost their lives shortly after graduation. There was, however, some bombast as well as belligerence about the young Assistant Secretary of War. Even some of his fellow Kentuckians felt that he had become a little too big for his breeches. Daniels was delighted with the story about Breckinridge's departure which Senator Ollie James, also of Kentucky, told him next day. He repeated it, as he often did the stories he heard, to the naval staff around his desk.

"Have you heard the sad news about Henry Breckinridge?"

"No."

"He is suffering from a cold. He hung his head out of the window all night last night expecting to hear the newsboys shout, 'Henry Breckinridge has resigned as Assistant Secretary of War. The government is in peril.' "

It was a small joke though a pointed one in a difficult time. Even in stress some things seemed funny. As an old-time anti-imperialist, Daniels felt awkward as the commander of the marines who occupied Haiti. Young Franklin would have been more comfortable about that. Indeed, in later enthusiasm he tripped over some of his pretensions about the Haitian occupation. Franklin's friend, Secretary Lane, who understood Daniels' feelings, loved to tease him about it. At Cabinet meetings, from which Garrison and Bryan were now both gone, Lane would rise, salute Daniels and say with mock solemnity, "Hail, King of Haiti!" That did seem funny. Daniels did not grin, however, when Lane casually spoke to him after one Cabinet meeting.

"Oh, by the way, Josephus, I've been going carefully over the Honolulu Oil case and I'm afraid you're going to lose. The Commissioner has approved thirteen of the claims of the company and denied four. I see nothing to do but affirm the findings of the Commissioner of the Land Office."

He went off plump and smiling, well-groomed and debonair.

NINE

"... A Vote for Daniels ..."

FRANKLIN ROOSEVELT PRESERVED IN HIS PAPERS THE RECORD OF
a good-natured exchange with his chief about Daniels' insistent
economy in the Navy Department. The Secretary was often
shocked by the casualness of naval officers with the taxpayer's
money, something which then and later did not bother Roosevelt as much as Daniels thought it should. Franklin wrote:

> Secnav
> 1. I beg to report
> (a) That I have just signed a requisition (with four copies
> attached) calling for purchase of eight carpet tacks.
> ASTNAV

The Secretary replied:

> Why this wanton extravagance. I am sure that two would
> suffice.
> J.D.

This "penciled memorandum" between the two men seemed
afterward to Elliott Roosevelt to indicate that "by the close of
1915 the friction between FDR and J.D. was gradually being
replaced by an intimacy that can be detected in this note."
Perhaps that was true. It was also true that not all their ex-
changes even at that time were so gay. Franklin was laid up
with another throat infection early in 1916. He went off
reluctantly in February with his mother to Atlantic City which

he described in astringent quotation marks as a "health resort."
It was "purgatory." It was "the place of departed spirits."
Also, Atlantic City then was a popular place for the ailing and
the convalescent. Admiral and Mrs. George Dewey went there
regularly. Mrs. Franklin Lane, who was not well that winter,
was there in February, too. It was to her there that Secretary
Lane in Washington, after a good luncheon and while he enjoyed a cigar of fine aroma, wrote about a reception at the
White House the night before. In Washington Lane was a gay
soul in purgatory, too. He covered with a joke his disappointment at not receiving the Supreme Court appointment which
President Wilson, to the outraged astonishment of the conservatives, had just given to Louis D. Brandeis.

"Neither the President nor myself alluded," he wrote Mrs.
Lane, "to the late lamented oversight on his part, and on meeting the members of the Supreme Court I did not find that by
the omission to appoint me on said Court the members thereof
felt that a great national loss had been suffered. No one, in
fact, throughout the evening alluded to this miscarriage of
wisdom."

Lane also wrote her with evident distaste that, when he
finished the letter and cigar, he faced an hour's discussion about
oil leases. He did not mention his proposed leases of some of
the lands in the naval oil reserves which at the time Daniels
had taken up with the President and the President had instructed Lane to hold up. Daniels was not in purgatory. He
had troubles enough to constitute even more than the inferno
which normally blazed around him. *The New York Times,*
along with assorted new preparedness, defense and security
societies, was sharply attacking him for his decision, in the face
of high bids from private companies, to build the newly
authorized ships in Navy Yards. He testified again in favor of
a government armor-plate plant. He wanted the Navy to have
its own oil refinery. Furthermore, he had ordered the incessant

Admiral Fiske to stop making speeches critical of the policies of the administration. In regard to the Navy's fighting readiness, Congressman Gardner said that Daniels had "first hoodwinked himself and then painted for us a delectable picture." The Massachusetts patriot compared Admiral Fiske to Lord Nelson, not at Trafalgar, but at the Battle of Copenhagen "where Nelson clapped his telescope to his blind eye and could not see his superior's signals." Insubordination seemed the basis of Gardner's patriotic plans. On the same occasion the Congressman praised Franklin, who had so often been so helpful in what Senator Lodge at that same time described to Theodore Roosevelt as "the struggle that Gus and I have been through to get the facts about the Navy."

Such standard opposition worried Daniels less than the divisions in the Democratic Party at the beginning of a Presidential election year. Ambassador Henry Morgenthau wrote in his memoirs that Daniels at that time "spoke hopelessly of the political outlook." Daniels himself later scrawled in the margin by that statement the word, "No." He could not have been in a state of confidence, however. The letters he was receiving from Bryan at his Villa Serena in Florida showed the Commoner to be still harsh about the President, though gentle toward his old friend Daniels. At the time Roosevelt set out for Atlantic City, Bryan wrote that he happened to be coming North early in March. If Josephus also happened to be in Raleigh at the time, they could ride and visit together.

"I shall not do anything at the present," Bryan promised. But he hardened. "My difference with the President is more religious than political. His course seems to me a repudiation of all that is essential in the Christian religion as applied to international affairs."

There is no record of a train ride with Bryan then, but Daniels did record the visit to him about the same time of tall, intense Kitchin in his dark clothes, his white vest, and black string tie. He was at least as disturbed as Bryan. At a White House conference then, about which there was later much dispute as to what was said and even as to when it was held, Kitchin had got the impression that the President wanted war. Daniels was sure he was wrong. He told Kitchin of the resistance of Wilson to the more belligerent members of his Cabinet —as well as to the peripatetic Colonel House. Kitchin was not convinced.

While Daniels worried about such divisions in the party and, to a lesser extent about criticisms from beyond it, he perhaps fortunately did not even know that he was the target of an operation within the administration itself. The renewed assaults on Daniels were attracting only less attention than the righteously indignant fight of the economic and legal respectables against the confirmation of Brandeis when Colonel House, after two months of high level diplomacy in Europe, got back to Washington on March 6. Nobody was happier to see House than Franklin Lane. House had not only put Lane in the Cabinet; after his conferences with him on his return, the Colonel regarded Lane as one of "two of the ablest men in the United States." (His protégé Houston was the other.) Lane had missed House's presence when the Supreme Court vacancy had occurred. He had missed House's presence when, with the support of Attorney General Gregory, Daniels had got the President to direct Lane to postpone his decision in the Honolulu Oil Company case. Now that House was back Lane undoubtedly talked to the Colonel about Daniels. It was while the open fight of the conservatives on Brandeis proceeded that Colonel House undertook what he called "the elimination of good Josephus Daniels." The forces against Brandeis and Daniels were remarkably the same. It seems highly probable that President Wilson did not miss that fact.

Wilson could not have been under any illusion as to the fight he was precipitating when he nominated Brandeis.

Colonel House had helped him decide, in 1913, that he could not put Brandeis in his Cabinet. In 1915, Wilson had had to intervene personally to get Brandeis into the Cosmos Club, on Lafayette Square in Washington, where some apparently regarded him as a radical as dangerous as he was considered on State Street in Boston. The respectables of Boston had been shocked by Mr. Brandeis' activities in cases against such solid companies as the United Shoe Machinery Company and the New York, New Haven and Hartford Railroad. It was almost overlooked that Brandeis had also been the lawyer for the conservationists when they believed the Secretary of the Interior in the Taft administration had improperly favored land claimants in the West. That was what Daniels was beginning reluctantly to believe Lane planned to do in connection with the naval oil reserves. Certainly in the secret fight against Daniels that spring, while the open fight against Brandeis raged, Wilson's official biographer found that much of the pressure for Daniels' dismissal "came from interests which were disturbed by Daniels' uncompromising attitude in regard to oil leases." The attacks on Brandeis and Daniels seemed to come largely from the East. East and West were not completely separate. One of those who came to see Daniels about oil claims in California which Daniels regarded as fraudulent was Senator Lodge, speaking for a company which "included honorable citizens of Massachusetts." Lodge was impeccable, as always, and when Daniels explained to him that his honorable constituents had purchased the worthless claims of squatters Lodge, Daniels said, did not press the claim.

The Brandeis fight was open and ugly. The more blatant defenders of respectability who regarded Brandeis as the man "largely responsible for the annoyances and oppression of the railroads" described his appointment as "a bald bid for the German, Jewish and radical vote." Also, it was whispered and then circulated by letter that Wilson had appointed Brandeis for unpleasant personal reasons. Wilson had named Brandeis, a clergyman said, as a reward for handling the payment of $75,000 to Mrs. Mary Hulbert Peck to get back indiscreet letters Wilson had written to her and to settle a breach of promise suit she threatened. She was the same lady Colonel House had named in his effort to prevent the marriage of the President a year before.

Mrs. Peck was undoubtedly a charming woman. I have a photograph of her standing, slim and gay in a wide sweeping skirt, on the porch of her cottage in Bermuda where Wilson first met her, in 1908, when he went to the island alone for a rest. As a pretty widow from Minnesota, she had married Thomas D. Peck, an older widower with several daughters, who maintained places for her in Bermuda and on Nantucket Island though his textile business generally kept him in Pittsfield, Massachusetts. When they were divorced in 1912 gossips thought that the action might have been instituted because she expected to marry the British Governor of Bermuda who, like Wilson, was certainly her friend. Woodrow and Ellen Wilson visited her. It was at her cottage in Bermuda that he relaxed after his election. She visited them at the White House in 1913. She said in her memoirs, which she was finally persuaded to publish, that the last time she saw the President before his re-marriage was on Memorial Day in 1915. She was fifty-two that year—nine years older than Mrs. Galt. There were gossips in Washington still betting she would be the second Mrs. Wilson, however, as late as the month before the announcement of his engagement to Mrs. Galt. Wilson did write her amazingly intimate letters, but letters which also contained endearing references to his wife. There is no evidence that she was party to any personal or political blackmail. Wilson did lend her, she said, $7,500 in 1915. There is no evidence that Brandeis had anything to do with the lady or the case.

Colonel House prided himself on his gifts in quiet dealings

with ladies as with gentlemen. Mrs. Peck was a lady in whispers; Mrs. Wilson was in the White House. The Colonel wrote in his diary that a month after his return from Europe and while the Brandeis fight raged, he was engaged in an operation to get rid of Daniels with Mrs. Wilson who was said to have resented Daniels' initial opposition to the promotion of Cary Grayson to an admiralcy over the heads of senior medical officers. In the midst of his courtship, in July 1915, Wilson had written Daniels, one of the few times he ever intervened in a naval personnel matter, to inquire whether he could do anything, "properly and legitimately to set forward Cary T. Grayson's chances of promotion." Colonel House wrote in his diary that Grayson had enlisted Mrs. Wilson's aid in the matter "even before she had ever met the President." Mrs. Wilson wrote me in 1953 that House's story of her participation in an effort to get rid of Daniels was *absolutely false.*

Certainly the Colonel's operation against my father that spring was so quiet that my father was never aware of it. Colonel House left his record, however, in his diary entry for April 6, 1916. He had had conferences with Lane that day about other matters. He talked to the President about someone's bright idea that once Brandeis was confirmed, he should resign and run for the Senate from Massachusetts in order to give the people a chance to rebuke the Brahmins. Wilson did not think much of the idea. However, House continued:

"The President had to go to another banquet, and Mrs. Wilson and I had a talk of an hour or more. We decided that the most helpful things that could be done for the President at this time, would be the elmination of good Josephus Daniels and Joseph Tumulty. She undertakes to eliminate Tumulty if I can manage the Daniels change. I do not know which is the more difficult feat, but I shall approach it with some enthusiasm and see what can be done."

There is confirmation for the enthusiasm. Wilson's official

biographer, Ray Stannard Baker, while identifying House only as "one close to the President," says that "he" asked Vance McCormick, of Pennsylvania, soon to be named as Democratic National Chairman, "to talk to Wilson about it, suggesting that McCormick himself should be appointed to succeed Daniels."

"Wilson ought to get rid of Daniels," McCormick was told, "and you should be appointed in his place."

McCormick was not interested in the suggestion. He and Daniels were friends and were to remain so all their lives. Furthermore, McCormick had already twice turned down Cabinet appointments and once an ambassadorship. McCormick's feeling about Daniels was the same as that of Wilson who, Wilson's biographer said, "neither budged nor doubted, supporting Daniels through to the end." Indeed, McCormick told Baker that had Daniels been displaced that year the political results "might have been damaging during the campaign, for it later developed that when moving pictures were used to illustrate the achievements of the various government departments, the Cabinet officer and the department that the theatre crowds applauded most generously were Secretary Daniels and the Navy." This was odd but a fact attested to by others as well as McCormick. In spite of the concerted press and other criticism of Daniels—perhaps in some ways because of it—Daniels constantly retained a remarkable popularity with the public at large which emphatically did not want war, yet wanted reasonable preparedness. With the people in general he was—after Bryan's resignation—probably the best known Cabinet member during the entire eight years of the Wilson administration.

If Daniels did not know of Colonel House's enthusiasm against him, he was warmly aware of Franklin Roosevelt's surprising rebuke to some of those whose attacks on the Navy seemed almost hysterical. Perhaps Gardner and others had been publicly praising Roosevelt too much in contrast with his chief. That was a danger which Colonel House sometimes feared in his relations with Wilson—though at the last not enough. Certainly, however, at a meeting of the Navy League which Daniels declined to attend, Franklin's speech must have astounded some of those who had been petting him most. What he said had about it the qualities of both militancy and reprimand.

"Every minute taken up," he said, "in perfectly futile and useless arguments about mistakes in the past slows up construction that much. Worse than that it blinds and befogs the public as to the real situation and the imperative necessity for prompt action. How would you expect the public to be convinced that a dangerous fire was in progress, requiring every citizen's aid for its extinguishment, if they saw the members of the volunteer fire department stop in their headlong rush toward the conflagration and indulge in a slanging match as to who was responsible for the rotten hose or lack of water at a fire a week ago?"

At that time the firehose metaphor, which Franklin was to use much later in his announcement of Lend-Lease, seemed only homely and effective language for the occasion. It marked, however, the beginning of a cohesion within the administration and among the Democrats which had not seemed possible at the turn of the year. Mrs. Wilson did not seem like a conspirator against Daniels when the "good Josephus" went with her and the President in May to North Carolina where Wilson made a patriotic address. The trip marked an important phase in the Brandeis fight, too. As it happened, two of the crucial Senators —and votes—in the Judiciary Committee were Senators Hoke Smith of Georgia and Lee S. Overman of North Carolina. Their wavering had been such that *The Boston Herald*, *The Boston Evening Transcript* and *The New York Sun* had predicted Brandeis' rejection by their votes. Hoke Smith had been the Secretary of the Interior who had brought Daniels to Washington in 1892. Both Smith and Overman had urged Daniels' appointment to the Cabinet in 1913. Daniels had worked first in the Brandeis vote on his old friend the Georgian. Also, he had something to do with Wilson's invitation to Overman to ride on his train with him to North Carolina. It turned out that a short platform speech on that trip was more important than the President's formal engagement. The President had been reluctant to stop in Overman's home town, but Daniels insisted. The President praised the Senator to his own people.

"Do you think Overman's vote is cinched?" Wilson asked as they departed.

"He will go back and advocate instead of merely voting," Daniels said.

Overman did. So did Smith. The vote in the committee was ten to eight for confirmation.

All the pieces seemed to be falling into place for the President. When that month the Germans agreed to modify their submarine campaign, Bryan could commend the President's efforts for peace and humanity. Claude Kitchin could at least momentarily believe that his impression about the President's belligerency was wrong.

That did not mean an amiable America in a campaign year. There have been few more cruel campaigns in American politics. Although Wilson's remarriage had not antagonized the country as his friends feared and his enemies hoped, it was necessary for the first Mrs. Wilson's brother to publish an article on the private life of the President. Daniels knew that some Republican emissaries had asked Mrs. Peck's former husband, then living in North Carolina, to come to Washington and tell the hoped-for story of the alienation of his wife's affections by the President. Peck consulted a lawyer who was one of Daniels' good friends as to what to do. "Go up there," he said, "and tell 'em to go to hell." He did. The Peck story was only one of the whispers. *Town Topics* blurted that Count von Bernstorff, in spite of his sinister activities, "is still with us and on terms, it is said, of considerable intimacy with the President and Mrs. Wilson at the White House."

That von Bernstorff slur was to be revived and sharpened after the war. Von Bernstorff himself wrote in his memoirs that it had been said, especially by Ambassador Walter Hines Page, that he "exercised a very strong influence on the President."

"This allegation is not true," von Bernstorff said. "The historic truth is that we went a part of the way together, because we both had *one single* aim, which was to keep the United States out of war."

The Count was a precious morsel for the serpent-tongued. He had been a popular as well as dapper figure before the war began. Leading universities (Columbia, Brown, Johns Hopkins, Pennsylvania and Princeton) had given him degrees. He was charming in society. He had a way of never letting a newspaperman leave his chancellery without a box of cigars or a bottle of wine. Even on the eve of American declaration of war, Lane wrote, he had his "little knot of society friends, chiefly women." *Town Topics* reported that Eleanor Medill Patterson, later publisher of *The Washington Times-Herald* which so bitterly hated FDR, sent twelve dozen American Beauty roses to adorn the von Bernstorff drawing room on the train which took the German diplomats away from Washington.

Meanwhile, under a placid surface no cruel thing was left unsaid about the Wilsons. The surface was placid. The summer which young Roosevelt had "expected to be full of excitement and action" was already turning out rather tame. All the same, as May ended, under a headline LET A ROOSEVELT SPEED, *The New York Times* reported that the police phoned ahead to all the towns he passed through to arrange for the Assistant Secretary of the Navy to break the speed laws when he went in a high-powered automobile from Harmon-on-the-Hudson across rich Westchester County to a preparedness celebration in New Rochelle. He did the twenty miles in fifty minutes though, even for those days, that does not seem a record run. He was a young man in a hurry. His young English friend, Nigel Law, saw that best a few weeks later when, at Roosevelt's invitation, they went together from Washington to the wedding in Hyde Park of Ruth Wales, niece of Elihu Root, and Harry DuPont who had been at Harvard with Franklin. They stopped in New York on the way.

"That night," Law recalled later, "Franklin took me to dine at the Harvard Club where the members were celebrating their victory over Yale in the Boat Race."

Obviously, Franklin's place that night was at the Harvard Club which was almost as much a center of his life as the Metropolitan Club in Washington. He understood its importance. That year he wrote to a friend about the Army-Navy football game that "during the last two years practically all of the spare seats of the Army were distributed from the Harvard Club and I think it did real good, because it was appreciated by the kind of people who can be of more service to the Army and Navy than the average complete outsider who goes to the Polo Grounds to see the game merely as a spectacle." That "kind of people" included many of the admirers of Theodore Roosevelt who had been, wrote Walter Millis (a Yale man himself), "plotting at the Harvard Club in New York (something of a center of these elegant, if subversive movements)" against the military and foreign policies of the Wilson administration. Both war and politics had sharpened differences that June, but no warlike sense of military austerity prevailed at the Harvard Club that night.

It was the perfect night for Franklin to be there, though I still do not understand how he missed the Boat Race itself at New London where so many of those friends with whom he was corresponding about the naval reserve were gathered. As a complete outsider from the traditions of either Harvard or the Boat Races, I can remember my own lively enjoyment when we went three years before to watch them from the *Dolphin*. Secretaries of the Navy were somehow expected to be at the

Boat Race. Also, I remember that I was for Yale as presumably the more democratic of the two Ivy League institutions. The sailors with whom I watched were particularly enthusiastic for Yale on the possibly prevaricated grounds that former Secretary of the Navy Meyer, a Harvard man, would not permit any sympathy for Yale to be shown by the crew. In the summer of 1916, however, Franklin Roosevelt was almost as much interested in the Yale yachtsmen as the Harvard ones, all of whom regularly had their schooners, cabin cruisers and speed boats lining the course. He was an inevitable celebrant, however, of the Harvard victory.

"It was naturally a gay evening," Law reported with British moderation. "Someone suggested that we should go over to the Yale Club and give them a friendly cheer."

The Yale Club, three blocks away on Vanderbilt Avenue, "the largest in the world and the first in the skyscraper class," had just been completed a year before. The proposed call seemed a good idea.

"A party of us with linked arms," Law continued, "every other man carrying a bottle of champagne, set off. Arrived there, we found that all the members had gone to bed except two who from the balcony had heard our approach. (I think we had a rudimentary brass band with us.) The two Yale men, with most hospitable courtesy, asked us all in for a drink, and this invitation, needless to say, was gratefully accepted.

"We then all went away, Franklin and I to spend the night, or what was left of it, at an hotel. The following morning we were called at 5 A.M. and set out for the Hudson River where we embarked on the *U.S. Torpedo Boat Destroyer No. 59.* Franklin, as Assistant Secretary of the Navy, then took charge and we proceeded up the Hudson at such speed that our wash nearly sank some barges moored to the bank."

The DuPont-Wales wedding must have been quite an affair,

but Law was more impressed by the Dutchess County evidences of Franklin's methods of work which he saw on that visit.

"Before we went to bed," Law reported, "I saw the newly added room with a dozen tables in it which Franklin explained were so arranged that, as each table got littered up with papers, he could move to another where there was room to write."

He needed plenty of room. That June in exuberant advocacy of legislation creating a Council of National Defense he had written to a gentleman who was working for it also that "without intending to throw bouquets at myself, I think I am the only person in Washington in the Administration who realizes the perfectly wonderful opportunities, nationally and politically, to accomplish something of lasting construction." He was impatient with delays in this and other matters. The Council of National Defense which was created that fall, after more careful consideration than Roosevelt felt was needed, differed in important particulars from the Council of National Defense which the Navy League among others had been urging. Their plan would have included ex-Presidents (Roosevelt and Taft; there were no living Democratic ex-Presidents) and representatives of railroads and great industries, but no representative of labor such as the American Federation of Labor's Samuel Gompers.

Franklin was working hard and happily, too, in connection with his well-loved naval reserve. He corresponded much about it with A. Lawrence Lowell, president of Harvard, who had joined fifty-five Bostonians in the opposition to Brandeis. He worked with John L. Saltonstall of Boston, "one of the best known yachtsmen and clubmen in the country" and a leader of the "year-round Beverly Farm Colony of smart young people." Down Philadelphia way Franklin had the help of Alexander van Rensselaer. Vincent Astor worked with him to organize owners of power boats. Astor and J. P. Morgan promised to donate their yachts in time of war. Franklin moved much

around New England shore places and stations. Twice during
the summer he went to Pride's Crossing, once to see Livingston
Davis who the next year was to come to Washington as his assistant in charge of naval reserve and other activities. There was
time for golf at Chevy Chase, dinners at the fancy Maryland
inn, Dower House, with Law and other British friends, for the
Follies in New York, for a good evening at Larz Anderson's big
house. But he sat long, hot hours, too, in the rooms of the
Appropriations committees in the Capitol helping with the
details of the bill embodying the Secretary's request for nearly
half a billion dollars for that "incomparably greater Navy."
Though it was more than ever asked—or secured—before in
time of peace, it seemed suddenly too little for the Navy League,
and, at the same time, outrageously too much to Kitchin and
others who felt they were fighting the crucial, final battle with
the jingoes. Suddenly, though the Navy League must have been
as surprised as he was to hear it, Daniels seemed to Kitchin the
war-traffickers' eager friend. So beset from all sides, it was amaz-
ing how cool the Secretary looked in his white linen clothes.

"Every doubt, every possibility," Kitchin said in closing the
debate on the bill, "has been resolved by this program in favor
of the shipbuilders and munitions-makers—the Morgans, the
Fricks, the Dodges, the Bacons, the Schwabs, the Perkinses, the
Thompsons and so forth. The war-traffickers' press already an-
nounces, with most flattering commendation, that the Secretary
of the Navy will be ready, almost immediately after the bill
becomes law, to ask for bids and award contracts to carry out
the program. They will have him to hurry, not that the country
is in any danger of a foreign foe, but that the shipbuilders and
munition-makers will be in danger of losing their high war
prices if the Secretary should delay until the end of the European War gets in sight. The people will find out sooner or
later that it is the profit to the contractors, not the danger to the

country, that has been one of the great incentives and inspirations to the speed and size of the program."

It was a hot August. When he could Daniels liked to go driving in the victoria in the evenings through the park and by the river. The greater speed and breeze of an automobile was not provided the Secretary by the government until the following year. Not a swimmer, he did not join other officials at the public bathing beach in the Mall where it was noted that "Washington Society . . . is finding some relief these torrid days." The Republicans seemed to be most confidently in possession. Alice Longworth had "a bathing suit which is a vision and a delight. It is sea-green, with broad bands of white. With this she wears apple-green hose and sandals and a beautiful head-covering, topped off with a big green bow." In the summer heat, "many a handsome young matron is not averse to taking a dip under the gaze of the hoi polloi."

Before August was over, Gussie Gardner was already out on the stump directing his Republican campaign speeches sharply at Daniels and the Navy Department. Gardner and his friends undoubtedly put much hope in the slogan, "A Vote for Wilson Is a Vote for Daniels." Even the Presidential candidate, Charles Evans Hughes, devoted a speech in Boston to an attack on the naval Secretary. Mr. Hughes reflected the views of some officers who had little patience with his ideas about education for enlisted men.

"We must pay less attention to punctuation and more to targets," the Republican candidate said.

Franklin, who had joined in some humor about the schoolroom Navy, answered Hughes this time in good swinging fashion, but he put his emphasis on the targets not the training.

"Does Mr. Hughes not know what the Navy knew, that the Navy in March, 1913, was a hollow shell, and that complete reorganization was imperative? . . . I can show him millions of dollars, item by item, saved through common-sense business

organization. I can show him an organization that would not
break down in case of war. I can show him long-range shooting with big guns that has surprised and delighted every officer
in the fleet. . . . The navy is growing; it must grow more. It
is using the appropriations wisely and honestly. All it needs
now is boosting and not knocking."

He did a good job, even if the eastern states in which he
spoke all went Republican. Also, in that campaign summer,
when he was valiant against the Republicans, he showed an
almost prescient-seeming fear of infantile paralysis. The epidemic was severe that summer. He warned Eleanor to swat
every fly. *"No one* is thinking of moving children by rail." He
was unwilling that the children come back by automobile from
Campobello. He was not alone in his fears. Villages in New
England were unwilling, he said, for motorists with children
to pass through. The Secretary, Franklin reported, was "scared
blue" not by the epidemic but by a charge in Congress that he
intended to use the *Dolphin* for political campaigning in
Maine. Daniels had sent his boys to Raleigh because he was
unwilling to use the yacht. In September, however, after the
Maine elections, Daniels told Roosevelt he saw no reason why
he should not use her to bring the children home. Even then,
however, Franklin wrote his mother to fumigate everything at
Hyde Park and make arrangements so that the children would
not have to use any of the Roosevelt cars and carriages in which
had ridden Mrs. Roosevelt's coachman whose own child had
been stricken with polio. Three days after he wrote, with every
precaution and without event, the young Roosevelts and off-
spring arrived in Hyde Park.

Just before the election the Lanes and their friends and the
Roosevelts' friends, the Adolph Millers (he was then a member
of the Federal Reserve Board) went, Lane wrote, to "the James
Roosevelt place up at Hyde Park on the Hudson . . . and had
an exquisite time." Lane was a wonderful companion. It did not

seem to disturb him when Roosevelt stood clearly with Daniels on the naval oil reserves matters.

Lane had not had such a happy summer, however. He had served effectively on an American-Mexican Joint Commission in which Colonel House was much interested. But Wilson still held up his decision in the Honolulu Oil Company case. Daniels had made an effective row in the Congress against oil-leasing legislation, introduced by Senator Phelan and backed by Lane, which Daniels thought would "seriously jeopardize the future supply of oil for the Navy." Lane felt Daniels had gone further than that. He was not quite placated when Daniels and Attorney General Gregory formally denied charges by Senator Phelan that they had instigated news stories saying that Lane was the friend of the big oil interests. That naked charge, however, was made in an "open letter" to Lane by Gifford Pinchot on whose side Brandeis had appeared in the conservation fight in the Taft administration. Pinchot, as an ardent conservationist, had rejoiced when Lane was appointed. He had completely changed his mind. He wrote: "The record shows beyond question that your program and the program of the Phelan amendment, for rewarding wilful trespassers with preferential leases at the expense of the Navy's reserves of oil, are one and the same." Lane told his friend, William Riley Wheeler, a California oil land operator, "I have no intention of saying anything in reply to Pinchot. He wrote me thirty pages to prove that I was a liar, and rather than read that again I will admit the fact."

Lane was unhappy and uncomfortable. When another vacancy on the Supreme Court occurred because Hughes resigned to run as Republican candidate for President, Lane was almost pathetically eager to be appointed in his place. He wrote to House's brother-in-law, Dr. Sidney E. Mezes, who often handled such matters for the Colonel, saying that he did not want to seem "cheeky or impatient."

"I'll stand guard all night without a whimper," he wrote.

"All I want is for you, in that superlatively tactful way of yours, to find out if my chances are worth considering at this time—and if they are, will the Colonel make them something better than mere chances. If they are not, I shall continue sawing wood, and whistling most of the time."

He could not have been very confident about his chances even when he wrote because on the same day he was "very much tempted" to run for the Senate from California "because things have been made so uncomfortable by some of my fool colleagues who butted in on my affairs." One of those fool colleagues was undoubtedly Daniels. Lane wrote his wife that he could get the nomination by merely saying that he would accept it and that "Phelan told me yesterday that he would see that all the necessary money was raised—that I could win in a walk." He did not run. The race would have been no walk against Hiram Johnson, who had been twice elected Governor of California by the Republicans and had been the Vice-Presidential candidate on the Progressive Party ticket with Theodore Roosevelt in 1912. Johnson won in a walk in the election in which Wilson carrying California, too, won by the skin of his teeth.

Lane and Roosevelt went down from Hyde Park to New York for the election returns and left the gloomy Democratic headquarters in the Biltmore Hotel at midnight convinced that Wilson was defeated. They were no more convinced than other Democrats. I remember that night in the offices of Postmaster General Burleson across Pennsylvania Avenue from the screen on which *The Washington Star* put the returns by lantern slides. Crowds filled Pennsylvania Avenue below us. No radio or television kept people at home. The evident defeat seemed more depressing when we went home through the dispersing crowds. That experience made the victory when the news came next day from California all the more exciting. I remember how pleased we all were when Father secured for framing from

Clifford Berryman of *The Star* his cartoon based on the Republican slogan, "A Vote for Wilson Is a Vote for Daniels." The cartoon showed a grinning Daniels saying, "My, what a lot of people voted for me."

Franklin Roosevelt, in a gaiety which freed him momentarily even of awe for Uncle Ted, quipped that "it is rumored that a certain distinguished cousin of mine is now engaged in revising an edition of his most noted historical work, *The Winning of the West*." The surprise victory, however, made him serious, too. He had a sudden indignant feeling about those whom he later called the "economic royalists," some of whom had been his active coadjutants in the Naval Reserve Program.

"The Republican Party has proved to its own satisfaction, I hope," he wrote, "that the American people cannot always be bought." Also, as if he himself had just personally escaped a danger, he said, "I hope to God I don't grow reactionary with advancing years."

He was nearly thirty-five, just a little older than Daniels had been as a Bryan first lieutenant at the convention which began the battle against the Goldbugs in 1896. Franklin was old enough, however, not to answer a letter which he received from the unabashed Colonel Thompson just two weeks after the election. He wrote Franklin asking if he would object to a Navy League campaign to make him Secretary of the Navy.

"You have mastered the details of administration," the confident Colonel wrote him, "you have shown a wide and strong grasp of the principles which must be employed in carrying on the Navy and . . . it will be impossible for President Wilson to find anyone else who can in the next four years do as much for the Navy and the country as you can."

To a supporter not quite so vividly labeled as Colonel Thompson, he wrote a tactful reply to a similar suggestion:

"I am having a perfectly good time with many important things to do and my heart is entirely in my work," he said.

"Personally, I have no use for a man who, serving in a subordinate position, is continually contriving ways to step into his boss's shoes and I detest nothing so much as that kind of disloyalty. I have worked very gladly under Mr. Daniels and I wish the public could realize how much he has done for the Navy. I would feel very badly indeed if friends of mine should unwittingly give the impression that I was for a minute thinking of taking his place at the head of the Navy."

In less guarded fashion he had written Eleanor in the Indian summer weather immediately following the victory: "I have any amount of work to do and J.D. is too damned slow for words—his failure to decide the few big things holds me up all down the line."

He was in a hurry but Colonel Thompson, of course, was a romantic. In the election people like Thompson had lost. People like Daniels had won. Even *The New York Times,* which had been as unenthusiastic about Daniels as Colonel House in April, said in November that hostility against him had diminished because of the character of his aides and his coolness under criticism. The ships were already building. Before the end of the year, Daniels always remembered with pride, "we had entered upon the biggest shipbuilding program ever undertaken by any navy at one time." The morale of the Navy was high. Perhaps Daniels had been pretty tough with some of those like Admiral Fiske who publicly opposed his policies. But there were stout aides around him. It made him feel best, however, to have old Admiral George Dewey's affection.

Dewey, who himself had been subjected to cruel attack when, after his victory, there had been talk of him for the Presidency, had profanely resented the criticism of Daniels. The old man had a temper. Once, indeed, he flared furiously at Admiral Benson in Daniels' office. Dewey had been told that Benson wished to replace him as the chairman of the Navy's General Board. Dewey was wrong. Late in the afternoon Daniels went to his home and told him so. Neither he nor the President would ever see Dewey put aside, he said, and the Admiral had been unjust to the younger officer. The Admiral listened. When the Secretary was through he walked out to the door with him and suddenly there the Admiral put his arms around Daniels and kissed him.

"You're a good dear boy," he said.

There was a quarter of a century between them. At fifty-four, Daniels did not feel like a boy but even with war coming beyond the turn of the year, it seemed a good, dear time.

The Last for War

"PLEASE SUE THIS SHEET FOR LIBEL!" FRANKLIN WROTE HIS CHIEF.

Nothing was more characteristic of Roosevelt in those years than the peremptory, underlined *"Please"* generally followed by an exclamation point. Even in the documents the word carries the sense of the head tossed back and the nose lifted under the pince-nez glasses. It was a word with which Daniels was familiar. In this case Franklin had scrawled it across a clipping from the *Detroit Free Press* in which an over-eager headline writer had written, above a dispatch which contained nothing to justify it, the headline: NO LESS A PERSONAGE THAN JOSE-PHUS DANIELS GAVE HINT THAT LED TO 'KILL-INGS' IN WALL STREET.

Daniels did not sue. He did not bother with the charge. Within six months he had been subjected to the allegation that he was concerned for the profits of war-traffickers as well as to the savage statement of Theodore Roosevelt, when he turned down high battleship bids by private yards, that "the dominant idea in the Navy is to get possession of and break down all private yards, not with a view to preparation but in order to advance on the road to socialism." The particular matter about which Franklin cried, "Please," of course, related to charges that Daniels' friend, Bernard M. Baruch, member of the Advisory Committee of the Council of National Defense, had made millions by short sales on a peace "leak." Baruch completely

refuted the charges as to himself. Nobody but a mislabeling
headline writer ever suggested that Daniels was connected with
the suspicions.

Roosevelt sent in his "please" with the Detroit clipping as he
prepared, in January 1917, to leave on an inspection tour of
marine-occupied Haiti and San Domingo. There seemed little
immediate prospect of war when he set out on that trip in a
congenial company, including two of his favorite golf partners,
Livy Davis and John A. McIlhenny. His mother then expressed
her feeling of the only apparent danger in her hope that he
"took dark glasses and a pith helmet for I know how you feel
the tropical sun." He was in good spirits. This time instead
of missing the dispatch of marines, he was going to join them.
Haiti, as a land long occupied by marines, was important to
him then and afterward. In 1943, he said that he expected that
when he died Haiti would be found written on his heart. He
had begun to remember then that "I myself sent marines to
Haiti through a period of great unrest in that Republic." Actually, when the marines landed in Haiti, in the summer of 1915,
he had been at Campobello. He certainly had a good time on
the Caribbean island during his two weeks' visit, in January
and February 1917. He was dining in the flower-filled court-
yard of a marine commandant when he got a message from
Daniels calling him home. The Germans had announced the
reopening of unrestricted submarine warfare. Wilson had
given von Bernstorff his papers and sent him home.

Franklin felt very let down after he hurried home. To one
of his companions on the trip he wrote that the "wild dash
north" seemed "more or less of a joke." It did not seem like a
joke afterward. In 1941 he recalled "distinctly that beginning
about the fifth of February, when I got back from Haiti and San
Domingo, with the approval of Mr. Daniels, we went ahead
ordering the guns with which to arm the ships." Admiral Ralph
Earle, Chief of the Bureau of Ordnance, at Daniels' instruction,

was already at work on that before Franklin returned. Franklin
did not get back from Haiti until February eighth. It was a
month later, March 6, that he commented on inaction which
gave him the let-down feeling. It was at that time, he said in
1939, that he went to see Wilson as Acting Secretary in "the
first week in March" 1917. Actually he was not Acting Secretary
during that time. Daniels was in Washington that week and
apparently during the weeks before and after it. All the same
Franklin recalled Wilson's refusal to let him as Acting Secretary
bring the fleet back from its Cuban base and what Wilson said
to him at that time.

"I am going to tell you something I cannot tell the public,"
the President told him. "I owe you an explanation. I don't
want to do anything in a military way, by way of war preparations, that would allow the definitive historian in later days . . .
to say the United States had committed an unfriendly act against
the Central Powers." Roosevelt was impatient then, but the
night before Pearl Harbor when Harry Hopkins suggested that
the United States might strike first, he almost repeated Wilson's
words when he said: "No, we can't do that. We are a democracy of a peaceful people. We have a good record. We must
stand on it."

Franklin was not content with that point of view in 1917.
He was impatient then with Wilson as well as Daniels. In a
diary which Roosevelt kept briefly at the time, he wrote less
philosophically about Wilson's attitude, in early March, when
Wilson faced the war as he began his second Presidential term.
Franklin noted: "White House statement that W has power to
arm and *inference* that he will use it. J.D. says he will by Mon-
day. Why doesn't the President say so without equivocation?"
Wilson's problem was not quite so simple as it seemed to young
Franklin, but the President had just said what he thought with-
out equivocation of "the little group of wilful men" in the
Senate who, on the eve of war, had by filibuster denied him

clear Congressional authority to arm merchant ships against the U-boats.

It was at that time that Franklin took his impatience with Daniels—not Wilson—to Colonel House. Roosevelt was in a very critical mood. In his diary he described the day on which he began his second term as the subordinate of both Wilson and Daniels, Monday, March 5, 1917. He was seated, he wrote, too far away to hear Wilson's address, but he observed "little enthusiasm in crowd." Even when he got on the President's protected reviewing stand for the parade his comment was that it was an "awful mistake to review troops from glass cage." Obviously the important part of the day to him was the late afternoon when he went to a confidential conference with Colonel House.

Since some of Franklin's close friends were the protégés, informants, and admirers of the Colonel, Franklin appreciated the Colonel's power. In his quiet way House did not conceal it. He was never before or after so conscious of his power as at that time. Even Admiral Grayson, in his position close to the President, seemed to the Colonel to have lost influence as a result of "pressing his own fortunes in an indelicate and objectionable way." Like a man rubbing his hands together, House wrote in his secret journal that "the little circle close to the President seemed to have dwindled down to the two of us, Mrs. Wilson and myself." The Colonel's enthusiasm to get rid of Daniels seemed to have diminished but he was glad to hear Franklin's criticism of him. Franklin described the confidential session briefly in his short diary:

> Saw Colonel House at White House at 6:00 and gave him guarded views about condition of Navy and opposed strongly sending fleet through Canal in event of war. Looks like running away. Bad for morale of fleet and country and too far to bring home if Canal blocked or German submarines in Caribbean.

That was not the problem about the fleet as Daniels recorded it in his diary. The choice in his mind and in that of naval officers was between the bases in Cuba and Chesapeake Bay. Colonel House obviously encouraged Franklin's reports. He checked with Franklin's friend, Frank Polk, new Counselor of the State Department, in whose office House's son-in-law, the always-rising Auchincloss, was soon to have a new and better job. Polk, who had been a little ahead of Franklin at both Groton and Harvard, kept House informed, the Colonel duly noted, not only about State Department matters but also as to what went on in the Army and Navy Departments in the same building. Polk advised House to "keep in touch with the Navy situation through Roosevelt."

After his talk with House, Franklin left Washington to inspect Navy Yards in Boston and New York. He was glad to note that the Boston naval district was ahead of others "on plans and enrollment of boats and men for reserve" which was the naval program closest to his heart. He lunched "with Class of '04 at the Harvard Club and spoke quite freely about the Navy." He paid particular attention to the naval reservists of Boston. He had a special conference with old social friends, Nathaniel Frederick Ayer and Robert Wales Emmons, II, members of his civilian naval reserve committee. They had had, he was shocked to find, no replies from Washington as "to authority asked for" in six days. "I got it by radio." He was pleased by the response of "young gentlemen," who, a society writer noted enthusiastically, were "willing to exchange the ballroom for the battlefield" (or the power boat).

Franklin came down from Boston to New York, where on Sunday he talked with Colonel House again for an hour. House was waiting for him. He had put in his diary the day before an entry about "prodding Daniels through Franklin Roosevelt and others." Franklin wrote in his diary of his second visit to House:

Outlined principal weaknesses of Navy—J.D.'s procrastination—Benson's dislike of England—failure to make plans with France and England and study their methods—necessity if war comes of going into it with all force—money, troops, etc. He was sympathetic and agreed to main point.

That main point was clarified by another confidential conference later in the day. That was a remarkable dinner at the Metropolitan Club which Franklin attended as a member of the Wilson administration. It would have been difficult to assemble a more powerful body of Wilson's or Daniels' critics. Those present, FDR noted in his diary, were Theodore Roosevelt, Leonard Wood, J. P. Morgan, Cornelius Bliss, Mayor John Purroy Mitchel, Elihu Root, and Governor Edge of New Jersey. Ray Stannard Baker referred to such a group at a similar meeting just a year before as "the Sanhedrin of the opposition." Bliss' father had been McKinley's Secretary of the Interior and long-time treasurer of the Republican National Committee. Edge had just been elected Republican Governor of New Jersey. Though Mayor Mitchel had been one of the bright young men to whom Wilson's eye was attracted in 1913, he was that year to be defeated for re-election on the grounds that he had become "too much Fifth Avenue, too little First Avenue" by a regular Democratic opponent whom Mitchel denounced as pro-German and possessing a "yellow streak." The elder Roosevelt had quoted Mitchel to Senator Lodge not long before as a witness to what they regarded as President Wilson's vacillating policy. TR then considered Wilson "purely demagogue" but was saying nothing publicly himself at the time because "war is possible, and as I have applied for leave to raise a division, I doubt the propriety of doing so."

Franklin at the time was as publicly quiet about the Metropolitan dinner meeting for similar Rooseveltian reasons, but he described it in his diary: "Condition of Army and Navy outlined." He alone among them could give official information about that. And he added: "Discussion of 1. how to make administration steer clear course to uphold rights. 2. how to get action increase Army and Navy. Decided to use Governors' Conference to demand this. Root inclined to praise administration's present course.—T.R. wanted more vigorous demand about future course—less endorsement of past. I backed T.R.'s theory. Left for Washington."

In Washington he found the Secretary in very serious mood. Daniels wrote in his diary that he called Roosevelt in to go over with him and Benson the final instructions to be given the officers commanding the gun crews which were being placed on merchant ships.

"It was a rather solemn time," Daniels wrote, "for I felt I might be signing what would prove the death warrant of young Americans and the arming of ships may bring us into war."

The week which actually though not officially brought America into war was already begun. Perhaps a longer war than anyone realized began that week, too. The Secretary of the Navy and Mrs. Daniels went on the first day of that week to a dinner party at the Bakhmeteffs'. There were no signs of impending change at the Russian Embassy then. The Bakhmeteffs had acquired the big house on Sixteenth Street which the Communists were to inherit. It seems almost to have been designed for such transition. It was built by the widow of George M. Pullman, the palace car magnate, in whose "model" industrial town in the 1890's had begun the railroad strike which had helped make the politics of Bryan in those days seem the politics of revolution, too. The house was, a contemporary critic of Washington architecture said, "the finest example to be found in Washington of how money can be spent without securing beauty, elegance or comfort." In the house in the Bakhmeteff days, according to Vice-President Marshall, who thought the Ambassador kept the best cigars in Washington, "all the flunkies were more than six feet tall. As they waited at table they wore their swords at their sides."

In his diary my father did not describe the scene. He recorded instead his conversation with an American who had lived long in Russia and returned with the assurance that Russia like America was democratic. "The aristocracy is a myth," he said. He quoted, and Daniels recorded, the statement of the president of a great Russian university that the two countries had more in common than any other two. It seemed to Daniels a very interesting point of view. He added, however, a note of his own.

"Just while we were talking," he wrote, "the Russian revolution was going on and the Duma was deposing the czar."

That "glorious act of the Russians," as President Wilson described it, came just six days before the crucial Cabinet meeting at which in effect the decision for war was made. After that meeting on March twentieth, Franklin Lane, who had some time before facetiously suggested that in terms of their belligerency he and Daniels should swap posts, wrote that, "The Cabinet is at last a unit." But the President, Lane said, "goes unwillingly." So, he indicated, did Daniels. The Secretary of the Navy was the last man for war. Daniels wrote his feelings in his diary:

"He [Wilson] opposed G[erman] militarism on land & E[ngland]'s militarism on sea. Both were abhorrent. He was disinclined to the final break. Spoke of the glorious act of the Russians, which, in a way, had changed conditions, but he could not give that as reason for war.

"Asked about Cabinet view. All declared for war except B[urleson] and I, & the President said: 'Burleson, you and Daniels have not spoken.' B said he thought we were already at war, & that unless President called Congress the people would force action. The Pres. said, 'I do not care for popular demand. I want to do right whether popular or not.'

"It was a supreme moment in my life," Daniels wrote. "I had hoped and prayed this cup would pass. But there was no other course open, & I said our present attempt by armed guard could not be wholly effective & if it succeeded we must co-operate with English & let them convoy our ships while we patroled this coast. Having tried patience there was no course open to us except to protect our rights in the seas. If Germany wins, we must be a military nation."

The mood of the time, however, was not one of resignation. Soon after that Cabinet meeting, on the afternoon of March twenty-fourth, President and Mrs. Wilson together came across the narrow street between the White House and the State, War and Navy Building to call on the Secretary of the Navy. A young White House clerk named Thomas W. Brahany, who was also keeping a diary at that time, thought it was "the first time in American history that a President's wife has accompanied the President in a purely business call on a Cabinet officer." As Daniels described it, it was a purely social visit. However Colonel House may have felt, Brahany noted that there was general rejoicing at the White House that Dr. Grayson had just been confirmed as an admiral. "Everybody in the Executive office likes Grayson," he wrote. It had taken "a good navigator," Daniels said in his diary, to get Grayson's confirmation through the Senate, however. The President and Mrs. Wilson were in a sociable mood on their visit to Daniels. Mrs. Wilson admired the office, "the most beautiful in Washington." The Secretary showed her John Paul Jones' sword. Wilson talked at length and with pleasure about Paul Nikolayevich Milyukov who was then Minister of Foreign Affairs in the new revolutionary Russian government. It pleased the President that he was a college professor. Daniels noticed the loving attention which Mrs. Wilson gave the President's talk and stories and that his word for her was "sweetheart." It seemed a happy visit in an unhappy time. Not all meetings in that office at that time were so amiable. Indeed, then, around the Secretary, the roughest row was going on between Franklin Roosevelt and the admirals.

Franklin had come back to Washington in an impatient frame of mind. The day he got back he wrote the last entry in the brief diary: "Asked Secretary in the presence of Benson that matters pertaining to Naval District Defense be put under me. To discuss tomorrow. Something must be done to organize and expedite work." Also, he began his enthusiastic campaign for 50-foot motorboats to patrol the shores. It was a campaign in which he ran into the opposition not so much of Daniels as of Benson; and of Admiral Hugh Rodman, then a member of the General Board of the Navy and later commander of the American battleships in European waters; the Navy's chief constructor, Admiral David W. Taylor; Admiral Robert S. Griffin, Chief of the Bureau of Engineering; and Admiral Henry B. Wilson, who was to be in command of American naval forces in France. They listened to Roosevelt and got the impression he thought it was a yachtsman's war.

Franklin's difference with the Secretary and the admirals was not about sub-chasers as such. The day he got back from New York, Daniels had a conference, arranged some time before, "with a score of men" in his office about the building of 110-foot sub-chasers. FDR's 50-foot boat idea was something else. He pursued it with the enthusiasm which he gave to brighter ideas. He may have discussed it the next day when Daniels noted: "Plans for organizing motorboat flotilla" and the next when he wrote, "Roosevelt, Benson and the ships for patrol service." Apparently the young Assistant Secretary was officiously persistent about his small boat idea, for the day after the decisive Cabinet meeting Daniels wrote a little impatiently, "Roosevelt urged motor boats to be used for patrol. Will order many, but are they valuable? How much of that sort of junk shall we buy?" And again four days later: "FDR & 50-foot boats—his hobby. Good in smooth water. I fear buying a lot of junk."

Roosevelt's persistence created an explosion the next day. Franklin on his own initiative went ahead and ordered some 50-foot boats. Officers in the Department recommended that the contract not be approved. Admiral James O. Richardson, then a young officer, remembered later that Roosevelt jokingly threatened to send one of them to Guam. Richardson also remembered that not all officers appreciated his joking. And when Louis Howe, who lacked Roosevelt's light touch, suggested to Admiral Rodman, then about to go to sea, that it might be to his advantage to favor the 50-foot boats, Rodman exercised his special gift for salty profanity. Also he took the matter straight into the Secretary's office. The Daniels diary said, "Rodman—angry—R had urged 50-foot boats and Rodman had opposed." Also an entry at the same time indicated that the 110-foot boats could be obtained. Franklin did not agree. He wrote a letter to the Secretary "most solemnly" protesting the manner in which Admiral Taylor and Admiral Griffin had handled the matter. He wrote:

> I am entirely dissatisfied with the manner in which the Bureau of Construction and Repair and Steam Engineering and the Division of Operations have handled the whole subject of building chasers.

When Daniels received this letter "roasting Griffin and Taylor," he called them and Roosevelt into his office. Afterward he noted of Roosevelt: "He wants 50-foot boats. I saw Captain Henry Wilson and he said he would not waste public money building 50-foot boats." And Daniels added: "Interview with R, G & T not very agreeable. Left a bad taste in the mouth."

In retrospect the taste is not sweetened by the background presence of Arthur P. Homer. He was a promoter, not a patrician, from Boston. Franklin found him fascinating. He let him use his name as a reference to J. P. Morgan. It was not until 1932 when a Homer scheme of getting campaign contributions from contractors with whom Franklin had dealt in the Navy Department was publicized that Roosevelt felt it necessary to repudiate him. Also, in those later years when Homer sued to collect a commission from a shipbuilding concern for getting a contract, he alleged that he had been put to the trouble and expense of bribing an admiral to get it. He must have been quite a figure ensconced in the Shoreham Hotel in 1917. Obviously he had a very persuasive influence on Roosevelt who sent him to Europe twice to get aircraft data. Franklin put two exclamation points after a sentence in a letter to Eleanor in which he reported that "last night Livy and I and Jim Wadsworth dined with the Homers!!" When Roosevelt was quarreling with the admirals upon whom Daniels depended Homer was advising him. He was after his fashion qualified to do so. He was a representative of Sterling Motors which his advertisement, in the Boston Directory for 1917, described as "The Engine of Refinement—For the Finest Boats That Float." Franklin's 50-foot boats were to be powered with Sterling engines.

The row over the motorboats was at its height when Wilson delivered his war message to Congress. Daniels wrote of it that he went up to "hear the President speak on Germany's making war on us." I went with my father to hear the President speak. I remember riding with Father after that great occasion in the carriage to the Navy Department and listening there to the sound of the hooves of the cavalry escort which had come back from the Capitol with Wilson. I remember, too, that on the ride that night to the Department and then home, Father was very quiet, but hard quiet which we understood in our family and respected.

The next day the President told him that "the applause in

the Capitol grated on him because he felt the gravity and seriousness of the situation made applause far from his feeling." Claude Kitchin closed the debate on behalf of those who even then could not vote for war. His speech reads in history like a brave if mistaken one.

"Profoundly impressed with the gravity of the situation," Kitchin said, "appreciating to the fullest the penalties which a war-mad moment will impose, my conscience and judgment, after mature thought and fervent prayer for rightful guidance, have marked out clearly the path of my duty, and I have made up my mind to walk it, if I go barefooted and alone."

Much as he disagreed with Kitchin at that moment, my father would have been angry if he had been there and heard the blatant Tom Heflin of Alabama, later so close to the Ku Klux Klan, when Heflin jumped to his feet and shouted:

"I say to you, Mr. Speaker, that had I contemplated such action as that committed by the gentleman from North Carolina, the majority leader of this House, I would have made out my resignation as leader first, then have made the speech and resigned from Congress."

It seems to me important in American history that, even at that passionate moment, Heflin was hissed. I am particularly glad now of the little note Father made about that war speech session in his diary at the time.

"Jonathan got in through kindness of Kitchin."

There was no hanging back. Even before the declaration Lane had written that the meetings of the Cabinet were "nothing less than councils of war." On April 6, watching while the President signed the declaration of war, Daniels' aide, a flag enthusiast and a driving destroyer builder, had semaphored the news across the street to the Secretary's office. The news went as quickly to every ship and station. The next day, however, when Franklin came in with a proposal for a twelve-hour work day in the Norfolk Navy Yard, Daniels disapproved it. He undoubtedly seemed to be disapproving many of Franklin's suggestions at that time. It was on that same day that Franklin wrote in longhand another of his "please" communications:

> DEAR MR. DANIELS—
>   Do *please* get through two vital things *today*:
>   1. Get that Interior Building or give it to the War Dept. & let us take latter's space here.
>   2. Authorize calling out Naval Militia or Reserve—It is essential to get them if we are to go ahead.
>   FDR

Across the top someone, perhaps one of those who felt that Daniels had been listening to too much talk about 50-foot boats and the naval reservists, penciled: "Do you always follow his advice?" Franklin did not think so. The Secretary was not disturbed by the peremptory "pleases." Properly, office space received much of Franklin's attention at the time. It was the sort of work for which he was primarily responsible and the quest for it remained a lively part of his memory afterward. When a similar problem arose in 1941 he recalled:

> Back in the fall of 1917 [sic], the Navy Department needed space, and I took up with President Wilson the possibility of building a temporary building—wooden building—down here on the Oval. And he said, "Why do you select that site?" I said, "Mr. President, because it would be so unsightly right here in front of the White House, that it would have to be taken down at the end of the war." "Well," he said, "I don't think I could stand all that hammering and sawing right under my front windows." He said, "Can't you put it somewhere else?" So I said, "Of course. Put it down in Potomac Park." "Well," he said, "put it there and we will get rid of it."

It was not quite so simple, then or later. He was not, however, content with getting office space, he crowded the day of his imperative memorandum with another request which Daniels noted more seriously: "FDR wanted me to sign order for Winslow to come here to assist him. Declined. Should not have a retired admiral for such service. Had a long talk with B[enson] at night. He thought it was aimed at him and R wanted W to advise as to operations. No division of power as to operations."

Admiral Cameron McRae Winslow was an excellent officer. Daniels himself had considered him for Chief of Operations before he named Benson, but found that his ideas on naval organization were too much like those of Admiral Fiske. Daniels had made him Commander-in-Chief of the Pacific Fleet instead, where Winslow had served until he retired the year before. Such facts and Winslow's rank gave color to Benson's suspicions, particularly after the sharp feelings just aroused in connection with Roosevelt's 50-foot boat argument with the admirals in the Department.

Two days later Daniels vetoed another Roosevelt proposal: "Benson went down on steamer to meet English and French Admirals at Old Point with Mayo [Henry T. Mayo, Commander-in-Chief of the fleet] and Wilson to discuss best methods of cooperation. R wished to go down to meet them as honor. I said No. He did not like it but—"

Only the admirals went to meet the admirals. Franklin stayed at home and went instead to see Theodore Roosevelt whose arrival in the capital had about it the qualities of both a march on Washington and a magnanimous but contingent support of the President. "Uncle Ted" seemed the epitome of vigor though he was blind in one eye and had never recovered from the tropical infections of his last exploration. He was ready, given permission, to raise and lead a division to France, to assure the President that "all that has gone before is as dust on a windy street." There was dust and there had been much wind. Senator Lodge was TR's first visitor and, his daughter Alice said, "the next day the house was overrun with politicians, personal friends and representatives of the press, at breakfast, lunch and dinner, and at all hours in between." Eleanor and Franklin were among the callers, and Eleanor remembered that "though he was kind to us, as he always was, he was completely preoccupied with the war" and after he had seen Wilson "returned in a very unhappy mood."

"I hated to have him disappointed," she wrote later, "and yet I was loyal to President Wilson." She was "much relieved" when the decision was made not to let him go. Franklin had arranged an interview for TR with Secretary of War Newton D. Baker, who had succeeded Garrison in March 1916, and tried to secure the decision TR wanted.

Much less attention was paid to the arrival of Bryan in Washington a few days later. He did not seem dramatic when he telegraphed the President on the day of the declaration, "enroll me as a private wherever I am needed and assign me to any work that I can do." He wrote Daniels:

"I do not want any command. Am too old to learn the art of war. I simply want to do my duty wherever I can when I am needed."

Bryan came to dinner at the Daniels house. He was not happy. He hoped, he told Daniels, that democracy would come in Germany and hasten the close of the war. Also he recalled that twelve years before, after a visit to Russia, he predicted it would be the first country in Europe to become a republic. Bryan's burlesquers would have been quick to wonder aloud whether he had ever heard of France or Switzerland. There seemed to be no end of innocence.

Action was all. One thing "Uncle Ted" had much on his mind was his strong feeling that Franklin should resign and go into uniformed service. He was "always urging Franklin to resign," Eleanor remembered. Franklin was thirty-five. TR had been forty and the father of six children when he resigned as Assistant Secretary to go to the Spanish War. Franklin's roommate, Lathrop Brown, after serving as Lane's war assistant, went into the tank corps. Henry Breckinridge, who had been Franklin's opposite number, became a major in the Army. Gussie Gardner resigned from Congress, saying that he had advocated preparedness so long and so strenuously that he could not stay out with a clear conscience or a straight face. Daniels' young son, Josephus, Jr., though his bad eyesight had to be waived, went into the Marine Corps as a private, not as an officer as Franklin thought he should. Franklin himself was advised to stay where he was by very different gentlemen. Daniels urged him to stay. Leonard Wood, who shared the prejudices of the militants against Daniels, wrote one of Franklin's friends that "Franklin should under no circumstances think of leaving the Navy Department. It would be a public calamity to have him leave at this time."

It may have seemed strategically essential to Wood that there be an assistant secretary ready to attend the secret Metropolitan Club meetings of the opposition. Daniels obviously was not anxious to keep Franklin for that reason. He wanted Franklin to remain because he not only liked him, but he trusted him and depended upon him.

Despite suggestions from the Congress and the example of the War Department, Daniels saw no need of adding additional Assistant Secretaries. He was not disturbed by the imperative "pleases." He was eager for anti-submarine craft—if not 50-foot ones. Though less confident of its practicality, he was as interested as Roosevelt was—and President Wilson—in the possibility of a mine barrage across the North Sea to shut in the submarines, and from the first month of the war was impatient with the reluctance of the British Admiralty to adopt this proposal. It was one of the aggressive activities which he had urged Admiral William S. Sims to impress upon the Admiralty when the Secretary dispatched Sims to England in civilian clothes in March to take command, as soon as war was declared, of U.S. Naval Forces Operating in European Waters.

Sims, Roosevelt said later, was suggested by him. Daniels had first offered the post to Admiral Henry B. Wilson, but that officer preferred command in the fleet. Sims had been selected quickly as a substitute. Daniels had not been impressed when he first met Sims with the Admiral's arguments that the American Navy should be organized like the British Admiralty. Also, he was aware when he named him to the British post that President Taft had felt it necessary to reprimand Sims, a Canadian by birth, for a speech in London in which he said, "If the time ever comes when the British Empire is menaced by an external enemy, it is my opinion that you may count upon every man, every dollar, every drop of blood of your kindred across the sea." Sims may have got the feeling for such belligerent speech when he was naval aide to Theodore Roosevelt. In 1917, however, his strong pro-British sentiments seemed to commend him for the task of quick co-operation with the British Admiralty. Daniels, however, took the occasion when he informed him of his assignment to say that he was selected not because of that speech but despite it. It was an assignment he was to regret deeply.

Many things had to be arranged then quickly. The Secretary of the Navy had other than purely naval tasks. As a member of the Cabinet and as senior member of the Council of National Defense, he had to consider all the major problems. These involved not only dispatch but debate. And in the debate it was remarkable in how many matters he found himself confronting Franklin Lane. The war pressure for petroleum gave new strength to those who wished to open the naval oil reserves in California to the private claimants. In a threatened railroad strike Daniels felt that Lane's proposal in the Council of National Defense "would have been equivalent to taking sides of RR owners against the employes." With the President behind them, Daniels and Secretary Baker opposed a coal price agreement Lane had negotiated. "I came to the brink" of resignation, Lane later wrote Lansing, when the President did that. Daniels and Lane differed on how to treat the IWW's who constituted a first and indigenous "red scare." Daniels had had his fingers burned on that matter early in the administration when a speech he made about the flag, to his shock and surprise as an old friend of labor, had been followed by an attack by sailors on the IWW headquarters in Seattle. He was opposed to any such ruthless roundup of the IWW's as some Western Governors suggested. At the same time, some large business interests might have suspected a lingering malice when, in trying to keep arms prices down, he noted in his diary after the President had approved a steel price agreement he urged, "Watch Schwab and Grace wince."

Daniels was expected to be against any man from Wall Street. That was one reason, his friend Baruch said, why people found surprising Daniels' steady support of the tall, blue-eyed speculator in the increasingly important war purchase and war industry jobs he was given. That may have been one reason why Baruch always regarded Daniels as "an extraordinary man." Daniels' attitude toward Baruch was completely different from that of Colonel House, who had many friends in Wall Street, but thought of Baruch still as "a Hebrew Wall Street speculator." Baruch was not, House wrote, "the type that inspires confidence." Like some others Baruch thought House was his friend but he was a little horrified when the Colonel, making a motion as if he were holding the earth in the palm of his hand, said to Baruch, "Isn't it a wonderful thing to be playing with the destinies of the world?" That was a kind of gambling the Jewish speculator did not care for. Also, years afterward Baruch remembered that the Colonel who tried to prevent his getting the war industries job was not averse to asking Baruch to give a job to a friend of his. Later, Baruch told me, the man came to him and said he was ashamed of the role he was playing, "that he had been put in there by

House as a spy." No such suspicions ever troubled Daniels and Baruch. It was later suggested that Baruch was one of those who wanted to get rid of Daniels. Baruch denied it flatly. He and Daniels had become, as he said, "fast friends" by April 1917, when the Wall Streeter wrote the Navy Secretary in the first month of war: "I feel you are making good and that the Navy, under your guidance, is going to be a source of pride to this country and an example to the rest of the world." Daniels had written in his diary a few days before, "Talked to Baruch about steel. He is fine. . . ."

Daniels, as the newspaperman in the Cabinet, had almost the single responsibility of working out for the President a system of censorship which he was determined should be as free and as sensible as possible. In that and war propaganda, Wilson depended upon the controversial but effective George Creel. Creel leaned much on Daniels. The head of the Committee on War Information was a fascinating talker who looked like a gargoyle and whose prejudices were as passionate as his loyalties. As Daniels' friend in war publicity Creel collided soon with Louis Howe, who Daniels always felt "would have sidetracked both President Wilson and me to get Franklin to the White House." Soon after Creel arrived in Washington, he said Howe came to him with the proposal that the information chief ask FDR to sit with him "from time to time as guide, philosopher and friend." The offer was declined with thanks. Then not long afterward Creel said he began to note a revival "of the old canards about Josephus Daniels' ineptitudes, rusticities and Billy Sundayisms. I put tracers out, and soon found that the whispers had their source in none other than Howe, whereupon I went over and let him have it right between the eyes. Of course, he insisted he was 'only explaining and defending Uncle Joe' but I told him if I heard any more of his phony explanations and defenses I would carry the matter to W.W. who had a very precise idea of what constituted loyalty."

There were many things to wish for and work for. In the early days of the second world war, when so many things were "on order" but not on hand, some wit suggested that in addition to the red routing slips on orders marked RUSH another was needed marked FRANTIC. There was the same feeling in 1917. Daniels' working day lengthened. His Sundays were less secure. For some, however, it was a gay as well as a strenuous time. There was almost a social blossoming for war. Some felt that Daniels did not give that social side of war a proper emphasis. It was a definite shock to a State Department official when he sent "quantities of drinkables" to the *Mayflower* for the entertainment of the French Commission, that the Captain refused to take them aboard and that Daniels on appeal said, "It is Final. Final." There was no lack of such ashore, however. There seemed to be an increase in elegance rather than austerity. The rich and fashionable arrived. Not all were deserving Democrats. The situation was somewhat similar to that in World War II when Roosevelt spoke of the second congregation of the Dollar-a-Year men: "I have searched the whole country. There's no Democrat rich enough to work for a dollar a year."

The Secretary of the Navy noted indignantly: "Everybody wants to be an officer and get a bombproof position." It was some time later before he got a report on "the Roosevelt young men—all entered as officers with commissions." Oddly, perhaps, one of the first jobs Roosevelt gave me when I went on his staff in World War II was to see how many rich and well-born young men had found safe and decorative places in Washington. He remembered well. One of his favorite stories was about Washington in World War I, when the tired official looking for diversions in the afternoons could take his choice on Massachusetts Avenue. There were houses where guests were served every kind of drink. There were residences where the intellectual and the artistic met for intellectual and artistic talk. There was a mansion where the music was soft, so were the sofas and the ladies were very pretty. Franklin knew them all.

"The saloon, the salon and the Salome," he described them in reminiscence during World War II. It seemed more than a joke about a time he had enjoyed.

Nigel Law, who was living then with other British bachelors on Ashmead Place, described the times:

> There are many entries in my diary saying "dined with Franklin" or "F dined with us." Most of these were in the summer months and referred to occasions when we went with a few others to such places as the Lock Tavern Club on the Potomac and walked in the woods or bathed. We had little time for diversion. You can guess how busy he was, and my own hours of work began at 9:30 AM and seldom ended until 2 or 3 AM, with a break of a couple of hours or so at supper time.

There were also weekends on the river on the blessed *Sylph*. One such party that summer included Franklin, his cousin Major Henry L. Roosevelt, U.S.M.C., Colonel A. W. Catlin, U.S.M.C., Franklin's good golf partner and friend John McIlhenny and his wife, Nigel Law and Lucy Mercer. They sailed at three on Saturday and Eleanor Roosevelt joined them down the river in the early evening. They went ashore to visit Wakefield where Washington was born. They swam in the river. They had fun.

"I was stung by poison ivy for the first and last time," Law recalled, "because I climbed a wild cherry tree in bathing trunks to pick the fruit for Franklin."

They were back Monday morning. Papers piled high on the Assistant Secretary's desk—as on all other desks in Washington then—and a hot summer was beginning. It got on people's nerves. Since some of the Roosevelt children had been deposited with Franklin's mother at Hyde Park, Eleanor got off a little later than usual for Campobello. She apparently left un-happily. After describing a bad cold which he had, Franklin wrote her reassuringly soon after she left.

"I really can't stand that house all alone without you," he said, "and you were a goosy girl to think or even pretend to think that I don't want you here all the summer, because you know I do! But honestly *you* ought to have six weeks straight at Campo, just as *I* ought to, only you can and I can't! I *know* what a whole summer here does to people's nerves and at the end of this summer I will be like a bear with a sore head until I get a change or some cold weather—in fact as you know I am unreasonable and touchy now—but I shall try to improve."

He was nervous. He may have been romantic in the midst of another war twenty-seven years later when he said that in the spring of 1917 the Secret Service found on a German list of those "to be eliminated" his name and that of his Groton and Yale friend, Frank Polk, who had been his close contact with Colonel House, leading all the rest. The Secret Service asked him to wear a pistol in a shoulder holster, he said. "Although a fair shot with a revolver," Franklin realized that he would not get the gun out before his assassin was half a mile away. He put it, he said, "in the top table drawer where it remained for twenty-five years." He must have had it out just after Eleanor left, however.

"Last night," he wrote, "I thought I heard a burglar and sat at the head of the stairs with the gun for half an hour, but it turned out to be the cat."

The heat was hard on the nerves of everybody in Washington. Colonel House was back at Pride's Crossing where it was cool.

Men of Vigor

FRANKLIN ROOSEVELT AND FRANKLIN LANE JOINED IN THE INVITA-
tion, early in the summer of 1917, to other government officials
in Washington to get up and exercise before going to work in
the mornings just as the boys were doing in the camps. Walter
Camp, the Yale athlete, clock manufacturer and picker of All-
American football teams, agreed to come to Washington and
direct them. William Kent, wealthy member of the Tariff
Commission, offered the grounds of his house at 1925 F Street,
which later became an exclusive club, as the scene of the
Cabinet and sub-Cabinet calisthenics. There they stretched and
jumped and squatted, and from there Camp led them on the
"double quick," running and panting through Potomac Park.

The intentions of Lane, Roosevelt and Camp were excellent,
but they almost disrupted the war effort before it was begun.
Lane had already had one attack of angina. Franklin was to be
laid up with a cold soon after he started exercising and with an
infected throat again before the summer was over. Daniels, who
kept his health and was not sick a day during the war, declined
the opportunity, after working grinding hours through the day
and night before, to give up an extra hour of sleep in the
morning to cavort with Mr. Camp.

The Secretary of the Navy was not an athlete. For middle-
aged men, he rather distrusted the strenuous life which
Theodore Roosevelt had made so popular in Washington.

Daniels felt about such exercise for himself and his tired colleagues as he had felt about giving military command to the confidently vigorous TR who was to be operated on twice during the war in which he wished to lead. Daniels stayed home and got his sleep. He had been willing, however, in the face of the enthusiastic pressure of Franklin and others on him to join the "keep fit" sessions, to take technical advice about the matter. He asked Sterling Ruffin.

"Joe," said the doctor, "you never took any exercise in your life. You never walked when you could ride. Stay away from that crowd and you'll live longer."

He did. He outlived them all. But he gave his blessing to the vigorous life by appointing Camp chairman of the Athletic Department of the United States Commission on Training Camp Activities. He understood the necessity of exercise for the boys. Indeed, he showed an acute, almost fatherly responsibility for the young men pouring into training stations. He was concerned for their morals as well as their muscles, so much so, indeed, that he was accused of "coddling the recruits a little too much." His determination to keep the boys from temptations "savors too much of the nursery" rather than the Navy, some robust citizens thought. The mayor of Newport denied Daniels' charges of immoral conditions surrounding the naval training station there. He said that the liquor laws with regard to men in service were being better enforced "since the Navy has at last been able to properly uniform the boys."

It was the day he had lunch with Camp and those who were going to exercise with him that Daniels also wrote about the "awful conditions" in Newport and a conference with the Governor of Rhode Island about them. Undoubtedly, the vice conditions there were bad but local officials, Daniels noted, were inclined to blame the Navy for conditions caused they thought by crowding and lack of adequate quarters. That conference may have been responsible for a note Daniels made a little later that a "Secret Service man in Newport wrote report quoting a gambler saying everything would be open soon for Governor Beekman had bought up Secretary Daniels."

"Roosevelt hahaed," Daniels wrote.

The vice situation there was not always going to be a laughing matter for Franklin. Daniels had told him to stop and investigate conditions when he went in June to Cambridge to become a Harvard Overseer. Franklin not only went but he was charged with approving the use of some sailors as decoys in the entrapment of homosexuals, a charge which was greatly to embarrass him later. That visit was only one detail in a varied activity which was to make that a strenuous summer for FDR.

Franklin was back at his office and his exercises before Eleanor went off reluctantly with the children to Campobello in the middle of July. He had already become one of the leaders of Mr. Camp's vigorous morning men. That summer Mr. Camp described him as "a beautifully built man, with the long muscles of an athlete." Also, he had his well-known sinuses and tonsils. Two days after Eleanor left he was so miserable with a cough and cold that he did not even feel like playing solitaire. It was that day that he apologized to her for being unreasonable and touchy. Two days later he kept his irritation within humorous control when he read a story quoting Eleanor in *The New York Times*. "The food saving program adopted at the home of Franklin D. Roosevelt, Assistant Secretary of the Navy," that paper said, "has been selected by the conservation section of the Food Administration as a model for other large households." *The Times* story suggested that Eleanor's plan would serve as a model for "fashionable summer resorts" and for such ladies as Mrs. Harry Payne Whitney and Mrs. Williard Straight.

"Making the ten servants help me do my saving," Eleanor was quoted as saying, "has not only been possible but highly profitable." The "cooks" (plural), the paper said, saved food scraps, the laundress was sparing in use of soap. The menus allowed only two courses for luncheon and three for dinner.

"All I can say," wrote Franklin of what he called Eleanor's "New Household Economy for Millionaires," "is that your latest newspaper campaign is a corker.

"Please have a photo taken showing the family, the ten co-operating servants, the scraps saved from the table and the handbook. I will have it published in the Sunday *Times*."

As a charitable husband, however, he knew that she was going to be mad. She was.

"I will never be caught again, that's sure," she said, "and I'd like to crawl away for shame."

The embarrassing elegance of Eleanor's patriotism did not disturb him long. It was also a summer in which, despite the piling work, there was time for fun. Old Admiral Cowles reported the feeling of his wife, TR's sister, when she came down that summer.

"She speaks of you as her debonair young cousin," the old Admiral wrote, "so brave and charming, but the girls will spoil you enough, Franklin, and I leave you to them."

That was a hazard. There were rumors, Dr. Freidel reported later, "apparently emanating from a prominent society figure who had the sharpest tongue in Washington, that FDR during this period was enamored of another woman, who, being a Catholic, would not marry him even if he got a divorce." That other woman was undoubtedly Lucy Mercer of whom he saw a great deal that summer of 1917. She was a Catholic. She remained devoted to him throughout his life. But that their friendship then ever came to a point where Franklin seriously contemplated divorce in order to marry her, if she would have married him, I do not believe.

No romance relaxed Roosevelt's young ambitions. And in those days, if he had obtained a divorce, any politician would have considered that action as terminating a career. It certainly would not have strengthened his position in the Navy Department. Daniels, as a Methodist, felt so strongly about divorce that when shortly before his own brother-in-law divorced his wife to marry another woman, he declined to let him continue as the business manager of his newspaper. Dr. Freidel, after scrutinizing the story, concluded that the divorce rumors were "preposterous." Romantic rumors at the time coupled Lucy's name with that of Nigel Law. Undoubtedly, however, there began in those years the story of an affection which ended only when Roosevelt died. Lucy was, as Grace Tully said in 1949 in her book, *F.D.R.—My Boss,* one of those visiting at Warm Springs on his last trip there.

Miss Tully said mistakenly that Miss Mercer (then Mrs. Winthrop Rutherfurd) had commissioned the portrait which Elizabeth Shoumatoff, the artist, was painting at the time of Roosevelt's death. Mrs. Rutherfurd was a friend and patron of the artist. She was interested in the two portraits of Roosevelt which Shoumatoff painted in his last years. The last unfinished portrait was designated by Roosevelt himself for Mrs. Rutherfurd's daughter Barbara, Mrs. Robert W. Knowles of Boston and Aiken. She had known Roosevelt most of her life and during the war when she was a student came sometimes among the "Off-the-Record" visitors to the White House to see him. Mrs. Rutherfurd came to see Roosevelt in South Carolina when the President was convalescing there from illness after the Teheran Conference in 1943. Once, during the war, Roosevelt's train was stopped on the way to Hyde Park for an afternoon at the Rutherfurd estate, Tranquillity, near Allamuchy in western New Jersey. Mrs. Rutherfurd, however, lived most of the time at the estate in Aiken which her husband, who died in 1944, had purchased from Congressman Gardner's estate. She was still a distinguishedly beautiful woman in her fifties—

and a very religious one—when she died in Memorial Hospital in New York in 1948.

She was lovely at twenty-six in 1917. Also, clearly, she was not only the employee but the accepted friend of both Franklin and Eleanor. A week after Eleanor left for Campobello Franklin spoke of her in a letter about a second trip down the river that summer on the *Sylph*.

"Such a funny party," he reported, "but it worked out *wonderfully!*"

Nigel Law and Lucy Mercer went along again. There were also the Cary Graysons, whom the President did not require on his cruise on the larger *Mayflower* that same weekend. Also there were the Charlie Munns. Munn, Harvard '10, was—or was to be—a naval lieutenant on duty in Washington. His wife, formerly Mary Astor Paul, of an old and wealthy Philadelphia family, worked closely with Eleanor in Navy Red Cross work and was, Eleanor wrote later, then "a young and pretty bride." Lucy Mercer and "Altrude" (for Alice Gertrude) Grayson had grown up as beauties in Washington together. With such ladies and Grayson in his new admiral's uniform, they must have made a decorative company—and a young one. Grayson, the oldest of the voyagers, was thirty-nine. Franklin was thirty-five. All the others were in their twenties. They had fun. Franklin reported: "We swam about four times and Sunday afternoon went up the James to Richmond. We stopped at lower and Upper Brandon, Westover and Shirley and went all over them, getting drenched to the skin by several severe thunderstorms. Those old houses are really wonderful but not *comfy!*"

Also: "I found much food for thought in the fleet—things not right and due to old lady officers and lack of decision in Department." They inspected the expanding fleet in a destroyer and had lunch on the battleship *Arkansas*. They visited the battlefield at Yorktown.

Law remembered their visit to the fleet safely based in York

River: "After lunch the ships passed in review, with bands playing. Most of them managed The Star-Spangled Banner successfully, but some auxiliary ships at the end of the line, presumably not trusting their newly formed bands to play the national air, went past to the tune of Alexander's Ragtime Band and other popular ditties. Franklin laughed heartily at the episode and the Admiral joined in after some hesitation."

At Westover, once home of the Byrd family and one of the earliest houses built on the grand scale in Virginia, Law remembered "an amusing incident."

"Franklin and I and some of the party," he recalled, "landed at the bottom of the garden and rang the bell. A darkie servant came out and he was told to say that the Under Secretary of the U.S. Navy would be glad to be allowed to visit the house and garden. The servant looked doubtful and soon came back with a curt 'No.' For a moment we were nonplussed, for we particularly wanted to visit this famous old place. Then Franklin had an idea. He said to me, 'Maybe they don't like Yankees in these parts. You send in your card.' So as a joke I told the man to take my card, on which I was described as 3rd Secretary of His Britannic Majesty's Embassy. To my surprise he came running back to say, 'The Master wants you all to come right in.' Franklin was much tickled by this Southern rebuff to Federal authority, and kept laughing over it all afternoon."

They came home by train from Richmond to a hot Washington, where Franklin had to appear before the House Naval Affairs Committee trying to get an additional $147,000,000. That year the Navy was to spend $2,257,000,000, in comparison with the $155,000,000 they spent the year before. That seemed some spending then. It involved as in earlier and later wars frustrations and bottlenecks, shortages and delays. Franklin wrote Eleanor that his hoped-for dash to Campobello would not materialize, as the weekend trip down the river had put him too far behind with his work. He had a dull time at a dinner party. Daniels at the same dinner party (given by General George Barnett, commandant of marines, and his wife, whose niece Wallis Warfield, later to be Duchess of Windsor, had just married the first of her husbands) was a little bored, too, by a lady who "wanted to know why we were not doing more about the war. She was violently anti-Wilson, pro-war and talked against taxes." It was a fairly familiar attitude even among those who came to Washington for the war. Senator Lodge was complaining to the eagerly listening Theodore Roosevelt that "we cannot carry on a war against American business and against Germany at the same time." Some of the taxes which Congressman Kitchin, who had opposed war, was industriously providing for its prosecution, seemed most astounding to some of those who had been most belligerent.

Despite his exercises, soon after that dinner, Franklin was sick again. A week after he got back from the holiday on the *Sylph* he wired Eleanor, "Throat vastly better." The next day, however, someone in his office sent him a memo that his mother was coming if he were not improved. It was Eleanor, however, who made the dash from Campobello. He was, he wrote later that month, "four days in the hospital with the same old abscess on my tonsil." There were no more *Sylph* trips that summer but later that month he was able to take a Sunday off to play golf all morning with Charlie McCawley and to drive in the afternoon "to the Horseys' place near Harper's Ferry."

"Lucy Mercer went and the Graysons," he told Eleanor, "and we got there at 5:30, walked over the farm—a very rich one and run by two sisters—had supper with them and several neighbors, left at nine and got home at midnight! The day was magnificent, but the road more dusty and even more crowded than when we went to Gettysburg."

The Horsey sisters, Elizabeth and Anna, lived much of the time in Washington and must have known Lucy and "Altrude" as children there. Also, though Franklin did not mention it, the richness of the farm may have been attributed to the nearby Horsey Distillery. In the 1850's, Franklin's Maryland WPA Guide writers were to report, the Horsey Distillery began the ingenious process of shipping its whisky in slow-sailing vessels around Cape Horn to California which was supposed to age it in a voyage. Like other distilleries in 1917, it was involved in that wartime prohibition which a little later explained FDR's report to Eleanor that after another round of golf with McCawley—thirty-six holes—they dined at "a very dry Metropolitan Club." It was in that same letter that he made the last reference to Lucy Mercer in the *Personal Letters:*

> No news, except that apparently Daniels has chucked the Comfort Committee entirely and is trying to organize a rival set under the Red Cross and to be directed by Mrs. Stotesbury. The end is not yet as the League (or at least the Comfort Com.) is I think going to fight back.
> *You* are entirely disconnected and Lucy Mercer and Mrs. Munn are closing up the loose ends.

Franklin's letter referred to the final and furious break that summer of Daniels with Colonel Thompson and his Navy League. Eleanor and Franklin's mother as active knitters for the Navy were much disturbed. Franklin's reference to "the Daniels-Thompson row" clearly indicated that it was no row of his. Colonel Thompson was still friendly to him. The fact that he told Eleanor she was "entirely disconnected" showed, too, that he was not standing with Thompson in the fight with his chief.

The declaration of war had not made Colonel Thompson or the majority of his members any friendlier to Daniels or the Wilson administration. The Colonel had been to see Daniels about what he regarded as a lack of co-operation shown the Navy League by the Red Cross in the League's efforts to provide comforts for sailors. In general he and many of the other members of the League shared Theodore Roosevelt's feeling that "the chatter about 'standing behind the President' . . . is sickening." It seemed intolerable that those who had shouted longest and loudest for war were not to be permitted to command it. Wilson had succeeded, the elder Roosevelt thought, "in putting Wood and myself on the sidelines; *because we both sought to save this country.*" (Italics by TR.) TR's opinion, which Senator Lodge received and shared after the war began, was that "the one real offender is Wilson. If our people were really awake he would be impeached tomorrow; Daniels, and Baker, and the General Staff are merely his tools." It was the sort of talk in which Colonel Thompson and the other old warhorses of the Navy League rejoiced and joined. In a press release, in August 1917, the Navy League charged that the investigation of an explosion in the Mare Island Navy Yard had been blocked at the demand of labor leaders.

"Benson indignant at N.L. statement," was Daniels' first entry in his diary about the incident.

The Chief of Operations was not far ahead of the Secretary of the Navy who carried his anger to the White House: "Went to see W about the charge of the Navy League & showed the statement and letter. Time for silence has ended. Speak out."

The Secretary spoke. In view of what he called "treasonable action by the League toward the government and a gross slander of the patriotic workers," he demanded that Colonel Thompson and other officers of the League "resign from what had come to be an unpatriotic organization." The suggestion that the Navy League was not patriotic must have seemed preposterous to the Colonel. He looked on himself as the model of the patriot. He minimized the League's mistake and debonairly replied that he would resign if Daniels would. The Secretary declined to be either amused or abashed. He issued an order excluding all officers and representatives of the League from all ships and stations.

In Eleanor's absence Franklin told the ladies in Washington who "handed in a record amount of sweaters and other wooleys" at the time "to sit tight, keep on knitting and not rock the boat!" With the exception of the knitting, that was the course he himself was following. There were, the editor of his *Personal Letters* said, "some 4,000,000" such knitters and members of the Comforts Committee of the Navy League. They might have made a stinging swarm. Fortunately for Daniels the reports of Secret Service men whom he put on the case and the findings of the Mare Island Board proved that the League, eager to criticize, had jumped to false statements. Also, fortunately for him, Mrs. Edward T. Stotesbury, as an indignantly patriotic lady, telephoned him from Philadelphia that she had resigned from the Navy League. It turned out that she would be very happy to head a new Naval Auxiliary of the Red Cross to take the place of the Navy League's Comforts Committee.

If Colonel Thompson's League had received, as charged, much support from the House of Morgan, Mrs. Stotesbury's husband was himself a member of that firm and head of the house of Drexel, Morgan & Co., of Philadelphia. Henry P. Davison, chairman of the War Council of the American Red Cross, who was ready to take over Daniels' new comforts organization, was also a Morgan partner. Mrs. Stotesbury was a strange, vivid and valuable ally for Daniels in that fight. When she came into his office for the first time, wearing her famous ropes of pearls, she murmured something to him about his "courage to issue the wine mess order." She was better known, however, as a hostess than as a reformer. Some Main Line ladies considered her jewels and parties in bad taste.

She had private detectives who carried her pearls back and forth between Washington and Philadelphia. Perhaps she needed a little prestige as well as pearls at that point. As a patriot, however, she was a perfect adversary for Colonel Thompson, and that was what Daniels required. The new

Naval Auxiliary was a great success. Colonel Thompson could no longer carry sweaters and wooleys into Navy Yards along with his own views about how the Navy should be run, namely, by the Republicans. Those who shared his views, however, were not rebuffed. Indeed, the Colonel's dismissal coincided with Senator Lodge's complaint to TR that Wilson would "not allow any Republicans if he can help it have a post of any importance." Wilson clearly—and almost incomprehensibly to Lodge and Roosevelt—meant to be his own commander-in-chief. He had greater troubles than the Republicans.

"G[reat] B[ritain] is very careful of her ships," Wilson had said to Daniels in June. In effect, through the Secretary of the Navy and Admiral Sims, he was already then forcing the acceptance by the British of the convoy system which was to prove so effective. Also through Sims—who seemed to send him back only the objections of the British Admiralty—he pressed the mine barrage scheme which had such enthusiastic support from Franklin Roosevelt that sometimes Franklin imagined he was in front of the President and pulling him. This idea of such a barrier across the North Sea was apparently first suggested (though the credit is certainly not clear) by so unlikely a character as Secretary of Commerce William Redfield, whose red mutton-chop whiskers seemed to tie him to the past. Redfield apparently got the idea from some long nets used in fishing operations in Alaska. A mine barrage across the North Sea, of course, presented incomparably greater obstacles. It was only made possible by the unexpected invention of a new type of mine, and it was not completed until almost the end of the war. Roosevelt—and Daniels—believed, however, that the terror it created in German submarine crews during the war's last days contributed materially to the Allied victory.

Franklin never had any doubts about the barrage. It was to become in his mind "my proposition" though the preliminary plans and blueprints had been drawn up by Admiral Earle, the

Navy's Ordnance Chief, and submitted by Daniels to the British Admiralty almost immediately after America entered the war. Sims cabled back that the Admiralty considered such a plan "quite infeasible." Daniels, himself, despite his pride in it later, was not completely convinced of the practicality of the plan even when he approved it in October 1917, after the British Admiralty and the General Board of the American Navy had at last accepted it.

"A stupendous undertaking," he wrote, "perhaps not impossible but to my view of doubtful practicality. North Sea too rough and will necessitate withdrawing all our ships from other work and then can we destroy the hornet's nest or keep the hornets in."

Wilson, in July, prodded Sims and expressed his impatience "at the failure of the British Admiralty to use Great Britain's great naval superiority in an effective way . . . every plan we suggest they reject . . . this is not a time for prudence but for boldness, even at the cost of great losses."

Franklin shared Wilson's impatience but not his feeling that the British Admiralty was entirely to blame. He had increasingly strong ideas about the "old lady" admirals in the Navy Department and about Daniels, too. The midsummer night on which he and Daniels were both so bored by the dowagers he was already engaged in more exciting conspiracy with the American Winston Churchill, a Naval Academy graduate and historical novelist, the owner of a New Hampshire estate which Wilson had twice occupied in the summertime. Franklin wanted Churchill to pass on to the President his feeling that there was "hookworm" in the Navy Department. He gave Churchill information which the novelist thought they ought only to discuss "away from the Department." Daniels had heard that Churchill "was going to criticize me rather severely," and was more relieved than disturbed by what Churchill actually reported. Yet it seems probable that the prod through Churchill to Wilson, which recommended, as Daniels knew, "putting power in operations in younger men," went into the secret speech in sharp criticism of the British Admiralty which Wilson made, in August, after Daniels had presented him to all the officers of the American fleet at its base in York River.

I saw the spectacle of that speech—the lean civilian Wilson talking naval warfare very earnestly and confidently to the uniformed officers before him. I had come down to the fleet with Father, and the next day, as an undoubted piece of special privilege, I went over to the *Texas* of which Victor Blue had taken command and became a fifteen-year-old supercargo when the *Texas* sailed for New York. Perhaps the favoritism was made less unique by the fact that Blue took along his own son, Stuart, who was fifteen, too. We thought we sighted a submarine on that voyage, but the truth is I was more troubled, as we sailed, by the fact that Stuart, who was an ingenious adolescent joker, saw to it that I got at every meal a glass with a tiny hole in it which made me dribble whenever I drank. It is sharp combination of memories to recall that that giggling Stuart Blue of World War I was one of the first naval officers to die heroically in the Pacific in World War II. Stuart and I were only interested in the spectacle of Wilson's speech. But a part of the spectacle was the eager attention which the officers gave their commander-in-chief.

"Every time we have suggested anything to the British Admiralty," Wilson told them, "the reply has come back that virtually amounted to this, that it had never been done before that way, and I felt like saying, 'Well, nothing was ever done so systematically as nothing is being done now.'"

He was very serious.

"The Secretary of the Navy and I," he went on, "have just been talking over plans for putting the planning machinery of the Navy at the disposal of the brains of the Navy and not stopping to ask what rank that brain has, because, as I have said before and want to repeat, so far as experience in this kind of war is concerned we are all of the same rank."

And he added: "America has always boasted that she could find men to do anything. She is the prize amateur nation of the world. Now, when it comes to doing new things and doing them well, I will back the amateur against the professional every time, because the professional does it out of the book and the amateur does it with his eyes open upon a new world and with a new set of circumstances. He knows so little about it that he is fool enough to try the right thing."

The President pressed hard again to urge new action against the submarines in a last conference before Admiral Mayo left for England to urge more aggressive naval measures on the Admiralty. Daniels attended with his chief admirals, and wrote afterward in his diary: "He [Wilson] spoke of the absolute necessity of finding and ending the hornet's nest and destroying the poison or removing the cork. He impressed upon them the need of an offensive and reiterated his view we cannot end the war by merely hunting submarines when they have gotten into the great ocean.

"Mayo said he hoped the President would not expect too much.

"No, but he expected plans by which America could lead and be senior partner in a successful naval campaign. He was ready to make great ventures for a chance to win but of course wished no policy that would mean suicide."

Later that day Daniels and Admiral Benson went over Benson's instructions to Mayo and talked about his mission. Daniels wrote in his diary after Benson had gone.

"Is Mayo hopeful enough?"

The next day Franklin wrote to Eleanor that he was encouraged to think that Wilson "has *begun* to catch on, but it will take a lot more of the Churchill type of attack." He must have felt unhappy about Admiral Mayo going to England while he stayed in Washington. Daniels wrote in his diary: "R said we would get nothing from naval officers who go to Europe. Needed a civilian on commission. Wanted to go himself. No." At the conference in the Secretary's office before Mayo departed, they talked about the news that the Germans had taken Riga, and that it would be comparatively easy for them to go to Petrograd. Franklin blurted his feeling about that situation and perhaps about himself.

"We ought to have sent TR over to Russia with 100,000 men," he said. "This would not have happened."

"It's strange how many folks TR has fooled," Admiral Josh McKean said.

Daniels undoubtedly made a wry face. Also, undoubtedly he smiled indulgently afterward. He knew that Franklin was disappointed. He knew that Franklin was tired. Despite the extra hour of sleep Daniels was getting every morning while Roosevelt and others flexed their muscles in the park, he was tired, too. The Secretary knew that his assistant shared the tension which he had felt until the destroyers had reached Queenstown and the first token transport of troops had arrived in France. They would not quite ever escape that tension until the Navy had finished the job of escorting four-fifths of the two million and more American troops which were moved to France before the Armistice. There seemed a never-ending need for more destroyers, transports, men and materials. Daniels had introduced the first women into the American armed services when he had discovered that there was nothing in the law which required a naval yeoman to be male. Sometimes young Roosevelt irritated him, but even when impatience snapped between Franklin and the admirals, occasionally between Franklin and himself, Daniels understood there was a propelling power in it. Fortunately, Franklin was getting away for at least a brief feel of the tides and the sea at Campobello even if he had sold the *Half Moon* and considered that there was at least one chance in five hundred that a German submarine might come into Passamaquoddy Bay and start to shell Eastport or the Pool. He wanted Eleanor and the children to watch out.

It was unusually cold when Franklin came back to Washington in September. That was the time of the detail—it was hardly more than that—when on a dreary day a sparse company attended the funeral of Lucy Mercer's father, Major Carroll Mercer, in old St. John's Church. Old Metropolitan Club cronies, including Colonel McCawley, who "had stood between the wolf and the sadly changed gallant of the Spanish-American War" acted as pallbearers.

It was a grave but gay time, too, in the capital. Even if their N Street house had seemed a model for large households in war savings, the Franklin Roosevelts moved into a larger house on R Street that fall. Eleanor came back much more active in society than she had been before, though she was also devoting more and more time to activity in war work. Indeed, society reporters said that she rescued Washington's "little season" from a crisis which threatened it almost to extinction by her plans for a Halloween dance at Rauscher's, for the benefit of the American Hospital at Neuilly on the outskirts of Paris. Mrs. Franklin Lane was helping "but all the management is in the capable hands of the wife of the Assistant Secretary of the Navy."

That dance came the evening after a day of triumph for Franklin which he made a day of explosion, too. The British Admiralty and the General Board at last in October agreed on the barrage. Daniels described the day in his office in his diary. Lord Northcliffe had called. Daniels had seen the British publisher before when he had first come over, earlier in the summer, as head of the British War Mission. Franklin had talked, also, with Northcliffe. The Britisher was highly critical of his own Navy.

"He hoped we would build fire under the British Navy," Daniels wrote of the English publisher. "Jellico had but one thought and that was to preserve the great fleet. Not accustomed to fighting & had no real engagement since Nelson's day."

After Northcliffe left, Franklin came in: "Roosevelt after reading report of General Board for a barrage across North Sea said, 'I told you so last May.'"

He did not merely say that, he wrote it also in what he called himself "a very stinging memorandum," sending a copy to the President as well as to Daniels, about the order as "nothing more nor less than a resurrection of my proposition." He felt that, while the British Admiralty might be blamed in part, "our own Navy Department is at least largely responsible for failing to consider this proposition seriously during all these months—May, June, July, August, September, and October— which have gone over the dam beyond recall." If approval at last was to be followed by performance, he felt that one American and one Britisher should be given authority to put it across: "You need somebody with imagination and authority to make the try." It seems pretty clear that he meant himself. It was not a suggestion followed by the President or the Secretary.

Franklin was eager to get abroad. After Admiral Mayo's departure he had felt left at home again when Daniels, with Wilson's approval, named Admiral Benson, of whom Franklin had been most critical, to go with Colonel House to the inter-Allied war conference in Paris. Young Gordon Auchincloss went as Colonel House's secretary. The Navy, Franklin felt, needed a civilian and an amateur to press the naval professionals. He felt a greater personal need to get where action was when Gussie Gardner, who had accepted demotion in military rank in order to get to France, died that winter in a Georgia camp.

Even Nigel Law got a chance to go back to the war zone late in 1917. He went to England, he explained later, to find additional staff for "our overworked embassy." While there he visited the front as guest of the British G.H.Q. He was missed in Washington. *Town Topics* was almost inevitably speaking of him in an item about a charming Washington girl and a delightful young diplomat "closely akin to the loftiest of British nobility." The young man, it said, had recently been to London "on an errand requiring both resource and delicacy in handling." The girl had "recently gone into retirement because of family bereavement." Nigel and Lucy Mercer might have been an "ideal match," as the item in the magazine suggested. It did not come about.

"On my return to America," Law recalled years later, "Franklin was anxious to have news of Europe and I lunched with him immediately."

Franklin listened eagerly. Law told him of the trench-cut and bombarded western front. The face of Europe had been torn since the young diplomat crossed it from Vienna to London in 1914 on his way to Washington. Law had seen the long convoys, watched the destroyers. In France the troops were beginning to arrive in strong thousands, but the Allies faced offensive and effective German strength. Listening to Law and others, Franklin was a restless young man.

"Not much likelihood of my going over," he wrote his mother after he had welcomed Law back, "though they ought to send me. You will have plenty of notice!"

There was plenty of work to do in Washington. Daniels was as aware as Franklin of the delays and difficulties. They constituted reasons why he kept Franklin on duty in Washington. They had not only to keep pressing the construction of destroyers. Also, old problems remained. Two of the men upon whom Daniels chiefly depended in the protection of the naval oil reserves died that year. He spent long war hours being grilled about the oil lands before the Senate Public Lands Committee. He and Franklin Roosevelt were harassed by indignant objections from Newport about the methods used under Franklin's supervision to clean up vice conditions around the training station. Daniels and Roosevelt shared enthusiasm about the reforms in the naval prison at Portsmouth, New Hampshire, where Franklin's friend, Thomas Mott Osborne, had been put in command. Sometimes Daniels and Franklin disagreed even about small matters. The Assistant Secretary wanted to give the destroyers coming down the ways Indian names. Daniels held out for the brave dead, of whom he feared there would be too many before the war ended.

In the midst of the pressure and strain, Daniels was pleased by a letter from Colonel House denying a story in *The Boston Transcript* that he had tried to get Wilson to remove the Navy Secretary. The Colonel had repudiated the story, he wrote, "but these things have to go a certain length after once begun." However, he regretted it "beyond measure because of my friendship and high regard for you." The Colonel followed his letter by a visit to Daniels' office a little later.

"In all this talk and criticism," he told Daniels, "the good condition of the Navy has saved the day."

In his diary Daniels quoted the Colonel: "He said everybody abroad praised the alertness of the men of the Navy. Benson was easily the first man of the military men in the Council—towered over Jellico & told them what to do & put them to doing it."

Daniels was pleased with the report about Benson. He knew, however, that the criticism had not ended. A new Republican Congressman from Illinois had taken Gussie Gardner's clamoring place on the Hill. The only change among the critics was an increase in savagery toward the Secretary of War. ("We need a butcher, not a Baker.") Daniels knew that his colleague on the other side of the big building was doing an excellent job. Also, he knew that the diminutive Baker was deeply hurt.

"Newton Baker came over," Daniels wrote, "to confer about a letter he had written to the President saying that he had but one purpose—to have the country united to win the war—and that in view of the criticism, he was ready to tender his resignation so the President could name a man as Secty of War who would unite the country. I told him the President would not permit it, that the opposition would be satisfied with nobody except TR, Root or Wood and the President would not name either. Instead of composing and uniting, his resignation would have the opposite effect. Looks five years older. I told him that within a few months his critics would see how unjust they were."

The Secretary of the Navy was right about Baker's critics, but he was too optimistic about the cessation of the criticism. Also, if there was not time for all the war tasks, needs, hopes, there was not time for justice either. History understood Baker's accomplishment. But Theodore Roosevelt, who had less time than he himself believed, was not waiting. If Washington would not let him go to France, he announced he was coming to Washington. There were plenty to welcome him as a man of vigor required in the capital.

Perhaps it was odd that one of the few places where TR's gentle wife was to go on that crowded, strenuous visit was the house of old Henry Adams on Lafayette Square. He looked "sadly little and old," Alice Longworth remembered. He was to be eighty in a month and dead in two. That winter warplanes flew over his house, where such a little while before they had been talked of as dreams of the future and old Adams was not alone then in "already wishing to heaven that they had remained dreams of the past." Only the oldest friends went to see the old man. He derived "a sort of stale satisfaction from having the wisdom of our philosophic President, Mr. Woodrow Wilson," read to him. Wilson, his near neighbor, was hardly aware that he was still alive. In the new militancy around the old square Adams was already more forgotten than the monument in Rock Creek Cemetery which he had had Stanford White and Augustus St. Gaudens design for the grave of his wife. She had killed herself in the midst of his *Education* thirty years before. The legend which lingered, long after Adams was gone, around the square (to the gossip of which on other matters Adams contributed so much) was that Mrs. Adams understood he was in love with young, lovely Elizabeth Sherman Cameron, wife of a tough, rich, dull Senator from Pennsylvania. Many people, including young men in uniform and the new crowded war workers in the bulging capital, went to look at the shrouded figure of bronze seated on the monument. St. Gaudens who made it referred to it as "The Mystery of the Hereafter." Adams himself called it "The Peace of God." But it was from a remark attributed to the sardonic and sentimental Mark Twain that it became generally known as "Grief." Adams had completed his *Education* long before that day when Mrs. Roosevelt and Alice came to lunch. And education had completed Adams. His nieces found him dead on the morning of March 27, 1918, two days before the Allies in the fourth year of the war at last agreed on one commander-in-chief of their forces in France.

Others were in the process of education. Eleanor Roosevelt recalled later how much she had learned that winter, working long and hard hours in the Red Cross canteen in the railroad yards.

"I think I learned then that practically no one in the world is entirely bad or entirely good," she wrote in *This Is My Story* in 1937, "and that motives are often more important than actions. I had spent most of my life in an atmosphere where everyone was sure of what was right and what was wrong, and as life has progressed I have gradually come to believe that human beings who try to judge other human beings are undertaking a somewhat difficult job. When your duty does not thrust ultimate judgments upon you, perhaps it is as well to keep an open and charitable mind, and to try to understand why people do things instead of condemning the acts themselves."

TWELVE

"Splendid Time"

NOBODY EVER ENJOYED A WAR MORE THAN LIVY DAVIS.
Perhaps one historian was correct in deciding that Davis,
FDR's classmate, golf partner, and drinking companion who
had made the trip to Haiti with him early in 1917, did little
after he came to Washington as special assistant to the Assistant
Secretary in the latter part of 1917 to lighten Roosevelt's load
of war duties. He was a delightful companion all the same, and
he left a diary about a delightful war. He was an inadequate
Boswell but the only one almost constantly beside Roosevelt
during 1918 and Franklin, a collector who never threw anything away, preserved Livy's diary for posterity. Perhaps he
should not have done so. Eleanor Roosevelt never quite trusted
Livy. She wrote Franklin's mother in 1919 that he was "lazy,
selfish, and self-seeking to an extraordinary degree with the
outward appearance of being quite different." She forgave him
in her memoirs and perhaps history will. She decided long
afterward that he was an "excellent executive and I am told
that he proved an extremely efficient administrator." Livy did
not look back at solemn accomplishment. He did not move
to greatness from that war, though he left Franklin at the end
of it to go to the grim center of Europe to help Hoover work
with starvation. Long after, however, when in 1932, as one of
"Brookline's wealthiest citizens," he killed himself in the wood-

shed of his estate, he left Franklin $1,000 "in grateful remembrance of joyful comradeship."

They had such comradeship in the cold winter and swift, warm spring of 1918. Livy lunched or dined or had cocktails—or all three—with Franklin almost every day. He began his diary in the dark winter of 1918 and, so far as he was concerned, filled it with the details of a Washington at war which was having a wonderful time. He and FDR saw a rich variety of interesting people. There were dances. Apparently all their old friends were there. Dick Crane, of Harvard '04, had a house big enough for a dinner dance for eighty people at which Livy danced until 2:30 and then took the band home.

He went to dinners; at one he "sat between Princess Ihika, a Britisher who married a Roumanian, and Countess Polignac who was Mrs. Jimmie Eustis—a screamer." There were old friends like Beck Winthrop, Joe Grew, Dick Olney, Toni Beal, Russell Sard, Harry Hooker. Mrs. Barnett, the wife of the commandant of the marines, Livy thought, "appeared bewitching in her daughter's bathing suit." It was a bewitching time for the thirty-four-year-old Bostonian: "dined at Montgomerys'. . . . Bully time. Danced till 3 o'clock. Champagne flowing like water." Sometimes after such an occasion he reported, "Broke out feeling like wrath." They swam often: "All motored out to the Canal and had fine swim. After which we picknicked on huge rock where I got the sillies and had a huge time." Sometimes work and fun were mixed as when young Hugh Gibson, about to go to Paris as First Secretary of the Embassy, came to Livy's house for cocktails and Livy and Franklin "pumped him full of dope to use over there." But there were nights when Livy and Franklin went to the Department and "worked until 1:30 A.M. over Sims' reports." Livy was with Franklin, too, when they went to the Secretary's office and under the big late-burning chandeliers Franklin "had a good talk with the Secretary" about their hopes for an inspection trip overseas. Work or play, as Davis remembered it, Washington at war was vividly lit.

It seemed darker to some, undoubtedly sometimes to Franklin, often to Daniels. Not all in Washington were gay and glamorous. Indeed, that February when Livy began his diary was the one time during Daniels' whole service in Washington when the outlook seemed completely desperate to him. The Rev. Billy Sunday seemed to meet a need that winter. His big tabernacle down by the Union Station was jammed nightly. New war workers who bulged all department buildings including, of course, the Navy Department, soldiers, sailors, many officials went to hear the slangy sermons of the ex-ball player turned muscular evangelist. One morning he preached at the Daniels home on Wyoming Avenue where we had moved, in 1916, from Woodley Lane. It was a tall, high, town house across the street from the house of Secretary Lane. There was a street lamp before it which every evening a lamplighter, armed with a little ladder, came and lit.

Franklin was at the Billy Sunday service in the Daniels house. Sunday was not the Reverend Endicott Peabody of Groton, who conducted Franklin's religious ceremonies during World War II. The evangelical prayer session at the Daniels house might have seemed a strange occasion for the young vestryman of old St. James in Hyde Park. However, that same day, even Alice Longworth listed the Rev. Mr. Sunday among the callers on her father, who had come to the capital with the air of a man on horseback.

Others, among the many who "stacked" the hall at the Longworth house on M Street, included Senator Lodge, and John King, whom Alice described as the "henchman" of Senator Boise Penrose and who, she said, did "the sort of work that really counts." Penrose and Lodge represented the partnership of the strong arm and the scholarly mind in the Republican Old Guard. FDR also called, and on the night TR went back to New York, Mrs. Theodore Roosevelt and Alice dined with Franklin and Eleanor.

Nobody, apparently least of all himself, knew how ill Theodore Roosevelt was then. He looked and acted the role of the man of vigor. The younger Bryan, who was in town at the same time, seemed more deteriorated. Both would have resented any suggestion of similarity. Bryan was failing to provide leadership for the extreme pacifists, as some of them had expected, like that which TR was providing for the extreme militants who felt that they had been cheated out of the direction of the war. Bryan, before the year was out, was to feel cheated out of a part in the peace he believed he had planned. If they were not equally innocent, they were equally futile. Apparently only Daniels noticed that Bryan was in town, and even he was more concerned about Roosevelt.

"TR came to town," he wrote, "to set up a rump gov—but failed."

Also, he wrote that same day of a meeting of the Council of National Defense at which he urged Baruch for chairman of the War Industries Board. Baker was inclined to agree, he said. Secretary of Commerce Redfield was opposed to him and Colonel House's protégé, Secretary of Agriculture Houston, was "decidedly opposed." Daniels was for meeting the TR tumult head on.

"I urged no man be appointed who was not devoted to success of Wilson administration. Chief trouble too many men in on war business who had no loyalty to Wilson."

The next day, however, he made an entry about the matter closest to him in connection with the Roosevelt visit.

"Oliver talked to FDR. He said speed was not made, etc. TR has been in town two days."

The reference obviously was to Congressman William B. Oliver, chairman of a Congressional Committee which investigated the naval conduct of the war at that time and issued a report showing "phenomenal" progress in warship construction and "efficient and expeditious methods" in various naval bureaus. Oliver had not been impressed by the Assistant Secretary's statements except as he thought the Secretary should know about them. Daniels attributed Franklin's criticism to TR's influence. Franklin's admiration for his famous cousin was no secret to Daniels and he did not hide his irritation with the aging but acrimonious elder Roosevelt from Franklin. He was pleased with the Congressional findings. Also he was happy to know that one of the arguments the President used in opposing a munitions ministry (which, along with a Super War Cabinet, was urged by the critics of the administration) was that in the Navy there were no avoidable delays. Daniels was not so sure of that himself. He was almost sick when shipbuilding schedules were not maintained. However, he was spared at the time the sharpest criticism of those who rallied around the elder Roosevelt.

He had no such Rooseveltian rebel in arms as Baker had in Leonard Wood. That general had taken advantage of a brief visit to the front as observer to get, Secretary Baker believed, the support of the British in a move to substitute him for General Pershing. Daniels did direct, with the President's approval, that Admiral Sims should decline a proposal to make him an honorary member of the British Admiralty. Before the war was a year old the British sometimes seemed as irritating to Wilson and his War Cabinet as Theodore Roosevelt. Perhaps naturally, the British trusted most those Americans who had been ready to join Britain in war when Wilson was till protesting about the British Navy's blockade of American shipping. Perhaps it was natural for an old nation to count on its own realism and to regard as innocents the officials of an American government which seemed almost garrulous about idealism in the world— including such an incomprehensible phrase to an island kingdom and sea power as "the Freedom of the Seas." Wilson had listed that among the fourteen points he regarded as essential to an intelligent peace in January 1918.

Actually, Franklin Roosevelt and Daniels never got along better than they did in these toughest months of the war. Where speed was not made—and the lags were as disturbing as they were in the bottlenecks and shortages of World War II—the only way to get it was to press and press and press more. It does seem strange long afterward that Daniels could get to so many of Billy Sunday's meetings. It seems remarkable, too, that in the toughest month of the war FDR could take all but a few hours' holiday on George Washington's birthday or spare a whole afternoon a little later to what must have been the fulminations of Leonard Wood. (When as President, Roosevelt contemplated the imperious demands of Douglas MacArthur he must have better understood Wilson's and Baker's feelings about Wood in World War I. Secretary Baker found Mac-Arthur a very useful officer in Washington in World War I, not averse to such a task as finding office space for George Creel.)

Not all the discouraging bottlenecks were naval. Altogether, indeed, and in more ways than weather the early months of 1918 seemed, as the harassed Baker said, "a winter the like of which none of us has seen since we were children." The blizzards seemed almost as savage as the submarines. Soon Herbert Hoover, as food administrator, Daniels said in his diary "could not get food for our allies for lack of cars." Henry A. Garfield, as fuel administrator, "could not get coal for lack of transportation." Edward J. Hurley, as chairman of the Shipping Board, "could not build ships because of the cold weather." Secretary of Agriculture Houston was "troubled about wheat. Transportation fallen down. Weather made it worse. . . ."

The same night Daniels recorded those adversities in his diary, he noted also the news that the *Tuscania*, a British Cunard steamer, with 2,300 American troops on board, had been torpedoed. The first report indicated that 1,200 men might be lost.

Daniels scrawled in his diary: "Is God on the side of the Germans?"

It was the bottom of the curve. Newton Baker had made so splendid a showing before the Senate Military Affairs Committee that tremendous Senator Ollie James had rushed by taxicab to the White House to report to Wilson: "Jesus, you ought to see that little Baker. He's eating 'em up." Daniels chose the day after his blurted desperation to state his determination (which was to seem a little impertinent in London) for the "incomparably greatest Navy." Later dispatches brought word that the sinking of the *Tuscania* had not been the disaster they had feared. Then Daniels received the best news that he had had in a year, that losses to submarines for January were down to 318,000 tons, although there was still a margin of tonnage destroyed over the tonnage coming from the world's shipyards. It was winter still. Daniels went to New York and reviewed the "N.Y. draft army in a snow storm," the same storm which in Washington, Franklin wrote to his mother, made "a holiday golf game impossible."

Stronger than the desire to play golf was his ambition to go to Europe. He brought it up again on March 20. Undoubtedly there may have been political aspects to his desire. TR still thought he ought to resign and get into uniform. A trip to the front might serve well at a time when there were a number of suggestions about his political future coming from New York including the governorship that year.

He was not an indispensable man. He had faults as well as drive. John M. Hancock, the banker and industrialist, then a paymaster in charge of Navy purchases, remembered that in making awards Roosevelt was "a sucker for anyone who was a classmate or a member of the Newport crowd. Riches or social position gave a man great validity." Homer, of the refined

Sterling engines, was much in evidence in his office. Howe had friends in politics who were interested in contracts. There was one little flurry in May of which Daniels wrote in his diary when a clerk in the Bureau of Construction and Repair "had written he had secured contract for certain parties at highest prices by using much bull on Assistant Secretary." At worst Franklin was only a sucker for a class. He had not lost Daniels' trust or affection. It was of Franklin on that same day that my mother used a revealing expression of affection, and she always knew pretty well my father's prejudices and suspicions. It was the day of the first air mail, on May 15, 1918. With the President, the Postmaster General and other officials including FDR, Mother waited on the White House lawn for the momentous arrival of mail by airplane from New York. The Danielses received three letters.

"Give me one of the stamps," Roosevelt asked her, "I want to add it to my stamp collection."

"Of course, he got it," my mother said. "Nobody could refuse Franklin anything."

That seems a pretty accurate report of the facts at the time. Roosevelt suggested that this generosity extended even to Tammany Hall. He wrote later that his old enemy, Charles F. Murphy, sent the secretary of Tammany to Washington to offer him the Democratic nomination for Governor. The nomination went instead to Alfred E. Smith—according to Roosevelt with his help and Howe's. Specifically Franklin said that Murphy and Smith himself brought up the fact that Smith was not only a Tammany man but a Catholic which might hurt Smith in up-state sections and that he dismissed the church question as an issue in wartime. Ray Stannard Baker, in his *Woodrow Wilson*, says that FDR brought up the question of Smith's Catholicism and that it was Wilson who said that the day to take political consideration of such a matter had gone by.

"People are every day reading the casualty lists of American boys of every creed," the President told him.

Everything did seem open to Franklin. At that time a photograph was taken of the Secretary and the Assistant Secretary, looking from one of the stone porches of the Navy Department at the White House across the street. Afterward Daniels explained Roosevelt's wider grin in the picture.

"You are saying to yourself, being a New Yorker, 'Someday I will be living in that house,'—while I, being from the South, know I must be satisfied with no such ambition."

Clearly it was a good time for FDR. On June 18, when it was finally agreed that Roosevelt should go to England, Daniels made a note about the New York governorship in his diary: "WW said, 'He ought not to decline to run for Gov of NY if it is tendered to him.' I talked to FDR who was pleased at the President's view."

FDR himself, however, "entirely forgot" to talk to the President himself about the governorship matter when he saw him about his trip abroad, on Sunday July seventh. But he wrote him a longhand letter the next day, the day before he sailed, that he sincerely hoped the proposal would not come up at the convention while he was gone. It would be a mistake, he was certain, for him to "give up war work, for what is frankly very much of a local political job in these times."

He was off to Europe—and that had taken some doing. After he renewed his request on March twentieth, he wrote to Daniels on April 5, "It is obvious from an inspection of these cables that while of course Admiral Sims has been magnificent in the way he has handled the work, it would be a great help to him to have me go over there for a short time to help him co-ordinate the business end of his work. . . . I could perfectly well catch the cruiser that leaves on Sunday."

Livy noted in his diary that day: "FD said he had written a memo to Pres. suggesting that we sail for Europe Sunday. Was taken up at Cabinet meeting at 4. Turned down as 'inexpedient at this time.' Home to lunch—rotten cold—but returned at 5. Walked home with FD . . . for c-tail. Early bed."

A month later on June 6, Daniels and Davis both reported to their diaries on the project. With regard to it Daniels merely added that "(FDR) wishes to go abroad" to a note that they had talked about "prison management and Osborne." Davis was not much more specific. He had lunch that day with Franklin and "dined at Roosevelt's and FD and I returned to Dept. where he had good talk with Secretary. Finally ended up in Operations where we finally broke out at 11:15." Daniels was in the mood for good talk that evening. His important diary entry was the satisfying fact that "Lodge gave warm defense of the Navy Department." That was understatement about a speech which the Massachusetts Senator had made in the Senate that day in answer to an editorial in *The Philadelphia Public Ledger*, which was read to the Senate by Lodge's Republican colleague and Connecticut neighbor, Senator Frank Brandegee. The editorial sharply suggested that the Navy was not providing adequate defenses for the American coast and coastal shipping from German submarines. As the Senate navalist, Lodge got up. From the Secretary down, he said that the Navy "has done everything that human foresight could suggest." He went on in a speech which always afterward explained Daniels' feeling that he could count on Lodge's support. At that moment certainly, he had it.

"I want the Senate also to remember," Lodge went on, "that when newspaper editorials ask what the Navy is doing I should like to have them consider why it is that we have sent all the troops we have sent—and we have sent a great many thousand —why it is that they have gone to Europe without the loss of a transport. Thank God, as I do. How is it that this has happened? It has happened because of the American Navy, which furnishes the convoys, and no other cause.

"I wish I could go on and tell you what the American Navy has been doing in the narrow seas. I can not. The Navy has remained largely silent about its work and its preparation, and it is one of the best things about it, but it has been doing the greatest possible work everywhere. It has not failed in convoying the troops. It has not failed in its work in the Baltic and the Channel and the Coast of France and the Mediterranean, and it will not fail here. It will do everything that courage and intelligence and bravery can possibly do."

Livy and Franklin could not have found an evening during the war when they could have more surely counted on "good talk" with the Secretary. Also, Lodge's speech only announced outside the Navy a satisfaction which the Secretary and others at last felt within the Navy. The time had come when a young assistant could be spared from his Washington work. The final decision to send Franklin, however, waited ten more days. And when he sailed on July 9, on the destroyer, U.S.S. *Dyer,* Daniels —and he—had the satisfaction of knowing that a million soldiers had already been safely conducted to France. Behind Franklin as he sailed, New York was in mourning for that other brilliant young man in politics, Mayor John Purroy Mitchel, who had fallen, by accident or design, from an air corps training plane in Louisiana. Livy, who was to follow on a liner, had a "perfectly delicious" dinner at the Racket and Tennis Club and then went to see *Rockabye Baby* which he reported was "worst show ever saw." While Franklin was at sea, TR's son, Quentin, was killed in an air battle over the German lines and the big American counter-offensive had begun in France. The naval war was not yet won. And nobody knew that better than Daniels. While Roosevelt sailed Daniels wrote in his diary: "Conference of builders of destroyers. Not more than half up to estimated time. Benson had told Allies we would furnish ships and companies had not lived up their estimates. I was ashamed to go abroad until builders kept their pledges. Must speed up."

There were other problems at home. It may not have been true, as Wilson's official biographer felt, that the criticism of Secretary Baker in 1918 was "largely traceable to the great business interests of the country which resent government control of the railroads and the mines, chafe under taxation, fear the growing power of labor." Certainly, however, if war had suspended reform, it had not changed the views of the reformers. Daniels wrote in his diary, late in July, that Wilson was grave at a meeting of the War Council when Baruch talked of both steel profits and the reluctance of the steel companies to admit labor unions in the industry. The President said that "if big industry does not invite labor to place on directorate and share in profits & responsibility, it will invite worse." Such talk might have justified Theodore Roosevelt's feeling before the war began that Daniels was putting the Navy "on the road to socialism." Certainly it would not have supported the suggestion of Franklin Roosevelt to Lloyd George that a firmer attitude toward labor on the part of the British government would receive hearty applause from the United States.

In mid-August at one of the regular weekly meetings in the War Department to discuss the progress of the war, Admiral Benson "explained in detail the barrage across the North Sea." Franklin, who regarded this as "my proposition," had already written Daniels from Europe about it. "I am a little amused," he wrote "En Route to Paris" on August 2, "by the fact that they are carrying out certain operations now, which you will remember I tried to have taken up for weeks and months in the Spring and Summer of 1917. As a result, the English Channel is now fairly successfully blocked against submarines and only one, or possibly two, have got through in several months."

It was later that month, however, that he inspected the mine barrage operations in the North of Scotland, and it was probably just as well that Livy Davis' report on that inspection trip was not sent back to the Secretary. The Secretary had sent Admiral Joseph Strauss there to begin the operations three months before Franklin and his party, including Livy and his naval aide, Captain Edward McCauley, arrived. The Admiral, a man a little older than Daniels, was awaiting the Assistant Secretary and his staff late in August. Livy described their visit in true Livy Davis style:

> August 30—Awoke in Inverness. After remarkable breakfast which was passed into train piping hot. Changed trains and arrived at Invergarden at 11. Inspected Navy Yard under command of Admiral Pearce. Saw "Mars" and "Temrairo" and "Ajax" in largest floating dock in world. Yard employs 5,000 men. Then boarded and inspected "Roanoke"—mine layer—and had buffet lunch "San Fran." Thence by motor to Alness where saw mine handling plant. Very efficient. Laurence Cunningham. Thence FD and McC, went to call on friends, so Brown, Jackson, Bangay and I started for Strathffeffer. Got puncture so walked back to pub for drink but no luck. Arrived spa hotel—Mr. Wallace—and after a few rounds of Scotch took walk around town. Returned for wonderful dinner at conclusion of which old man Wallace brought out some real Chartreuse. Had private parlor so sang and told stories till 1 A.M. Wonderful time going to bed, FD finding a fox in his bed, Jack dressed up and Brown coasted downstairs.
>
> August 31—Up at 5:30. Breakfast at 6:00 consisted of oatmeal, cream, sugar, butter, fish, eggs, ham, marmalade and mushrooms. Brown, FD, Jack and I with Wallace drove out to Black Water belonging to Sir Arthur Mackensie in pouring rain in a dos-a-dos. Gillis [ghillies] late in coming so all had some Scotch and had a fine sing-song. All in regular clothes, low shoes. I in my new brown suit for first time. Lovely stream, falls, pools, etc., but no one got a strike. Weather was so dour all had to keep it out with copious draughts of sublime Scotch so all sang all the way home. While clothes were drying Wallace concocted a brew of hot Scotch, honey, and oatmeal served in beakers. All had at least two, and on descending found all guests and servants assembled so all hands to parlor, formed circle and sang Auld

Lang Syne. Left Strathffeffer at 12. FD, McC. took long way
round and got puncture. Rest arrived at Inverness with glorious buns at 1:10 to find Admiral Strauss spitting mad as he
had knocked his men off work at 10 A.M. and had had many
false alarms of our arrival, getting them out in pouring rain.
FD and McC. finally arrived at 1:45 just time to beat it to
Admiral's house for luncheon and beat it to train at 3:15.
Brown buying some tweeds on way. Found our car again.
Route very picturesque. More Scotch and all got out at Perth
for delicious and extremely jolly dinner. Had sing-song in
train till bed time at 10:30. One of the jolliest days of my
life!

Franklin left his aides after that jolly trip and went to an
English country house to visit old friends. It may have been on
that occasion, as he recalled in 1942, that prominent Britishers
spent a whole evening indoctrinating him "on all of the terrible
hardships that people in England had gone through. They
hadn't had this to eat or that to drink, and so forth, for a long,
long time. They hadn't had any butter, and they hadn't had any
bacon. They had to really tighten their belts enormously."

Roosevelt felt that they were stressing the facts to him because
he "was the first 'near' Cabinet member to go to the other side
during the war." (Actually Secretary Baker had made a thorough tour of the European front that Spring.)

"The next morning I was late for breakfast," Franklin related, "and sat down, and suddenly realized that all the food
was on the sideboard like most British breakfasts. And I went
over to it, and the first hot dish I took the cover off was just
piled high with bacon. So I filled my plate with bacon and sat
down. And the hostess said, 'What! Only bacon?' I said, 'Yes.
You know at home I have gone without bacon for a year and a
half, in order that you good people might have it.' "

The European inspection trip was coming to an end and Livy
described their last day—and night—in London:

Sept. 6—All lunched upstairs. Worked at hotel then went to Coliseum to see Russian dancers in "The Good Humored Ladies." Thence to H-2. at 6 FD, Lt. Heyden and I went to American Officers Club in Lord Beaconfield's house on Curzon Street. Several rounds of delicious c.ts, and saw many friends. Returned to hotel where had very rough dinner with a man named Thomas as guest. At Hadock Lt. Com. Jack Garde, and John Roys brought in Prince Axel of Denmark and his staff consisting of Thicle, Korwin and Laube. Came in. Everybody got drunk. All finally faded away except FD, Brown, Jackson and I. Stayed up until 4:30 pitching coins, playing golf, etc.

Sept. 7—Up at 7 to pack. All feeling very rocky. . . ."

On the *Leviathan* Franklin collapsed with flu and double pneumonia. Livy, who had not been enjoying himself on the voyage, saw Franklin again for the first time when he left the ship by ambulance. "Looked rotten," he noted briefly. Franklin did not get back to Washington until the middle of October.

Reverberations of his trip did, however. At a Cabinet meeting even before the sick Franklin had sailed from England, Lansing reported that the French Ambassador was disturbed because Franklin had said that the United States favored the British Admiral Jellico as Allied commander in the Mediterranean. Admiral Sims had urged that the American government take that position but this country had insisted, Daniels said, that the decision be made by the Allied War Council. Wilson shortly afterward asked that he be given the names of any persons, except those on strictly military service, who were going abroad. Too many people, he said, were presuming to speak for the government. Roosevelt himself was to have a similar feeling about many official World Travelers in World War II.

If he stirred up the Mediterranean, Franklin also made apparently well-justified reports about the bad condition in which airplanes were arriving at the naval base in France. When he was well enough to press the matter in person with the admirals in charge in Washington, they disagreed with his reports. His earlier cable was the sort of productive prod which the war effort needed to the last. The sharp reaction in Washington, however, to his apparently unauthorized intervention on the British side in Mediterranean naval command matter, fore-shadowed the fact that British and American naval differences were to constitute a crucial item in the making of the peace.

The same day in mid-August when Benson discussed the mine barrage at the War Department meeting, the President had left for another visit to the Massachusetts North Shore with the confidence of a man already planning the peace. He had drafted a constitution for a League of Nations and wanted to discuss it with Colonel House. Everybody wanted to talk with the Colonel. What he called his "little farm cottage" on the shore must have been often crowded. Shortly before Wilson came, House and J. P. Morgan, Jr., had "sat under the trees and discussed international finances." A little later the Presi-dent's son-in-law, Francis B. Sayre, was to call to ask House if he could arrange a place for him "in the Peace Inquiry." House told him he could—and did until Wilson, who had a greater prejudice against nepotism, canceled the arrangement. George Harvey, Wilson's sharp critic, dropped in at the little House cottage that August, too, and, as House recorded, "even praised Daniels highly." And House added, "Remembering the almost scurrilous articles he had written about Daniels, it seemed to me he would be ashamed to mention the subject." In his judg-ment of others, House was a sensitive man about such things.

Wilson came on his visit on August 14, 1918. It was not his first visit. He had been there also just a year before. On that earlier occasion, House suggested "an arrangement with Great Britain at this time looking to our securing some of her capital battleships after the war in consideration of our abandoning

our shipbuilding program of capital ships in order to build
submarine destroyers." Wilson considered such an agreement
"impractical." It was not a new idea. In the month in which
America entered the war Daniels had made a diary entry:
"R[oosevelt] proposed we send destroyers to England and tell
her we would expect her to furnish in return some of her best
dreadnaughts."

The idea may have contained some germ of what was later
called lend-lease. Certainly there was a similarity to the Rooseveltian swap of American destroyers for air bases in 1940.

Daniels did not like the idea in 1917-18. "We are in this war
for what?" he asked in his diary. "To crush autocracy and ruthless murder or nothing. And we suggest some return in ships.
L[ane] had made the same suggestion to Cabinet & President
had not approved."

No such idea was mentioned apparently on the 1918 visit
when Wilson and House discussed the League of Nations.
Clearly, however, in plans for peace the increasing American
Navy was of high importance to Britannia, which had so long
ruled the waves. Sir William Wiseman, whom Mrs. Wilson
later so bitterly disliked and described as "a secret agent" and
a "plausible little man," was staying with House on the North
Shore during the President's visit. Wiseman was practically
assigned to House throughout the war. His actual assignment
then was obscure. House's editor referred to him as British
chief of the Secret Service. He became the chief adviser on
American affairs to the British delegation at the Peace Conference. It was he who brought to House, soon after Wilson's
1918 visit to the North Shore, news of the stormy sessions in the
British Cabinet over Wilson's peace terms. They rebel, he told
House, against the "Freedom of the Seas." It was in that atmosphere that Sir Eric Geddes, First Lord of the Admiralty, though
he had not mentioned the possibility to Franklin in England a

few weeks before, proposed to Daniels in September a special mission to Washington.

Though he was occupied much with it, Daniels put little about the Geddes visit in his diaries. Long afterward he was puzzled by a memory that Geddes, at a time when the prospect of peace was bright, warned of a possible greater German U-boat campaign "in the early spring." Undoubtedly, Sir Eric and the impressive naval staff he brought along with him then stressed the possible dangers ahead. Unquestionably, however, he was as concerned about post-war naval problems as wartime ones. In his report to Prime Minister Lloyd George, Geddes said significantly that: "In talking of his Fourteen Points, the President's views on the Freedom of the Seas appeared to be unformed." Sir Eric had pointedly asked Wilson to clarify that question at the conference. Wilson may not have made himself clear to Geddes. His position was no secret, however. Within the month of Sir Eric's visit his cable to House in London on the subject was, House said, so "intemperate" that if House had read it to his European colleagues he felt it might have led to serious trouble. House sent word through Wiseman to Lloyd George that unless the British Prime Minister "would make some reasonable concessions in his attitude upon the 'Freedom of the Seas' . . . all hope of Anglo-Saxon unity would be at an end." Lloyd George's immediate reply was, House said, "that Great Britain would spend her last guinea to keep a navy superior to that of the United States or any other power, and that no Cabinet official could continue in government in England who took a different position."

"I countered this," House wrote, "by telling him it was not our purpose to go into a naval building rivalry with Great Britain, but it was our purpose to have our rights at sea adequately safeguarded, and that we did not intend to have our commerce regulated by Great Britain whenever she was at war."

On October 8, the day after Sir Eric's visit to the White House, Daniels scribbled in his diary: "WW came into Cabinet room whistling."

And: "In response to inquiry said he whistled because he thought he had done right in answering German note." The German note to which Wilson referred laid the basis for negotiations with Germany and Austria "for a peace for which the fourteen points . . . should serve as foundation." One of those was specifically "the Freedom of the Seas." At that time, too— on the Monday after Geddes' departure on Saturday—Daniels had a long conference with the General Board of the Navy which urged a naval construction program to give the United States "the biggest Navy in the world by 1925." The President, however, thought it "not wise while discussing reduction of armament in case of peace to increase our program. Therefore, did not favor General Board's 7 year program to give us Navy as big as Great Britain's, but approved another three year program. . . ." However, a few days later Daniels wrote: "Discussing GB's selfish policy WW said, 'I want to go into the Peace Conference armed with as many weapons as my pockets will hold so as to compel justice.'" It was at that time, when it began to be clear that the growing Navy might be a weapon not merely of war but of peace, that Franklin was able to get back to work for the first time—on October 18—looking, Livy thought, "fairly well" and very anxious to get into uniform.

"In September 1918," Franklin wrote Daniels a quarter of a century later, "I think I wrote you or cabled that after I had come home and reported to you, I wanted to go back to Europe with an assignment in uniform, to the Naval Railway Battery."

He did write it in pencil in London on September 4, between Inverness and the *Leviathan* but never sent it.

That fall, Eleanor recalled later, she met TR at the funeral of a relative and was angered by his reproaches because

Franklin was not in uniform. The letter the elder Roosevelt wrote after that meeting did not sound reproachful:

DEAR FRANKLIN:
We are deeply concerned about your sickness, and trust you will soon be well. We are *very* proud of you.
With love,
Aff. Yours
THEODORE ROOSEVELT
Later, Eleanor will tell you of our talk about your plans.

It seems a little strange that the talk about his plans could only be reported orally. Old TR was tired. Also, at that time he and Cabot Lodge were already as concerned about the Democrats making peace as they had been about their making war. They shared the feeling that "the American people want a complete victory and an unconditional surrender. . . ."

That was a phrase which stuck in Franklin's memory. He used it in his joint press conference with Winston Churchill at Casablanca in January 1943. Some feared then that it would delay peace by stiffening the resistance of the enemy. But Roosevelt said, "Practically all Germans deny the fact they surrendered in the last war, but this time they are going to know it. And so are the Japs."

In Washington Daniels agreed with Franklin that he could no longer conscientiously ask him to stay on as Assistant Secretary. Roosevelt went from the Secretary to the President about the matter and recalled later that Wilson told him that "in his judgment I was too late—that he had received the first suggestions of an armistice from Prince Max of Baden, and that he hoped the war would be over very soon."

Apparently Roosevelt talked so much about his determination to get into uniform, however, that the rumor that he had resigned was published. He was not resigning but he did want earnestly to go back to Europe. And so apparently did everybody else except the soldiers who were already there and wanted home—quick. The major traveler, of course, was Woodrow Wilson about whose proposed journey abroad there was considerable debate, as there was also, particularly since the Republicans had won the Congressional elections, about his colleagues at the Conference. Colonel House, of course, was going and taking along his son-in-law, Gordon Auchincloss, and his brother-in-law, Dr. Mezes, as part of a congenial staff. Secretary Lansing also was going and would have with him both his nephews, the Dulles boys. Enough members of the Fly Club of Harvard were going so that on the morning after one of their parties Livy was to notice that Eleanor was "very cool" with him and with Franklin. One man who wanted desperately to go, however, was not to be there. Bryan was apparently aware that peace was near before President Wilson told Roosevelt it was.

"Peace prospects improve," Bryan wrote Daniels on October 14. "A commission may be needed soon. I hope you will not consider me immodest if I say that it is a task for which I am especially qualified. If I understand the terms as stated I am in hearty accord with all of them. I say this so that you may know if the question comes up in the Cabinet."

Daniels passed on the "consuming ambition" of his old friend to Wilson. The President in reply expressed his own "cordial feelings toward Mr. Bryan" but suggested that at a time when many were "too much in love with force and retribution" the public might feel that "he would be too easy . . . and pursue some Utopian schemes." Even after Wilson sailed, however, Bryan sent Daniels his itinerary "in case the President should inquire about me." Also, there seemed in that letter the scarcely hid, threatening bitterness of an old crusader who felt, as strongly as Theodore Roosevelt did about war, that he was entitled to a place in the front ranks of the making of the peace.

"I shall not conceal from you the conviction," Bryan wrote Daniels, "that I am entitled to a place on the commission appointed. Not that the Democrats will expect it in view of my part in the campaigns of 1912 and 1916, but because of my interest in peace. I expect to attend the conference—at least to go to the place where it is held in order to urge the adoption of our peace plan as a part of the plan to prevent future wars but it would be much more pleasant to go as one of the official representatives of the government.

"I would have more influence and it would save me considerable financially but as I said I shall feel it my duty to go in my individual capacity if the President does not think me worthy to go in a representative capacity."

Bryan wrote that in pencil on a train "en route." He seemed always "en route." Bryan's letter worried Daniels more than Franklin's suggestion that "an Assistant Secretary" be sent to Europe to deal with the "enormous number of contracts, claims, both personal and property, readjustments, etc., etc." The work was too much scattered in young officers without much experience. A civilian was required. He was eager, he told Daniels, for "your administration of the Navy to continue without scandal or criticism." He wanted the Navy to take its departure from Europe with the good will of the Allied nations.

Daniels was reluctant because he felt that while the business abroad was important, the task at home would "require the united work and effort of both of us." Then, less than six weeks after he had got back to work from illness, Franklin was sick again. He added a sick man's asperity to a young man's eagerness in his importunities. Daniels finally acquiesced on December 15, but he did not sign Franklin's travel orders until the day before Christmas.

Before Franklin sailed, he and Daniels went to New York to review the returning fleet of American battleships under Admiral Hugh Rodman, which had served with the Grand Fleet of Britain in war. From the fleet review to the parade of the sailors up Fifth Avenue, it was a busy day for Daniels. All he wrote in his diary was, "Naval review at New York."

But Livy Davis, who was on his way to Europe again with Franklin, set down a fairly full report of that final item of the great war as he saw it. He wrote:

> Dec. 26—Arrived at New York at 7. Breakfasted with Roose-velts at Penn Station. Took Navy car to 97th Street where boarded Aztec. Lots of people on board—De Rhams, Gibson, Blisses, Governors, Naval Cons. Ed. and others. Anchored at Statue of Liberty at 9:30. Fleet consisting of NY, Wyoming, Texas, Okla., Ark., Fla., Penn., Ariz., and appeared promptly at 10 through blinding snowstorm saluting as they passed. Then proceeded upstream and passed each side of 22 ships each saluting and playing Anthem each time. FDR stand-ing bareheaded nearly froze to death. No lunch came aboard so beat it ashore with De Rhams and stopped at Childs for a gulp and arrived at reviewing stand at Library. Saw whole parade. Thence to R[acket] & T[ennis] for Turkish Bath. Dined with E. Davie and to "Better Ole." Bully. Thence to Plaza. Splendid time.

THIRTEEN

Innocents Abroad

BEFORE WILSON SAILED ON HIS TRIUMPHANT TRIP TO EUROPE, IN December 1918, he wrote Daniels that he hoped he would keep his "eyes skinned against anybody getting the better of us while I am on the other side of the water." In Washington it was not necessary to be very sharp-eyed to see the dangers. Having won the Congressional elections, the Republicans were waiting impatiently to take over both Houses of Congress in the spring. They not only questioned the propriety of a President's going abroad to make the peace—no President had ever done so before. Also they complained because, after the Republican victory, there was no Republican on the Peace Conference Delegation except the wealthy career diplomat, Henry White. Perhaps the departure of the Peace Delegation was as Franklin Roosevelt described it later. He told a press conference in March 1943, when he was determined not to let such a thing happen again, that "very little work had been done on post-war problems before Armistice Day.

"Everybody was rushing around trying to dig up things," he said. "The tempo seemed to be that of the lady who is told at noon that she is to accompany her husband on a month's trip that afternoon. Well, I have seen ladies trying to pack for a month's trip in three hours, and that was a little bit the situation over here, and everywhere else, in making preparations for the Versailles Conference. Everybody was rushing around

275

grabbing things out of closets and throwing them into suit-
cases. Some of the large things taken out of cupboards were
not needed at all."

And he added: "I have forgotten how many experts we took
to Paris at that time, but everybody who had a 'happy thought'
or who thought he was an expert got a free ride."

It was as a man left at home by that exodus that Daniels
promised to watch. With Wilson above him and Roosevelt
below him both off to Europe, he had a good deal on which
to keep his eyes. The confusion did not seem to him quite as
great as Franklin described it. Indeed, Daniels felt momentarily
rather odd, being popular in the aftermath of victory. That
was not grounds for complacency, however. In the mounting
Republican confidence and determination, he could expect
again to be a special target. In his own case, the first sharp post-
victory attack came, he thought, from a personal rather than a
political direction.

On the last day of 1918, *The Washington Post* published a
long story about the Secretary of the Navy's plan for an in-
comparable American Navy in any armed world. On the first
day of the new year *The Post* was editorially strong in support
of the idea:

"Build the big Navy.

"Mr. Daniels in reply to a query stated that President Wilson
coincided with this view.

"So do 100,000,000 Americans."

On January 2, however, Secretary and Mrs. Daniels went
with their friend, Mildred Dewey, widow of the Admiral, to
the District Court. She was suing her nephew, Edward Beale
McLean, publisher of *The Post*, on the grounds that his father,
who was Mrs. Dewey's brother, had cheated Mrs. Dewey out of
her rightful share in a "flourspar mine" in Illinois. The elder
McLean, whose financial behavior Mrs. Dewey was questioning
in the courthouse, was that John R. McLean, whom, though a

nominal Democrat, Henry Adams had called the "cheaper, fatter, commoner" measure of the Cincinnati regime which departed with Taft. His son, Ned, already had a lurid reputation. By 1919 he was more restrained in his behavior as both the inheritor of his father's millions and the husband of Evalyn Walsh, who owned the Hope Diamond and wrote her biography under the title, *Father Struck It Rich*. Young McLean then had not become one of the early supporters of a new Ohio regime headed by Harding.

Daniels did not like the Dewey-McLean suit. In his diary he noted, "Dirty linen washed in public. Hoped to avert it." But he and my mother both loved Mrs. Dewey and felt a certain naval guardianship for her as the Admiral's widow. I remember that she was a delectable old lady. Her hair was as white as her lace collar. She made a delicate satin sound when she walked, and a just perceptible perfume seemed a proper part of her mourning. She was perfect in her role as the Admiral's widow. Also, my memory of her is illuminated now by the realization that she enjoyed the role as she had enjoyed others before it. She had been twelve years a rich and pretty widow when Admiral Dewey came home a hero and a widower from Manila. A nation which soon tired of its heroes became indignant, however, when the Admiral gave her the house which the people of the country had given him. A good deal of the indignation came from politicians who did not want Dewey to run for President and from bigots who were shocked by Dewey's marriage to a Catholic.

Mrs. Dewey had been converted while her first husband was a military attaché at Vienna. Even in that waltzing capital, historians reported, she vied with the nobility in the splendor of her apparel. Henry Adams blamed her for the ridicule to which Dewey was subjected. She behaves, he said in 1900, "like a heroine by marriage, and has thrown Lady Jane Grey's social exigencies into shadow." She was, however, undoubtedly a target at which some people shot to hurt the Admiral. Certainly, standing beside her Daniels was a target at which McLean shot when the Secretary seemed by his protective presence to interfere in a family quarrel.

Admiral Samuel McGowan, the Paymaster General, who Daniels thought had done such a wonderful war job in purchases and contracts, also went to the courthouse as Mrs. Dewey's friend. And in his diary Daniels wrote that McLean told McGowan that he would make it hot for them for coming with Mrs. Dewey. He did. *The Post* carried no story about the lawsuit. Readers had to get that in *The Washington Star*.

Even on the morning of the trial *The Post* carried a sympathetic news story about the Secretary's appearance before the House Naval Affairs Committee urging Atlantic and Pacific fleets. On the same day there was a story that Daniels declined to comment on a statement by the *London Graphic* characterizing as "unfriendly" his statement that the United States should have a navy second to none unless the peace conference limited armaments. Then Daniels and Admiral McGowan went with Mrs. Dewey to the courthouse. *The Post*'s very clear position on the naval program the following morning was that the Secretary "combines an incurable ignorance with a stubborn belief in his own super-wisdom."

The Secretary's friends were indignant. Undoubtedly, however, there were others who were impatiently waiting for Daniels' wartime popularity to subside to start shooting at him again as a familiar target. Daniels was at the time less worried by them than by some of his friends in Congress who were troubled by his Big Navy proposals. That same January Congressman Padgett of Tennessee, Chairman of the House Naval Affairs Committee, came to Daniels' house at night to ask a question for himself and other friends of the administration. They "wished to ask if the President thought in view of the recent situation in Europe it was necessary to authorize the three year program of construction."

"If there is to be a League of Nations, why build other ships?" Daniels wrote in his diary.

He had resolved the question himself—as had Wilson—in the belief that while there would be no need of a greater Navy if there was a League, there might be less disposition to support a League or build a peace on the basis of Wilson's Fourteen Points unless America offered strength as the alternative to such peace. Republicans were already interpreting Daniels' plan as "a paper Navy" with which to bluff Europeans. He did not think it should be a bluff but a reality, a real steel Navy or clear determination that neither under the water nor on top of it should any nation deny others full freedom on the seas. However, in deference to the difficulties of the Congressmen, he cabled the President. Four days later he had his answer. "Cable from the President that it would be fatal not to build the three year program."

It was on the basis of that cable, undoubtedly, that the House committee unanimously approved the program. The leading Republican on that committee was as close a friend of Daniels as any of the Democrats. But on February 24, 1919, the day of Wilson's enthusiastic first welcome home in Boston, Daniels, noting the delaying tactics of Republicans, wrote that it "looks as if Senate Naval Affairs Committee not going to let bill pass this session." Senator Lodge was not then rising to defend the Navy's plans. The lame duck session in which the Democrats had majorities in both Houses was expiring. After March 4, the situation would be reversed.

Despite the acclaim of Europe, that was clear to Wilson when, with young Franklin and Eleanor Roosevelt as minor traveling companions, he came back on the *George Washington* to the United States for the last days of Congress in February. Eleanor remembered the "funny incident" that Wilson, who at that time had had six years' experience with naval etiquette, still refused to go ahead of his wife on boarding the ship, "a situation unheard of in Navy regulations." In her *My Memoir,* written after FDR became President, Mrs. Wilson said of the Roosevelts, "We found them very delightful companions." Eleanor's observation was that Wilson "seemed to have very little interest in making himself popular with groups of people whom he touched, though he had such a remarkable sense of the psychology of the people as a whole." He seemed to stir only when he spoke of the League of Nations.

"The United States must go in," she remembered him saying, "or it will break the heart of the world."

Their landing was the occasion of Wilson's triumphant home-coming in Boston where even Calvin Coolidge, whom Lodge regarded as "a very able, sagacious man of pure New England type," committed himself to the extent of welcoming Wilson "as a great statesman . . . to whom we have entrusted our destinies." Mrs. Wilson thought the reception in Senator Lodge's state "almost equalled those abroad—perhaps not so picturesque but just as warm." For the moment, despite the elections, Wilson seemed the only leader. When Daniels had sent Franklin a radio message of sympathy in January on the death of his "Uncle Ted," the leadership of the opposition appeared confused. The fight, however, against Wilson and his League, as TR's daughter Alice reported with much enthusiasm, had already begun in the Senate and in the drawing rooms in Washington. Sometimes it was more venomous among the women. Before the Wilsons landed on that first return, some of the President's enemies were already talking with an evident sneer about Mrs. Wilson's reception abroad "as the consort of a reigning sovereign" and reporting that in England her secretary had been called her "lady in waiting." That sudden devotion to democratic simplicity by Wilson's opponents was only a bland beginning.

If Wilson met tumultuous welcome, he also met determined filibuster in the Senate, so soon to be Republican. The Navy bill was not the only legislation caught in the tactics of postponement. Those tactics might make Wilson, as he told Daniels, "feel like swearing." He had more to swear about on March 5, the day after the old Congress expired, when Senator Lodge announced the opposition of thirty-nine Senators to the League as drawn.

It was while Daniels was preparing at last to sail for Europe himself that Franklin Roosevelt and Nigel Law had their last dinner together on March 2. It was the last time they ever talked. Though it was reported then that Nigel's "heart is no longer his own," he was returning alone to London for duty in the Foreign Office, later in Paris.

Daniels confidently left Franklin behind and in charge when he sailed on the *Leviathan* on her thirteenth troop crossing in March. Though laid up with the gout, Lord Reading, the British Ambassador, had paid him special attention as he departed. Also, before he left he had without any difficulty impressed upon Franklin the necessity of moving forward with the big navy program which the President felt so essential to the possibility of his success in Paris. If the Senate filibuster had temporarily killed any new three-year program, much building was still authorized under the old one which would not expire until July 1, 1919. It was Franklin's job to get the ships started. He did. He ran into the same pattern of identical high bids for steel which Daniels had found when he arrived in Washington in 1913, and took drastic post-war action in commandeering 14,000 tons under a wartime statute still in force. After his return to Paris on March 14, 1919, Wilson was going to have an increasing Navy for bargaining purposes in Paris.

"Wilson went to Paris," Daniels said, "resolved that the ancient ambition, from the first triremes of Rome to the dreadnaughts of Britain, that one powerful Navy should rule the waves must no longer prevail."

In some British circles that seemed not only an impertinent point of view but an innocent one. It seemed neither one to the old Catholic puritan Admiral Benson who was waiting for Daniels in Paris in a state of both stubbornness and indignation about British insistence that the United States halt its naval building program. Benson was an innocent. The solemn Admiral must have seemed dour in contrast to the supposedly blithe spirit of Paris. If Paris in the winter and spring of 1919 was cold and damp it was also gay. Earlier in the winter Eleanor Roosevelt had written home that the city was "full beyond belief and one sees many celebrities and all one's friends." Then, she had written her mother-in-law that it was "no place for the boys, especially the younger ones, and the scandals going on would make many a woman at home unhappy." However, with amusement she had noted that Mrs. Benson was "much disappointed and wishes she could return to Washington!" (Franklin's exclamation marks were contagious.)

Daniels was less solemn than his Admiral but no more worldly. He and Benson blushed together when they attended an official occasion where entertainment was provided, Daniels recorded, by a "ballet of women in such scant costumes as to be indecent. Benson and I agreed that such exhibitions to our young soldiers were disgraceful." The Admiral suggested that they leave, but Daniels felt that since they were the guests of the French government, they could hardly do that. It was going to be some time, however, before he could joke about the occasion as "a navel review."

In the mazes, if not the scandals, of peace-making, Daniels and Benson may have seemed very innocent or just unsophisticatedly stubborn to their British opposites in their insistence that, short of an effective League, there was no reason why

America should not have—and good reasons why it should have —"the incomparably greatest Navy" which Wilson and Daniels had advocated. The British had told Benson quite candidly that they did not know what Wilson meant by "the Freedom of the Seas." The American Admiral felt that the British were interested in continued "command of the seas." The suspicious old sailor told the Secretary that Britain was "trying to dictate naval matters in order to control commerce." He thought that if Britain were to be given, as it wished, an agreement to its permanent naval supremacy, "the League of Nations instead of being what we are striving for and most earnestly hope for, will be a stronger British Empire." Daniels wrote his view in his diary, "No Minority stockholder." Wilson agreed with him particularly at a crucial point in the Peace Conference, while Daniels was in Paris, when in the face of what the President regarded as the obstructions of Lloyd George and Clemenceau, neither of whom liked the idealism of his Fourteen Points, he ordered the *George Washington* and threatened to go home. Undoubtedly, that must have seemed rather imperious. Also, it may have seemed an impatient part of the American innocence to which some Europeans and Americans attributed the failure of Wilson and his League at home and in the world.

The persisting picture of the innocence of the Wilsonians in Europe does not take its pattern from the bumptious irreverence for an old civilization presented by Mark Twain. The new realists in America and Europe preferred instead the pattern of Daisy Miller, the tragic young lady created by Henry James. Perhaps Wilson's tragedy was, as H. G. Wells wrote, like Daisy's, "the pathetic story of a frank, trustful, high-minded, but rather simple-minded American girl, with a real disposition toward righteousness and a great desire for a 'good time,' and how she came to Europe and was swiftly entangled and put in the wrong, and at last driven to welcome death by the complex tortuousness and obstinate limitations of the older world."

Wells, who, in his *The Outline of History,* took a long view of the Peace Conference in a very short time, tied that image of Daisy Miller to Woodrow Wilson—and to old-fashioned American idealism. Maybe, as he said, Wilson failed to draw upon the moral and intellectual resources of the States, as embodied in the Republicans. Perhaps he made the issue too personal and surrounded himself only with personal adherents. It could be that his bringing Mrs. Wilson to Paris added, as Wells said, "a social quality, nay, almost a tourist quality" to the peace settlement. It is pretty clear, however, that Wilson was impatient with the social, tourist and ceremonial delays before he could get the conference down to work. And it was the almost celestially critical Mr. Wells who reported that Lloyd George, who had made the alliance with the British conservatives which Wilson declined to make with the American Republicans, came to the Peace Conference with "an urgent necessity for respecting the nationalist egotism of the British imperialists and capitalists who had returned him to power." Wilson met those forces in Paris, but, innocent as he might have been, he did not meet them there for the first time. He did not have to take a trip to subtle, intricate, sophisticated Europe to discover them.

When the Secretary and Mrs. Daniels lunched with the Wilsons immediately after their arrival in Paris, the President gaily showed them all over their house on the Place des Etats-Unis. Wilson seemed in high spirits about it as Daniels described him in his diary. The house, Mrs. Wilson wrote, was less ornate than the palace of the Prince Murat where they had stayed on their first trip, "and more homey." The President, Daniels said, "took us all over the house, showing the wonderful bathrooms."

" 'Now,' " he quoted the President, " 'let me show you the refrigerator where I sleep.' "

The innocent Secretary of the Navy was glad he was staying at the Ritz.

"The only exercise I get," Wilson told him, "is to my vocabulary."

Exercise was one thing Daniels could dispense with at home or abroad. He moved, however, at a swift pace. Undoubtedly he found time to indulge in the "tourist quality" of the American officials of which Wells complained. He sought out John Paul Jones' burial place. He helped dedicate a marker on the house where Jefferson lived. But he had the American situation as Wilson's Cabinet saw it to report to the President. He had much to discover in Paris, too. His well-loved and well-trusted friend, Baruch, who afterward somehow seemed both a realist and a Wilsonian, was troubled Daniels noted: "The more he saw of Great Britain, the more he felt the United States was the only nation that approached unselfishness and our best hope to protect the peace of the world was a strong American Navy." And from Baruch he learned of differences within the American delegation. Baruch said that House's young son-in-law and secretary, Auchincloss, was referring to the President as "Woody" and saying that his batting average would be better after House recovered from a slight illness. Apparently Auchincloss did not minimize the President to Daniels when he called on Colonel House, but he did tell him there was no point in going to see Secretary of State Lansing since House handled all important matters.

Daniels saw the Colonel soon after he arrived. He recalled in his diary House's phrase, "Between us and the angels," in his description of difficulties in the peace negotiations. That was a favorite expression with the Colonel. He gave the impression that, while he was a man of the greatest discretion, he kept nothing from the angels and that the angels kept very little from him. It was effective flattery when he seemed to let a Cabinet member into their company. Daniels spoke to House of the naval negotiations, about which the British were very impatient, as an apparent prerequisite to any agreement on the peace. He quoted House in his diary, "Talked about naval program, 'Nothing more important here than the question you have touched.' " In House's diary, which was then available only to himself and the angels, the Colonel wrote more about Daniels than Daniels wrote in his diary about House. Wickham Steed, editor of *The Times* of London, was about to interview Daniels, but House said, "I caught him [Daniels] just in time to tell him what to say and what not to say. It was a dangerous interview because he does not know how thoroughly Lloyd George and the British dislike him, and how much they resent the foolish things he has been saying in the United States about our naval program."

House also wrote that he urged Wilson to keep Daniels away from Paris and discussion of the naval questions with the British, but that "the President flatly refused this when I put the matter to him." House did not indicate to Daniels any opposition to the President's determination to have a great Navy or "Freedom of the Seas" for all shipping without any one nation dominating the oceans. He did, however, state the proposition negatively. Daniels wrote that House "thought we could afford to have no program of naval construction now if others would do likewise." On a very friendly, even intimate basis, House was dealing with the British on the question and apparently wanted to be the only one to deal with them. However, since that was impossible, the Colonel wrote, when Daniels prepared to go to England, that "I again went over the matter of his speeches in London. I even got him to phrase certain sentences which I thought it would be advisable to use. I hope he does this thing well, for its importance is greater than appears on the surface."

No agreement was reached in Paris with the British on the American building program. Daniels wrote afterward that the

fight in Paris between the Secretary of the Navy and the First
Sea Lord and their admirals ended in a draw: "John Bull did
not get from Uncle Sam his recognition of Britain's primacy or
agreement to cease construction of a Navy that would be the
equal of the greatest in the world, or any let-up in the construction of a merchant marine which Wilson believed was
essential both to enlargement of markets for American goods,
and to the international trade that lay near his heart. And
Wilson was unable to secure an acceptance of the second of his
Fourteen Points by Britain"—the Freedom of the Seas. If, however, the British considered Daniels "unfriendly" in his refusal
to stop building, he was never treated more hospitably anywhere else in his life than he was in Britain.

Like Colonel House, Admiral Sims had been a little disturbed by Daniels' visit to England. Under the circumstances,
he suggested, Daniels would not be very welcome. The Secretary did not find himself unwelcome. If it be the mark of an
innocent that he have a good time abroad as Daisy Miller
wanted to do, Daniels was innocent on that trip. He went to
the Orkneys where Franklin and his party had been on such a
lively excursion the summer before to see Admiral Strauss'
mine-laying station. He had a cup of tea in the cold weather
there, but noticed "we had taken over Old Glen Albyn distillery
here and another one in Scotland. I told naval officers war
ended too soon. My purpose was to make Great Britain dry
by taking over distilleries for naval bases."

The officers laughed appreciatively. He went to Scapa Flow,
where the surrendered German fleet was anchored and where
Vice-Admiral Sir Roger Keyes pointed out scornfully that three
trawlers were guarding the entire fleet. They were still guarding it presumably when two months later the German crews
of the fleet opened the water valves of the imprisoned battleships and sank them before the Allies could decide what to do
with them. Everywhere, not only at naval stations but in cities,

there were ceremonial welcomes. Daniels was delighted to lunch with the King and Queen, and noted that he ate plover's eggs for the first time. Also, he observed in Victoria's Windsor that "all smoked including the Queen." But he did not miss the chance to go to John Wesley's tomb.

Probably the high point of his visit to England was the dinner which Walter Long, then First Lord of the British Admiralty, gave for him in the House of Commons. On that occasion he had "private talk with Churchill." The Rt. Hon. Winston, at forty-five then, was Secretary of State for War and Minister for Air. He did not argue about American naval construction. He stated a fact. Daniels noted his statement: "GB would build as big ships & guns as any." It was not an argumentative occasion. There were no reporters. There were serious speeches on the war behind them and the peace before them. But Lord Curzon emphasized Anglo-American brotherhood with a bit of doggerel:

> There was a man who had two sons,
> And these two sons were brothers.
> Josephus was the name of one
> Bohunkus was the other's.

Daniels sailed home undoubtedly as much an innocent as when he had gone abroad. The sea was pretty rough as the *Mount Vernon* sailed homeward. He noted that two thousand people, including at least two generals, did not show up for meals on the big, crowded transport. He himself was feeling fine. He read a life of Nelson: "Interesting volume & just. Excoriates Nelson for his infatuation for Lady Hamilton which caused him to linger at Naples and was the only blot on his career." As puritan, however, he was under no illusions that the only place on earth where innocence might be dangerous to Daisy Miller or anybody else was the continent of Europe. The Republican Congress was convening in special session, on

May 19, two days after he got home. Franklin Roosevelt and many others from the Navy Department met him at the train.

"Department will be *up to the minute* when the Sec'y gets back," Franklin had written Eleanor. The ships authorized under the old three-year program were being hurried into construction. Also, that week he wrote his mother, "J.D. is back and I will have less work to do—tho' that is not an unmitigated blessing." There were few unmitigated blessings that year in young, simple, unsophisticated America. A people who had so long resisted war turned in irritation away from the purposes for which it had been fought. The Ku Klux Klan was being organized in America. There were race riots in Washington that June, and I can remember the fear on the faces of our servants when Father sent them home in his car each evening.

Early in June, soon after Daniels returned, the house of the new Attorney General, A. Mitchell Palmer, was damaged by a bomb. The blast killed the unidentified bomber, who was presumed to be one of the Reds against whom Palmer was conducting a strenuous and highly popular campaign which some thought might make him the Democratic nominee for the Presidency. Alice Longworth, who depicted herself as a sort of first feminine assistant to Senator Lodge in his fight on Wilson, rushed over to see the bombing and the body, both of which fortunately were located just across the street from the house of her still well-loved cousins, Franklin and Eleanor. It was not the only explosion in which Palmer was involved that summer.

In February, while Wilson was still on his first trip abroad, Daniels had written him urging that he appoint Palmer, who had been one of the President's strong political supporters since 1912, as successor to the retiring Thomas Watt Gregory as Attorney General. One of the first things Daniels discovered, however, on his return to the United States was that Palmer had dismissed an assistant attorney general who, under Gregory, had been fighting the Honolulu Oil Company claims on the naval oil reserves. John Ise in his study, *The United States Oil Policy,* says the assistant attorney general had "accused Lane of trying to push some fraudulent locations to patent" and in general criticized the Secretary of the Interior "so severely that he was dismissed by the succeeding attorney general." So while Wilson was in Paris the threat to the oil reserves was revived.

Wilson had held up oil reserve decisions Lane had wanted to make for a long time. For two years Lane had been complaining to Colonel House that the President no longer trusted him. A year before, Colonel House had carried the Californian's complaints to the President.

"Lane has stood still," Wilson said.

Apparently House did not argue when Wilson said that Lane had become a conservative and had tried to lease oil lands contrary to the administration's policy. Wilson in Europe had other matters on his mind in 1919, when at Lane's complaint Palmer fired the assistant who had opposed Lane's leasing plans. Daniels went straight to his old friend former Attorney General Gregory. Afterward he wrote in his diary that Gregory said that Palmer was a candidate for President. Palmer had told Gregory that Daniels was unreasonable while Lane was reasonable.

"Palmer will line up with the oil men," Gregory said.

That was one of the things Daniels, sure of support, had to bring to the attention of Wilson when the President came home on July 8. It was no longer necessary for anybody to have his eyes skinned to see trouble. Undoubtedly the enthusiasm of crowds in America as in Europe may have deceived Wilson. He was in high spirits. When Daniels waited at the dock for the *George Washington* to come in, Wilson wirelessed facetiously, "Why do we not come in?"

"Tide, like time," Daniels noted, "waits nor hurries for no man."

The crowds were enthusiastic when the tide did let Wilson come in. Even Hoboken, where the *George Washington* docked, looked lovely to him, he said. Daniels was pleased to notice that some of the crowd's cheers were directed at him. The New York reception was good. That night, as they came into Washington, the welcome, Daniels noted, was "beautiful." My mother expressed regret to the President that everything was illuminated but the Capitol.

"It never is," he said.

From his point of view that was increasingly clear. His fatal western campaign to illuminate it began less than two months later. It is hard, long after, to conceive the bitterness of his enemies. Alice Longworth said, after he was stricken, presumably exempting herself for the record, that "some of the comments were noticeably lacking in the Greek quality of Aidos—the quality that deters one from defiling the body of a dead enemy." Apparently not even Alice's Greek scholarship put any limits on what might be said of a live enemy or about his lady. The venom in Washington had been whispered as far west as the Pacific Coast. An unhappy lady whom Wilson was to see in Los Angeles had heard it there.

Daniels, who had been on an inspection tour of the great post-war Navy as far west as Hawaii, met the President in Seattle. Wilson reviewed the fleet and afterward he and Mrs. Wilson were awed as they looked at it in the night from their suite on the top floor of the Washington Hotel: "straight out as far as the eye could see, lay the entire fleet, every ship ablaze with light. Surely America should have been proud of such a sight." Wilson was proud of it. As a seventeen-year-old boy in the crowded Hippodrome, I was proud of him. He seemed to me to make a great speech. My father thought so. But an admiral with us remembered that "something seemed to be

wrong with President Wilson. . . . He appeared to have lost
his customary force and enthusiasm." Afterward, of course,
that seemed prophetic. The Presidential train moved on southward to Los Angeles and there on Sunday, September 21,
though much in need of rest, he did a very kind thing. He and
Mrs. Wilson invited Mrs. Peck to lunch. The President's invitation to Mrs. Peck at such a time seems the best evidence
not only of the emptiness of the gossip about them but of his
sympathy for her. She was having a hard time. Her only son's
health was not good. He was unable to get a job. Mrs. Peck
apparently supported herself by gradually selling all the things
she had had in better days. She had sold a house she owned on
Nantucket. She sold her personal effects, keeping to the last
some beautiful lace which she told a friend had been intended
for her dress at her wedding in the White House. She apparently stayed then only a few dollars ahead of those publishers
and partisans who wanted to pay her well for a story which
would reflect on Wilson. Both Mrs. Peck and Mrs. Wilson have
described that luncheon. Mrs. Wilson thought Mrs. Peck was
"a faded, sweet-looking woman." Mrs. Peck found Mrs. Wilson
"junoesque, but handsome, with a charming smile that revealed
her strong, white teeth."

At the luncheon, Mrs. Peck wrote later, conversation was
"gracefully diverted from subjects disturbing to digestion."
That was not the story that she told to a North Carolina friend
of hers who afterward brought Daniels into some awkward and
abashed negotiations with Mrs. Peck for Wilson's letters to her.
She told that friend, who told me, that at the luncheon Wilson
spoke of how deeply he regretted the pain which must have
been caused her by the gossip of his political enemies. Mrs.
Peck said that Mrs. Wilson spoke then. Apparently she meant
to be amusing in a strained situation.

"Where there's so much smoke, there must be some fire."

The "faded, sweet-looking" Mrs. Peck burst out in anger with one of the ridiculous canards in a continental whispering against the Wilsons which attended the loud, open League debate. It was silly but it was a symptom of a sick bitterness which moved as secretly as plague. Four days later Wilson's serious illness began on the train between Pueblo and Wichita. His train, at Grayson's insistence, turned back to Washington from its canceled tour on September 26. Daniels noted in his diary on September 28, when Wilson's train arrived in Washington, that Wilson "walked out unaided." But, on October 3, there was no doubt about the seriousness of his illness. Joe Tumulty was in tears. Daniels could not work. Perhaps the item about Wilson's illness which impressed Daniels most was told him by King Albert of the Belgians, who arrived on a ceremonial visit at almost exactly the time the President was taken ill. Albert's coming was marked by Franklin Roosevelt's irritation, apparently because he was not included among those to meet him. It was "stupid," he thought, but Daniels "advised FDR to drop it & save embarrassment." Later, after King Albert had seen the President, he told Daniels that Wilson had "a full beard on his face and it was white." The Presidential door was closed.

It would have been hard to conceive, beside the lively but fuming Franklin in 1919, that the country was narrowly to miss the same situation during his Presidency in 1945. I remember an at least half-closed door on a sick President seemed not so much inevitable as advisable when Roosevelt came back from Yalta. He was not incapacitated as Wilson had been. Apparently, however, at Yalta even his daughter, Anna, who had accompanied him, realized for the first time how serious his condition was. The approach of peace piled Roosevelt's duties high as his staff in effect disintegrated. Louis Howe was long dead. Harry Hopkins was sick at the Mayo Clinic in Minnesota.

Roosevelt's shrewd and jovial secretary, General Edwin M. ("Pa") Watson, died on the voyage home from Yalta. His secretary, Stephen Early, had resigned to go into private business. James F. Byrnes, unhappy because Roosevelt would not make him Secretary of State, was retiring to South Carolina. The suggestion was made—apparently with Roosevelt's approval—that more and more matters which had received his attention before, be handled and briefed by others before they were brought to his attention. It was an impossible plan. Roosevelt must have known that from Wilson's day. The most blessed thing that ever happened to Roosevelt and the country was that when he was stricken he was struck down forever. Fate dealt less kindly with Wilson.

Not all great foreign visitors like King Albert saw Wilson. Viscount Grey of Fallodon arrived in New York on a special mission to Wilson on the day the President fell ill in the West. Colonel House had helped arrange the Grey mission after Wilson's return to the United States. Grey came "with the greatest reluctance," House wrote. Before Grey came House had discussed the purposes of his mission with him and listed as first among them "the naval building programme." Grey brought with him the same Sir William Tyrrell, whom he had sent before the war to talk so "boyishly" about a German-British naval building holiday. Wilson had been enthusiastically candid with Tyrrell then. There was no Englishman, at the beginning of his administration, whom Wilson had admired more than Grey.

On the 1919 mission neither Tyrrell nor Grey saw Wilson to discuss the naval building program with him. Before Grey arrived, it is pretty clear from House's own diaries that the Wilson-House friendship was broken. Late in August and again early in September, reporters had been asking House about it. Wilson's failure to receive Grey has been ascribed to Wilson's sick petulance. Grey himself at the time was half blind and taking advantage of his visit to receive treatment at Johns Hopkins. Though he was "abroad" he has never been described as an innocent. During his visit he and Tyrrell were in constant touch with House, but Tyrrell suggested that House not let even Assistant Secretary Phillips know Tyrrell was seeing him because there was so much jealousy in Washington of House's influence that "he thought it well to take this precaution." It was not jealousy, however, that caused Wilson's refusal to see Grey and his final fury with Colonel House.

At a dinner party in Washington, Wilson was told, Major Charles Kennedy-Craufurd-Stuart talked scandalously to Mrs. George Thomas Marye, wife of Wilson's first Ambassador to Russia, about Mrs. Wilson. Major Craufurd-Stuart—or Stewart as he was sometimes referred to in the correspondence—was Grey's secretary. He was a gentleman who kept his age out of *Who's Who*. He was old enough, however, to have gone into military service in 1900, win decorations in the Boer War and to serve afterward with the military police in Burma. During World War I he had served in the Sudan "on special service." He was a man of many accomplishments and apparently a man of the world, not an innocent though he came from Rye, Sussex, where the American author of *Daisy Miller* had lived so long. He was a polo player, an amateur photographer who had exhibited at the London Salon of Photography and the author of such popular songs as "At Gloaming Tide" and "Make-Believe Land." He played the piano and that was what he was mostly doing, he said, at the party at which—so Wilson was told—he cavalierly repeated the same canard about Mrs. Wilson which Mrs. Peck had blurted out.

In a formal statement of defense, now in the archives of the State Department, Craufurd-Stuart said that all he did was "ask Mrs. Marye if she had seen an article in *The Tribune* of that morning, which as far as I can remember now criticized the

President's powers and ability when compared with Mr. Balfour, Mr. Asquith and Mr. Lloyd George. It was not my opinion nor was it given as mine. I said nothing further. After dinner I did not join the ladies as I played piano accompaniments for Mr. Constantinidi" (an Italian diplomatic attaché who sang).

The important correspondence about the matter, long buried in State Department archives, came from London. A cable to the Secretary of State, signed by Ambassador John W. Davis, in November, said:

> Personal for Lansing from Davis: Curzon tells me informally that Grey is much exercised about request to dismiss Crawford-Stewart *(sic)* and has threatened to resign if compelled to part with him. Represents that services at Embassy are essential to his comfort.

And two days later:

> Strictly confidential for the Secretary of State from Polk: Curzon and Reading have both spoken to Davis and myself in regard to Crawford-Stewart. They seem to fear that Grey would come home if we insist on Stewart being withdrawn. I know nothing of the situation at Washington in regard to this case but unless you consider it a matter of importance it would seem advisable to let matters stand rather than create another cause of possible irritation.

Secretary Lansing commented in a letter marked "Personal and Very Confidential" to Admiral Grayson:

> I enclose a paraphrase of a telegram I have just received from Ambassador Davis in regard to Lord Grey's support of Major Stuart. Lord Grey casually mentioned something of the kind to me but I did not take it seriously.
> I presume that the Ambassador has returned from New York after seeing the Prince off on Saturday. When he makes an appointment with me, as I expect he will this week, I am going to ask you to be present. My own disposition is to in-

sist on Stuart's severance of his relations with the Embassy, whatever the effect on Lord Grey's continuance as Ambassador may be as I think he is taking a very wrong attitude and that we should not establish the precedent of having imposed upon us an attaché of a foreign embassy who is *persona non grata* by the threat of an Ambassador to resign unless the demand for his recall is withdrawn.

If you think it is advisable of course you can show this letter to the President and see whether or not he agrees with my views.

Colonel House left his version of the incident as he got it from Tyrrell on November 20, after Grey had been waiting in America for nearly two months. House wrote in his diary:

> One Craufurd-Stuart, of the British Embassy entourage, seems to be the storm center. First Lansing demanded that he be sent home for talking disrespectfully of the President. When this was cleared up, the President sent a demand that he be sent home for talking disrespectfully of Mrs. Wilson and this is now under process of being worked out. Neither Grey nor Tyrrell believe the President sent the message and they have some corroborative evidence from Mrs. Wilson's secretary, Miss Benham. It all seems trivial to me and unworthy of the grave situation facing us at this time.

In December, after talking with Grey himself, House gave a strange version of the incident in his diary in which he suggested that the woman who carried the report of Craufurd-Stuart's wagging tongue to the White House was "a lady friend" of Baruch. Baruch and Dr. Grayson, House suggested, were using the lady's reports in an effort to hit Grey incidentally and House in particular.

Baruch told me later that he had nothing to do with the incident but that House "as he felt himself slipping physically and mentally, made all kinds of moves which incurred the displeasure of the President." Displeasure had clearly been incurred. House himself commented on what he called a "sensational article" by Louis Seibold which appeared in *The New York World* at the time when he was steadily conferring with Grey and Tyrrell on the Craufurd-Stuart case. If the article was sensational, it had an authoritative sound. Seibold "did not state a single truth," House said. The Colonel himself particularly emphasized one item: "He said the President was dissatisfied at my abandonment of the 'freedom of the seas.' Of course, the facts are the President abandoned it himself and so announced to newspaper correspondents at Paris." Daniels always believed that the Seibold statement was true.

Later that month, on December 22, Tyrrell called and told House that he believed "the Craufurd-Stuart incident has been dropped." Undoubtedly the musical major "ceased to be a member of the official embassy staff," though in *Who's Who* he reported that he continued to be Grey's secretary until the following year. Apparently he was not punished as he feared for the incident. His obituary noted that after his return from service with Grey in the United States he was made a commander of the Order of the British Empire and of the Victorian Order. Later he was made military secretary to the Viceroy of India.

While Grey waited and House wrote in his diary, Daniels, who did not discuss the naval building program with Grey, had dinner with Franklin Roosevelt at his house on November 19. It could not have been a very gay party. After mentioning the dinner, Daniels noted in his diary of that day, "Senate defeated the treaty. Lodge has one passion. Hatred of Wilson." Others were gay, however, that night. "We," Alice Longworth recalled, "and by we, I mean the irreconcilables," were happy. She had sent word ahead to have "eggs ready to scramble at any time we arrive." Mr. Lodge came to join the party. And "Mrs. Harding cooked the eggs."

Lord Grey did not take part in that celebration. He did see Lodge. Also, when he went home soon afterward and published a letter approving ratification of the treaty with the Lodge reservations, Secretary David Houston remembered standing within a foot of Grey and Lodge and "overhearing him sympathetically commenting on Lodge's handling of the treaty and on his reservations."

If neither Wilson nor Daniels saw Grey, however, the Franklin Roosevelts saw a good deal of the British statesman, which was natural, as Eleanor wrote, because of Grey's affection for Uncle Ted. It was also a little ostentatiously Rooseveltian in Washington where Wilson's refusal to see Grey was well known and even the Craufurd-Stuart case was slyly referred to in gossip columns. Neither seemed to bother Franklin. Indeed, three days after Tyrrell last spoke to House about the Craufurd-Stuart matter, he and Grey came to Christmas dinner with the FDR's. Franklin's mother was there and so was Louis Howe, who, Eleanor said, "was of English descent and always got on well with our English cousins." Alice Longworth also came to join the party. The only drawback was that young James went down with measles, but Lord Grey said "that he did not think he was subject to childish diseases." Apparently all had an innocent, merry Christmas-time.

Franklin was sick again at that year's end. Daniels wrote him:

DEAR FRANKLIN:
It is heartening to know you are better and I beg you to try to be content to stay in until this beastly weather is over. . . .

For both of them the worst weather was yet to come. On Christmas Eve, Admiral Sims began an attack on the Secretary of the Navy and the Navy Department and their conduct of the war. His charges were picked up eagerly in the Republican Senate where Lodge was the leader. The mounting fight in an election year arrayed old enemies and old friends. Mrs. Dewey, looking more fragile than ever, put her small hands on Daniels' shoulders.

"Give them hell," she said. "That is the message George Dewey would give you if he were here."

She kissed the Secretary on the forehead.

"This Is Not Goodbye"

FRANKLIN ROOSEVELT WAS STILL SICK WHEN DANIELS WENT TO THE
Jefferson Day Dinner in Washington in January 1920. There
still seemed, without Franklin, plenty of enthusiastic Democrats
as the Presidential election year began. For the first time, two
hotels and two banquets were required to seat the guests. The
increasing conflict with the Republicans had apparently created
a greater Democratic solidarity. From his sickroom, Wilson
sent a message urging that the 1920 election be made a "great
and solemn referendum" for the ratification of the League of
Nations without reservations. There was applause but there
was also Bryan.

As a man who understood the necessity of Bryan's support in
that referendum, the Secretary of the Navy in his speech that
night praised his old friend by declaring that "the principle
and spirit of the Bryan treaties are embodied in the Treaty of
Peace." Daniels' praise fell short of its purpose. Bryan spoke
last and, though his speech was awaited with little interest by
the big room full of sleepy men, he practically blew up the
banquet and, some thought, the Democratic Party. He urged,
if necessary, a prompt ratification of the Treaty and the adoption of the League with the reservations Wilson had rejected
as destructive of his purposes, in order that the world might get
back confidently to a condition of peace. He "thrust his knife
home," said *The Baltimore News*.

Daniels described the Bryan explosion in his diary:

> He was in a militant mood and when somebody called out: "Stand by Wilson," his eyes flashed fire and he said, "If you can guarantee victory, then I will not speak," etc., or words to that effect. Most of his speech was fine but he was deeply in earnest when he opposed delay in ratification and opposed making it an issue in the campaign. He got much applause and warmly praised Wilson about National Reserve Act & said no man since Andrew Jackson had so withstood the money power.

There was not unity even about the old money power. Daniels also noted in his diary that Governor John J. Cornwell of West Virginia, who was later to be general counsel of the Baltimore and Ohio Railroad, spoke "so much, as it seemed, against labor that another Democrat present murmured, 'That's the kind of talk I have been hearing from Republicans all my life and I did not expect to hear it at a Democratic banquet. It was because of such talk I left the Republican Party.' "

Daniels wrote, "Got home at 3 A.M." It was a late and dark time of night for him to be up. It was a late and dark time altogether. He was not, however, as surprised at the Bryan break with Wilson as some of his Cabinet colleagues. Next morning at one of their meetings which Secretary Lansing was calling in the absence and sickness of Wilson, Daniels wrote that "all were critical of Bryan." Daniels himself felt, he wrote, that no compromise such as Bryan proposed would be possible, "if President made proposition they would say he weakened, refuse to accept, and would then make the issue on the two or three points instead [of] upon their hostility and early opposition to the League."

Daniels went to see Bryan that same day, however, and found him adamant. He could not have been surprised. He had lunched with Bryan not long before the banquet and found Bryan hard in a final bitterness against the President. That had surprised Daniels at the time because, though Wilson had declined to take Bryan to Paris, after the President was stricken Bryan had written Daniels that he trusted the Senate would "cheer him by ratifying without reservations." At the luncheon, however, Bryan had been fixed in hostility. He told Daniels then that he believed Wilson had not only not regretted but had actually arranged his resignation from the Cabinet. Daniels did not quarrel with Bryan. Indeed, a week after his Jefferson Day speech he went with Bryan to a watch night service at a Congregational Church to celebrate the arrival of national prohibition—the same night on which, in different spirit, Franklin went to a Harvard '04 class dinner "to celebrate prohibition." A week later, however, Daniels issued a statement sharply disagreeing with Bryan's attack on the Democratic National Chairman because the chairman had attended a dinner in honor of a "wet" candidate for the Presidential nomination.

More bitterness had been brewing than was shown by Bryan's outbursts. Two days after his luncheon with Bryan in December, Daniels had made the first entry in his diary about the charges brought against him and the Navy Department by Admiral Sims. He referred to a "roast" given him by Ned McLean's *Washington Post* about the awards for gallantry and distinguished service in the war by Navy men. The diary entry did not mention Admiral Sims, but it was obviously based on that officer's blast in refusal to accept the decoration given to him. Daniels had revised some of Sims' recommendations and had made himself seem vulnerable by the fact that one of the awards he had approved went to his brother-in-law, Commander (later Vice-Admiral) David W. Bagley, whose destroyer had been sunk by a submarine in European waters. The Republican majority of the House Committee declined to have anything to do with the Sims charges. But a full-scale investigation was set up by the Republicans in the Senate, under the direction of Senator Frederick Hale (Groton and Harvard) which ex-

tended to charges from Sims and his friends that "failure of
the Navy Department to immediately send its full force of destroyers and anti-submarine craft [to Europe] prolonged the war
four months and occasioned the loss to the Allies of 2,500,000
tons of shipping, 500,000 lives, and $15,000,000,000." That in-
dictment had first been made in the Senate by Senator Boise
Penrose who had none of Senator Lodge's distaste for seeming
partisan in attacks on Daniels.

Fortunately for Daniels, the very dimensions of the charges
hit practically the whole Navy. Admirals Badger, Benson,
Mayo, Rodman, Wilson, Niblack, Strauss, Fletcher, Pratt and
McKean, whose activities in the war had been hardly less significant than Sims', all resented the extreme charges. Furthermore, the public could understand the fact brought out, when
Sims first took the stand, that he had not recommended a medal
for a single enlisted man, and had given great preference in his
recommendations to those officers who had served on the staff
ashore over those who had served at sea on ships. Daniels
heavily stressed the faith which he had had when he first came
to Washington that "the Navy exists on the sea." He hit hard,
and in a way that the public could understand, when he said
that "the position of Admiral Sims in placing shore duty above
sea duty in the danger zones is no doubt influenced by his own
record." Admiral Sims, he said, had "demonstrated ability of a
high order" as naval attaché at Paris and St. Petersburg during
the Spanish-American War, but he emphasized that Sims had
only nine years of sea duty in twenty-five years of service.

Mark Sullivan, in his history of those times, said that "to Secretary Daniels the Sims charges constituted a challenge which
he seemed only too eager to accept. 'We are so well fortified,'
he said in a statement to the press, 'not with perfect wisdom but
in the things accomplished by the Navy, that the more people
learn about the work of the Navy in the war the more satisfied
they will be that we did a good job. We are proud of our

record.'" By the middle of January, Senator Key Pittman of Nevada, who conducted the Democratic side of the argument in the committee, told Daniels he thought Sims was on the defensive. Undoubtedly, Sims' charge that the Navy Secretary was anti-British had renewed suspicions that Sims himself was too pro-British. There were independent attacks on Sims as a "political admiral," and James B. Connolly, a well-known sea writer, turned on the Admiral a phrase of "Fighting Bob" Evans, "He's a politician—in everybody's mess and nobody's watch." Paymaster General McGowan reported to Daniels his optimism about the public's reaction to the Sims hearings and Rollin Kirby drew a cartoon for *The New York World*, which Daniels always kept, showing Sims shooting at the Navy's war record under the heading, "Something the Enemy Never Did."

Daniels did not know that, in December when the Franklin Roosevelts were having a merry Christmas with Grey and Tyrrell, Franklin wrote a letter to Mrs. Sims soon after the Admiral began to make his attack. Roosevelt wrote her, that "strictly between ourselves, I should like to shake the Admiral by the hand." Soon after the Jefferson Day Dinner a society columnist reported that Franklin, "showing the same independence of spirit that was such a marked characteristic of his cousin the illustrious Theodore," was "getting up a big feast for Admiral Sims." The same item reported that Franklin and his friend, Frank Polk, were "getting ready to snap the ties that bind them to the Wilson regime."

That certainly exaggerated Franklin's position as Daniels understood it at the time. Indeed, just before that item appeared, Daniels wrote in his diary, on January 18, that "FDR came to see me and said he and Frank Polk thought I ought not to wait till called before the committee to say that the Department and I had made no such statement as Sims attributed to somebody in the Department." That statement undoubtedly was one which Sims said had been made to him when he was dispatched to England just before the American declaration of war.

"Do not let the British pull the wool over your eyes," the Admiral said somebody (presumably Daniels or Benson) told him. "It is none of our business pulling their chestnuts out of the fire. We would as soon fight the British as the Germans."

Daniels agreed with FDR's suggestion and prepared a letter. "Showed it to FDR who approved. So did Tumulty." Roosevelt's intervention at that point, of course, reflected Polk's concern about the possible effect of such a statement, undenied, on already irritated British-American relations. However, nothing in Roosevelt's attitude suggested the speech he made in Brooklyn, on February 1, which almost brought an end to his association with Daniels in the Navy Department. It was full of fireworks but it ushered in the blackest February in Roosevelt's life. Daniels wrote an almost incoherent diary item about it:

> FDR had made speech in New York saying the President had not wanted preparation for war prior to our entrance.
> He had risked impeachment by spending $40 [sic] [millions] for guns etc. sixty days after we entered the war. I sent for Earle who said I had given orders for guns for merchant ships while FDR was in Haiti—& all orders had been made after conference by me.
> Also we had no plans.

The Secretary also wrote that Franklin, perhaps a little appalled himself by the news report of his speech, "wished News Bureau to send out explanation that did not explain." Daniels told Marvin McIntyre, then a special assistant to the Secretary of the Navy in charge of public relations and later one of Roosevelt's campaign assistants and Presidential secretaries, not to send out any statement without the Secretary's approval.

The speech, made at a time when the Republican attack on the Navy and the administration was in full swing, seemed almost deliberate support of their enemies. The Associated Press dispatch as printed in Daniels' own Raleigh *News and Observer* began:

New York, Feb. 1—In describing alleged conditions of unpreparedness in the American Navy prior to the war with Germany Assistant Secretary of the Navy Franklin D. Roosevelt declared tonight in an address at Brooklyn that as a result of his efforts to obtain an adequate program he had "committed enough illegal acts to put him in jail for 999 years." He said he undoubtedly would have been impeached if he had made "wrong guesses."

"Two months after war was declared," said Mr. Roosevelt, "I saw that the Navy was still unprepared and I spent forty millions for guns before Congress gave me or anyone permission to spend any money."

The Assistant Secretary said that before the war he "was opposed by the President, who said that he did not want any overt act of war, but who added that he was following a definite course to avert war."

In March 1917, Mr. Roosevelt said, he suggested Admiral Sims as the head of the Inter-Allied fleet. . . .

Daniels was mad, but for Franklin Black February had arrived. Possibly when Franklin made that speech in full powers of voice, after a recent and belated tonsillectomy, he was, as President Wilson once said of himself when he was discussing naval matters, "intoxicated by the exuberance of his own verbosity." He could not, however, have exploded at a more unfortunate time for himself. The letter of his friend Lord Grey approving the Lodge reservations had just been reprinted in the American press. Three days after he spoke Eleanor received word that her Aunt Pussie (then separated from her husband, Forbes Morgan) and her two little girls had been burned to death in a converted stable in which they had lived on Ninth Street in New York. She had to go to a New York tied up by blizzard and take the bodies up the Hudson to Tivoli for burial. At the same time, in Washington, Franklin found himself involved in alleged scandals which were less pleasant than the Sims broadside against the Navy. One involved vice clean-up investigations to which Daniels had assigned FDR in the summer of 1917. Franklin was charged with authorizing the use of enlisted personnel as decoys with which to trap perverts. An Episcopal clergyman, who had been arrested by Navy investigators, had been acquitted in court and Bishop James DeWolf Perry of Rhode Island was demanding punishment for those who brought about the minister's indictment. Republican papers amplified his Episcopal wrath.

Many of Franklin's troubles then seemed to be coming from Newport. Admiral Sims, back on duty at the War College there, was, *Town Topics* reported, "extremely popular with Americans of the Newport type." Apparently Franklin suddenly was not. Admiral Sims had advised Commander Joseph K. Taussig to take the facts about an unpleasant dispute with Roosevelt to *The Providence Journal,* which was already attacking Roosevelt for his alleged approval of the use of young sailors as decoys in entrapment of homosexuals. Taussig's quarrel with Roosevelt was over the question of the return to service of prisoners by Roosevelt's old friend the prison reformer, Thomas Mott Osborne, whom Daniels had put in charge of the naval prison at Portsmouth, New Hampshire. Taussig, who had taken the first American destroyers to England in 1917, felt that too many depraved and unreformed prisoners were returned from Portsmouth to the fleet. In a dispute about it with Roosevelt he felt that his veracity was questioned and he was put in a bad light. He asked to be relieved of his duties as director of enlisted personnel and demanded a court inquiry to look into the whole matter.

Furthermore, at that time Franklin's old friend Homer of Sterling engines was in evidence about the Navy Department with an oil-for-the-navy plan which some officers felt smelled fairly high. As presented a little later by Franklin, the plan called for the Navy to put up $3,500,000 for an oil refinery in Louis Howe's home town of Fall River, Massachusetts, from which the Navy would get a supply of cheap Mexican oil. Daniels learned, he wrote, that Homer "would get $250,000 if the contract went to that firm." Commander H. A. Stuart, oil expert in the Bureau of Engineering, "learned that R had some interest in it." Actually, a careful study by Dr. Freidel produced nothing to indicate that Roosevelt had any personal investment in this New England Oil Corporation, though he did take a $5,000 flyer in a Washington Oil Syndicate, organized by Homer to buy oil lands in Oklahoma and which Homer, after Roosevelt had sold his stock, merged with the New England Oil Corporation. Roosevelt was financially hard up. He wrote his mother, on February 11, thanking her for a check which came "at the critical moment in life." His letter presented a picture of sick children, doctors' bills and fixed domesticity.

The day before he wrote that letter Lucy Mercer was married in a very quiet ceremony to the widowed Winthrop Rutherfurd, who was old enough to have ridden after the hounds with Theodore Roosevelt before she was born. The wedding of such a prominent society man and sportsman and a poor young lady of aristocratic lineage did not go unnoticed. One society writer noted that Rutherfurd's first wife "became a Roman Catholic before her death, and her husband is also a convert to that faith, and I believe the second Mrs. Rutherfurd is of the same religion." Rutherfurd was, as Elliott Roosevelt states in the *Personal Letters*, "a descendant of the first governors of New York and Massachusetts, Peter Stuyvesant and John Winthrop, and a leading figure in society for more than a half-century." *The New York Times* later said Rutherfurd was believed to be the gentleman Consuelo Vanderbilt had loved, as she alleged in seeking a papal annulment of her marriage, when her mother Mrs. O. H. P. Belmont forced her to marry the Duke of Marlborough. Rutherfurd had been regarded as "the handsomest bachelor in society" when he had married the tallest and fairest of the daughters of Vice-President Morton in 1901. He liked the rural life at his ancestral estate at Allamuchy, New Jersey, and his Ridgeley Hall on the acres which he had recently bought from the estate of former Congressman Gardner in Aiken, South Carolina.

Apparently that month, however, Roosevelt did not realize the proportions of Daniels' resentment. It was deep and real. Not only Roosevelt's loyalty to him was involved, but also Daniels' deep sense of loyalty to the sick Wilson. A week after the Brooklyn speech, the Secretary wrote obviously with some surprise that "FDR came in as usual." Also, on the same day he mentioned a "letter from Taussig roasting Roosevelt about prisoners going back." He seemed pleased when the officer and the Assistant Secretary "fixed up their differences." But he was clearly contemplating a break with his young assistant. He considered pointing it by declining to accept an invitation to dine with the Roosevelts. His diary recorded his feeling.

February 16: "Saw Mrs. Dewey and McGowan and they were glad we were going to the FDRs."

He had not quite relented, however.

February 17: "Dinner FDR. To go or not to go? Mrs. D and McGowan."

Suddenly, however, he was startled by a bitterness against Franklin across the street in the White House greater than his own. He jotted down on February 21:

> "I hate L," said E. Wanted T to tell L that Major S must be sent back or would not receive. T refused. Must put it on other grounds.
> FDR persona non grata with W. Better let speech pass.

The code of those capital letters is not hard to decipher. Daniels had talked with Joe Tumulty, whose position was obviously both increasingly important and increasingly difficult at the White House. He had told Daniels in post-mortem discussions of the sudden removal of Lansing as Secretary of State that Edith Wilson had hated Lansing and had wanted Tumulty to tell Lansing that Major Craufurd-Stuart must be sent back to England or the President would not receive Lord Grey. Tumulty insisted that they must put the recall of Craufurd-Stuart or the refusal to see Grey on some other grounds than the talk at the dinner party. The matter obviously had been taken out of Tumulty's hands. Apparently Tumulty had not known that Lansing was entirely sympathetic with the White House feeling in the Craufurd-Stuart affair.

What is not so easy to explain is the immediately following statement in the diary about Wilson's current antipathy to FDR. It could merely have been the Brooklyn speech. It could have been resentment about FDR's friendship for Grey and other British Embassy men at that time. The whole business was a matter which Daniels did not mention in his memoirs or even in conversations with his sons.

"Better let speech pass," however, is pretty clear. The situation was one in which he did not want to involve discipline or administration in his department. It was not time for a change. Wilson's dismissal of Secretary of State Lansing had already provided too much evidence of irritation within the administration.

Daniels had never admired Lansing. All the same that February he wrote, "Occasion unfortunate," of Lansing's dismissal. The explanation from Wilson's sickroom that Lansing had presumed to call Cabinet meetings during the President's illness seemed to Daniels less reason than excuse. In his diary, though he was devoted to Mrs. Wilson until he died, he mentioned the fact that she was very bitter. Also, he was astonished to learn that she thought the broken President might have to run for the

Presidency again. It was no time for an explosion in the Navy Department.

Apparently his colleagues shared Daniels' feelings about the irritability in the White House.

"I will never attend another Cabinet meeting," said Burleson, "unless I get a written letter from the President asking me to come."

And Daniels wrote that another member asked Burleson, "Why not require him to send a White House car after you?"

They joked at a luncheon Franklin Lane gave, on February 26, to his colleagues on his retirement from the Cabinet. Lane was taking a job with Edward L. Doheny as vice-president of the Pan-American Petroleum Company at $50,000 a year. He was not ever going to feel the "dishonor" of being poor again. At that moment, he told close friends later, he did not have enough money to buy railroad tickets back to California or to move there the furniture that he owned. That was irrelevant at last. He was in high spirits for the first time in years. Daniels was gay, too. Before the luncheon he had already talked with Lane's successor, John Barton Payne, and had written in his diary that the oil leasing bill which the President was soon to sign "safeguarded better than any former bill the naval reserves." It was impossible not to like Lane, with whom he had fought so long.

Neither was it possible for him long to be angry with Franklin Roosevelt. Franklin was increasingly and energetically cooperative in the defense of Daniels and the Department in the Republican Senate hearings which proceeded from the Sims charges. Early in March, the Secretary wrote that the Assistant Secretary had been very helpful in recalling what had been said when he gave Sims his instructions as he dispatched him to Europe. Franklin sat in the conferences with the Secretary and his chief naval assistants in the Department when plans were made as to how the evidence of the Navy's effective activity in the war should be presented. By March in another speech he was saying that he did not claim the Democrats won the war, "but I will say in spite of ninety-seven investigations, costing more than $2,000,000, they still have to unearth an embalmed beef or a paper shoe scandal." Roosevelt told Daniels that he had told Senator Hale that if Hale called him to testify the Republicans would regret it. Franklin strongly supported Daniels' opposition to greater staff control of the Navy. He agreed with Daniels' idea that the radio system which the government had built in the war should be kept as a government monopoly. Franklin no longer wanted to shake Admiral Sims warmly by the hand. He was holding on firmly and loyally. Later he thought that Sims had done a good job in London, but that "during my two months abroad I saw more sea-service with the American Navy than Sims did in two years."

From February forward, Franklin was actively engaged in the presentation of the Navy's war story which his son and editor later reported led to the result that "after more than three thousand pages of testimony, the hearings were concluded with the repudiation of Sims' charges, and the Navy's contribution to the war effort was praised by both Republican and Democratic leaders in Congress."

Not all was smooth, however. Daniels kept his doubts about the Roosevelt-Homer oil proposition which Franklin continued to press. He still questioned it after Franklin finally convinced Admiral Griffin and other officers of its merits when oil was high priced and hard to get.

"I ha' me doots," Daniels wrote, "but Griffin and all the others agreed and I agreed voting against it, but saying I have only one vote."

His doubts were justified. By the time the New England Corporation produced any oil it cost more than the open market price. There was no question early in May, however, as to whether or not the Secretary and Mrs. Daniels would go to the Roosevelts for a dinner party. Daniels and Roosevelt were working in close co-operation. There was no split between them when Daniels put in General John A. Lejeune, who had led the marines in France, as Major General Commandant in place of George Barnett who had held the post since 1914. General Barnett, and particularly his socially prominent wife, began to scream charges like those Sims had made. But even *Town Topics,* which had been shrilly outraged at Daniels earlier in the year, remarked that "everyone is tired of these affairs."

Franklin was on the reservation as a loyal Democrat and increasingly interested in Democratic politics in a political year. He liked to come into the Secretary's office, stretch out his long legs and talk to his chief about the approaching conventions. Daniels undoubtedly told Franklin that when he made a speech saying that the next President would be "the man who embodied the best platform that secures to all men a fairer proportion of what their brains and toil have wrought," three candidates thought he was talking about them. It was the sort of joke he liked to share with Roosevelt. Probably he did not tell him about a visit from former Governor Glynn of New York, who had made the keynote speech at the 1916 convention. Glynn felt neglected.

"None of our people are deemed worthy to sit in the councils," Daniels wrote in his diary that Glynn said of the Irish Catholic Democrats, "and it is about time to let the Democratic Party leaders know what a great defeat means. If we are not good enough to hold positions of importance we ought to assert we will not vote the ticket. Frank Polk and Frank Roosevelt carry no votes and no strength and yet they are recognized. Woodrow Wilson is an ingrate."

Daniels did not think so, but he understood Glynn's disappointment. Also he understood that there were increasing divisions and angers. He had watched some politicians trying to dodge such issues as woman suffrage, prohibition, peace. Of

one he said, "It is the longest straddle for a short-legged man
that I ever saw." Franklin urged him to be certain to go to the
convention in San Francisco.

"He said I might be of great service in getting along with
harmony," Daniels wrote. "Tammany sullen but friendly to me
as was also Bryan."

His friend Senator Swanson, who was to succeed him as
Secretary of the Navy in FDR's time, rather advised him to stay
in Washington. Swanson thought he would be more embarrassed than helpful in the fight that was certain between Wilson
and Bryan. He went. He could hardly have stayed away. He
did not miss a Democratic Convention in half a century. His
chief preoccupation at San Francisco as it turned out was in
trying to prevent Bainbridge Colby, who had succeeded Lansing
as Secretary of State, from pressing the renomination of Wilson.
Daniels and other older members of the Cabinet believed that
could only result in tragic injury to the President's reputation.
The Secretary of the Navy convened his Cabinet colleagues at
a conference on a battleship in the harbor to veto Colby's plan.

Daniels had been delighted at the convention, however,
when Franklin, seizing the standard of the reluctant New York
delegation, carried it into a great demonstration for the President. Daniels thought the nomination of James M. Cox of
Ohio was brought about by "delegates who were anything but
Wilsonian, including nearly all the city political bosses." He
was pleased when Franklin was nominated as Vice-President
with the reluctant consent of Boss Murphy of New York. When
Governor Cox took him to see Wilson, FDR in dark coat above
gleaming white pants and shoes seemed the shining example of
the young man fighting for Wilson and his ideals. On that visit
to the paralyzed President in his wheel chair on the White
House portico, Cox and Roosevelt promised to make the election a "solemn referendum" on the League which Wilson
wished. Franklin's choice was made and his wavering was over.

The correspondent of *The Boston Globe,* who had also been a Massachusetts Republican Party functionary, described Roosevelt on that occasion acting as the master of ceremonies "ushering Cox into Tumulty's room where the correspondents had assembled" and looking "bright and boyish and a little silly in his exuberance—the thing has gone to his head."

Senator Lodge, to whom that description of Roosevelt was sent, replied: "He talked well in the early years of the [Wilson] administration. He is a pleasant fellow whom I personally liked, but now that the administration is coming to a close we can see that when it came to the point, he did exactly what Daniels wished him to do. He is a well-meaning, nice young fellow, but light."

If Daniels and Wilson had known of Lodge's prompt relegation of Roosevelt to the company of inconsequential pleasant fellows, nothing could have bound them tighter to Franklin. They did not. Two weeks after the session of the Democratic candidates with the President, Daniels made a strange entry in his diary set off by itself in lines on the page:

> After Cabinet I talked of FDR's resignation & asked if President had any man in view for vacancy. No.
> I resent & deeply resent, etc., he said.

Wilson was clearly referring to Roosevelt. The only explanation I can think of for my father's diary entry is that Wilson had not forgiven Franklin for the merry Christmas with Lord Grey or for the Brooklyn speech. Wilson was not then a very forgiving man.

Franklin certainly was not aware of any continuing resentment. Wilson had not shown it when he and Cox called. Roosevelt felt confident in his relationships to the administration. From the West he wired Daniels: "In regard to successor I think I have solution which will appeal to you." Roosevelt's suggestion was that no assistant secretary be appointed for a while. It was at that time, too, that Roosevelt told Daniels that Louis Howe, whom he wanted as an aide in the campaign, had an offer of a $20,000-a-year job outside the government.

"He believes it," Daniels wrote and added: "I have a great big swallow but I cannot swallow that."

Daniels did not follow Roosevelt's suggestion. He named instead Gordon Woodbury, of New Hampshire, a solid, unexciting man only a year younger than himself and, like himself, a newspaperman. Daniels may or may not have been aware that in disregarding Roosevelt's suggestion, he disregarded other things, too. Woodbury had been one of those Democrats who fought Bryan—and Daniels—in the great campaign of their youth in 1896. He was a comfortable man, however, to have around in the unraveling post-war job. In the tired time of an administration Woodbury was undoubtedly a rest after Roosevelt.

Daniels was not disregarding Franklin, however. The day Franklin made his suggestion in the Secretary's office in the new Navy Building was the day also of his official farewell. The Department gave Franklin a fine send-off. There was music. It pleased the Secretary that organized labor, with which he had taught Roosevelt how to deal in understanding fashion, gave him a loving cup as he departed. At the request of its leaders Daniels made the presentation. There were, he said, only two compensations for men in public office, consciousness of giving one's best to the public weal and the friendship of co-workers. Roosevelt, he said, had both. Franklin said his good-bys to all "from our chief here to the most recent comer in the ranks." The ceremonies were not all. He wrote that day:

> DEAR CHIEF:
> This is not goodbye—that will always be impossible after these years of the closest association—and no words I write will make you know better than you know now how much our association has meant. All my life I shall look back— not

only on the *work* of the place—but mostly on the wonderful way in which you and I have gone through these nearly eight years *together*. You have taught me so wisely and kept my feet on the ground when I was about to skyrocket—and in it all there has never been a real dispute or antagonism or distrust.

Hence, in part, at least, I will share in the reward which you *will* get true credit for in history. I am very proud—but more than that I am very *happy* to have been able to help.

We will I know keep up this association in the years to come—and please let me keep on coming to you to get your fine inspiration of real idealism and right living and good Americanism.

So *au revoir* for a little while. You have always the
Affectionate regards of
FRANKLIN D. ROOSEVELT

Daniels wrote him a long, affectionate answer. Also, a little later he wrote a shorter, more formal letter which went to Franklin signed by Woodrow Wilson. But it was in his diary that the Secretary wrote his private feeling about his departing assistant.

"He left in the afternoon," he said, "but before leaving wrote me a letter most friendly or almost loving which made me glad I had never acted upon my impulse when he seemed to take sides with my critics."

Roosevelt left no contemporary footnote on their exchange of good-bys. He had been taught well even if the teaching and learning process had not always been so simple or so gentle as he described it. His arrival at appreciation of the meaning of such a man as Daniels was more important than anything he had learned under Daniels about dealings with labor, with steel and other magnates, with power in democracy in terms of the backcountry as well as the shore and of men in the forecastles as well as the wardrooms. To the young aristocrat, there had been about Daniels almost the same deceptive appearance which a plain, strong, democratic America so often showed to the supercilious who suddenly confronted it in history. Roosevelt's greatest attainment when he departed was that he was no longer self-deceived in democracy—and would not be so deceived again.

Daniels followed Roosevelt almost immediately to Hyde Park for the ceremonies at which Franklin was formally and oratorically notified of his nomination as Vice-President. Eleanor met him at the train. He sat with Franklin's mother during the exercises. He thought Franklin made a good speech. But he "came back with the McAdoos and we had a jolly time. McAdoo was disappointed that FDR made no reference to WW." Daniels himself was having a little trouble "trying to get into the campaign spirit. . . . I feel like the man from Maine who said, 'I am going up to Boston to get drunk and, O Lord, how I hate it.'" He went. He spoke. At fifty-eight, though he had more than a quarter of a century of useful life ahead of him, he felt old. The voices had changed. Theodore Roosevelt was dead. Wilson was silenced. It was the first campaign in forty years in which Bryan did not make a Democratic speech.

He followed the young Roosevelt on his campaign train with his encouragement: "You are hitting the bull's eye in every speech." That was a cheer for encouragement. Daniels did not agree with everything Franklin said. Roosevelt's campaign in the West came into the Navy Department explosively when in enthusiastic ad libbing at Butte, Montana, he boasted, "You know I have had something to do with the running of a couple of little republics. The facts are that I wrote Haiti's constitution myself and, if I do say it, I think it is a pretty good constitution."

Afterward he always denied he had said that. The clear evidence, however, is that he did. He was trying to answer the Republican argument that in the League of Nations Great Britain would have with its dominions five votes to the one of the

United States. Roosevelt's argument that small Caribbean republics would vote with the United States got a blast back from Harding, who promised that he would not "empower an Assistant Secretary of the Navy to draft a constitution for helpless neighbors in the West Indies and jam it down their throats at the point of bayonets borne by United States Marines." Also, Franklin pulled the little republic into politics just a week after Daniels noted in his diary that he had brought up in Cabinet meeting "the propaganda to try to make people believe conditions were bad and the government was killing people" in Haiti. Daniels was never happy about the situation in Haiti. The Uruguayan Minister was making complaint. Also, General Barnett, whom Daniels had replaced with General Lejeune as Major General Commandant of the Marine Corps, instead of defending marine occupancy of the island, was suddenly and vividly remembering aspects of American despotism. Long before, Daniels had grimaced in distaste when Franklin Lane had hailed him as "King of Haiti." It did not help him when Franklin on the stump claimed the scepter and held it high.

Franklin's old friends showed no reluctance at using him as new target. Senator Lodge encouraged the continuation of the investigation of the Newport vice case which, even after the election was history, brought a *New York Times* headline: "LAY NAVY SCANDAL TO F.D. ROOSEVELT—Details Are Unprintable." And Theodore Roosevelt, Jr., speaking in Sheridan, Wyoming, cut even closer ties.

"He's a maverick," he said of Franklin. "He does not have the brand of our family."

All the same on the campaign tour Franklin wrote that he thought that "things are looking better all the time." Marvin McIntyre, who went with Franklin on that political tour, used to recall that campaign to me when he was an ailing and bird-thin secretary at the White House. He said that Roosevelt was still the too-untousled Harvard man, but one who was learning fast in his first national campaign. Also he said that, in the face of Roosevelt's apparently increasing confidence, he asked him if he had any illusions that he might be elected.

"Nary an illusion," he quoted Franklin as saying.

Perhaps not. I am sure my father had none. The tide to the Republicans had set as solidly as Henry Adams said the social tide had set toward the Allies in Washington in the fall of 1914. Now it was set solidly against both internationalism and reform. I was surprised. I remember that in those days, before radio and television, I watched the returns chalked on the blackboard of a physics amphitheater at the University of North Carolina in the little town of Chapel Hill. The lines of communication were sufficient to make it clear long before it was late that an age had ended. Outside as a young Democrat I found the campus very dark. My father, like reform, seemed suddenly very old and out of date, defenseless and innocent. My own education as a democrat seemed to have only led to disaster.

The last months in Washington, while the Republicans waited, elated and impatient to take over, could not have been easy for my father. A gentleman came from Los Angeles to suggest that since he and his associates were Democrats, it would be well to let them have leases in the naval oil reserves before the Republicans came in and leased them to Republicans. My father was not amused or moved. He expressed his confidence that the new administration would do nothing of the kind but, he said, he had a newspaper and he would be watching.

Thomas A. Edison wrote irritably to "Friend Daniels" about the plan to put the experimental laboratory for a more and more technological Navy in Washington and in the hands of naval officers. "However, as it is done," Edison wrote him, "you must not be angry with me if I go to members of Congress and give some facts about this affair and the utter inefficiency of the whole naval establishment from a technical standpoint." Daniels did not agree with his friend, the old inventor. That laboratory became the Naval Research Laboratory in which by 1924 the first crude radar was developed.

Admiral McGowan, the Paymaster General, who had closely watched the sharply partisan Senatorial investigations, came to tell Daniels that he wished to retire. "They will not pick my bones," he said.

Franklin returned to Washington as the old administration was expiring. Daniels noted a few days later: "That New England Oil Co., wants us to take bonds on secured mortgage and release our first mortgage." He told Roosevelt to take the oil matter up with his successor Woodbury. Franklin was not pleased when he found the unexciting Woodbury's attitude about it such that he wrote that Woodbury must be "either crooked or a pin-head." Franklin was also anxious that the Navy complete its record in the Newport vice charges before Daniels left office. Daniels wrote him as the administration drew to its end, "I am sweating blood over the Newport case." He did not bring it to an end. Franklin had trouble getting the two Republican members of the investigating subcommittee even to let him put a statement into the records. Despite the Republican Senators, however, the charges of improper methods were dropped as in simple decency they should have been long before.

Soon after Franklin's visit, in February, Daniels learned that young Theodore Roosevelt, Jr., was to become Assistant Secretary of the Navy in the Harding administration. It amused Daniels.

"Carry the word to FDR," he wrote in his diary. Also, of the ineradicable Roosevelts he noted at the time that a German doctor, who had obtained release from the Alien Property Custodian of his property, complained that it "lacked a priceless possession—the appendix of Alice Roosevelt Longworth in alcohol."

At that time, too, Admiral Taylor came in shaking his head.

Daniels not only wrote in his diary that Taylor was "the ablest man here." Also, the Admiral had the distinction of having made the highest marks of any graduate up to his time at both Annapolis and at the British Naval College at Greenwich to which he was sent for graduate work. He had served with Franklin Roosevelt and as the Navy's chief constructor had been the chief opponent of his 50-foot boats. He had served as well under Theodore Roosevelt, first when he was Assistant Secretary of the Navy and then a President who regarded the Navy as particularly his own.

"I have had to stand two Roosevelts," Taylor said. "I cannot try another."

Daniels worked on the Newport case at Franklin's request until the night before Harding's inauguration. In his last letter as Secretary to him he mentioned that matter but emphasized his affection:

DEAR FRANKLIN:
. . . Tomorrow I follow you to private life. The record of the years here is made up. As we grow old I feel sure we will look back upon the days we were in this great adventure together as the golden days of our lives. . . .

The Danielses spent their last night in Washington with Mrs. Dewey in her house on K Street. In the old house, Washington did not seem much changed. Indeed, somehow nothing seemed to have happened. General Lejeune had kept Colonel McCawley on his eternal Washington duty and it was suggested that the new commandant would "no doubt avail himself of the latter's knowledge of the depths and shoals of social Washington." Also, society column readers noted that "Mrs. McCawley, who had been so ill, seems on the mend, and will spend a part of the summer with Mrs. George Cabot Lodge on the Massachusetts North Shore."

Colonel Thompson of the Navy League opened his house in Washington and was inaugurating spring gaiety with a large musicale at which Mlle. Bori and Alberto Silva of the Metropolitan Opera Company would sing. "The Thompsons now feel tremendously relieved," *Town Topics* said, "for they did have a disagreeable time with Mr. Daniels and the other malcontents about the Navy Club. . . . Mr. Thompson approves of the more tolerant attitude of Secretary Denby about the contents of lockers at the Army and Navy Club, and also the dull olfactory sense of head waiters when innocent-looking cups exhale the headiest odors." The *Journal of Society* added an item of similar significance soon after: "How thoroughly Secretary Denby understands his job, the spirit of the Navy and the attitude of the people toward the service is evident from his restoration of the full-dress uniform for officers of and above the rank of lieutenant-commander. . . ." That appeared in May when Secretary Denby also transferred the supervision of the naval oil reserves to Secretary of the Interior Albert B. Fall, the old friend of Edward L. Doheny.

Franklin Lane, the vice-president of Doheny's Pan-American Oil Company, died that same month on May 18. He had been almost steadily ill since he left the Cabinet. He could have been religious, he thought, if he had always lived on a ranch in California "and not been too hard driven for a living." He sent his greetings in March, as the Wilson administration disappeared, to Franklin's mother, "the Ducal lady at Hyde Park," and also to what he called the "young lord lover" Franklin himself. Also, he sent word to an old subordinate in the Department of the Interior: He hoped he would like his new boss. He was glad that boss was a Westerner and a Senator: "they care for their own."

Washington hardly noticed Lane's death. The event did not mar the new gaiety in Washington with the return to power of a new regime from Ohio. Ned McLean, publisher of *The Post,* was described as "one of the most intimate of the coterie" of the new President, though some, remembering his youthful dissipations, regarded him as rather wild company for so conservative a gentleman as the new President. His downtown mansion became a crowded place of call for those who hoped to be recognized with places in the new administration. Ned's wife, Evalyn, wore the Hope Diamond at the more glittering receptions. And in the Decatur House on Lafayette Square, which was the one house Daniels had wanted when he came to Washington, "Mrs. Truxtun Beale, brown as a berry from golf, horseback riding and general open air life at her summer place in San Rafael, California, was . . . ready to lose all her dairymaid robustness of health by keeping up with the social whirl and turning night into day."

When Daniels got back to North Carolina the long agricultural depression had set in. Times were already hard in the country around his newspaper. He consulted Bryan about some Chatauqua activities. Also, he worked for the first time as Roosevelt's subordinate in the campaign which the younger man was heading to raise funds for a Woodrow Wilson "memorial." Wilson himself in his house on S Street seemed better. He joked with Daniels about the fact that his new house was so situated above the residence of the wealthy Senator from California, who had been so much interested in opening the naval reserves to private claimants, that he could "look down on Phelan." In similar mellow mood Wilson wrote Roosevelt:

"I have noticed," the former President told Franklin in a letter on July 4, 1921, "that the fund is frequently referred to as a 'memorial,' which suggests a dead one; and inasmuch as I hope in the near future to give frequent evidences that I am not dead, I have ventured to formulate a title—not as gratuitous attempt at self-appreciation—but with a desire to put into words the purpose I have understood my generous friends entertain."

The fund became a foundation, not a memorial. Wilson, however, did not get better as he had hoped. But Franklin was young and striding still. He was very busy that month. His desks (plural) were piled with mail. It was going to be wonderful to have a long free holiday at Campobello. It gave him a lift like the tides of Fundy when he thought about it in New York. He wrote Eleanor to be sure that the boats were rigged. And he hurried north to Campobello and to polio. He was brought back almost surreptitiously by Louis Howe, who did not want anybody to know that his health or his legs had been impaired.

Josephus Daniels did not realize that Franklin was hopelessly and permanently crippled until he came back East after speaking day after day and night after night in hot halls in little towns. After that he went to see him every time he came to New York. He came fairly often. He did not go to see Colonel House, but the Colonel was seeing the world statesmen. Also the Colonel was already looking for another possible President whom he could selflessly serve. Every time Daniels came, however, he also saw his tall friend Baruch. He quoted in his diary with approval Baruch's statement to him that "the world must decide between the constructive radicalism of Woodrow Wilson or the destructive radicalism of Lenin."

That was one way of stating the problem. Daniels, who loved Wilson no less than Baruch did, would not have limited the alternative he preferred to Wilson's radicalism. The good radicalism seemed to him to include also the purposes of the antique Jefferson and the Bryan he had known when he was young. I doubt if he hoped then that it might include Franklin Roosevelt, too. What troubled him most was that in America, which had brusquely discarded the visionaries, the choice was not confronted at all.

FIFTEEN

The End of Innocence

THE YEARS MOVED VERY SWIFTLY. THEY BROUGHT ME TO THAT afternoon in the White House when the news came that Franklin Roosevelt was dead. I telephoned my father in Raleigh. He had, of course, already heard. John Gunther, one of the many visitors who constantly came to see him, later wrote about being with Father that afternoon in the big house where Father lived alone. It was a stone house on a hill and Father liked to say that he had built it with the rocks people had thrown at him. A good many had been thrown. He and Gunther, the writer said later, had been talking about the nature of power in America when, at almost the exact moment of Roosevelt's death, Father started talking about Roosevelt and "about how the three greatest mysteries of life—birth, love and death—were mysteries beyond control." Father may not have mentioned it then, but his faith was in the greater mystery still that the innocent would inherit the earth. That is all any democrat needs to believe.

When I phoned him from the tumultuous White House, Father already had his tickets to Washington. I expect he had Gunther working on his arrangements along with his secretary and his servants. At eighty-three, as always before, he sometimes seemed an innocent about such things as telephones, tickets, and —even as an editor—typewriters. Gunther told me that he found hardly anyone else, however, with a better understanding of the

327

anatomy of power in America. Father often saw it denied and diverted, but he never doubted that it resided, for their ready use, in the hands of all the people all the time.

That was a dark afternoon. It would have been impossible for me to understand then that it was a good time for Roosevelt to die. Though enmity was nothing new to him, reaction had already begun to set in at home against his world leadership. He had been, many were sure, an innocent abroad at Yalta. The realistic Russians were already "acting up." The time had clearly come, as Colonel McCawley's best friend, Larz Anderson, had said in 1920, for the people to "return to the sane constitutional government under which they had thrived in the past" and away from "all sorts of radical experiments in legislation." Harry Truman gave an immediate deceptive impression that Harding was back in town. If General Leonard Wood was not running for President, General Dwight D. Eisenhower, as Robert Sherwood reported, was about to mention the possibility of his candidacy to Harry Hopkins when Hopkins passed through France on a mission to Russia. But for his loyalty, Hopkins might have been a sort of skeleton Colonel House. It was, of course, sad that Roosevelt could not see the mushroom flowering of his audaciously pursued ideas in the atomic bomb, the unconditional surrender he demanded, the United Nations which, I think, he wanted to set up in the Azores with himself as its first Secretary-General. He died in greatness and in good luck at the right moment in history, nevertheless.

I did not see much of Father in Washington in the overwhelmed time of transition as well as tragedy. It seemed to me I hardly saw him at all until after the funeral, at Hyde Park, when, as the train moved down the Hudson shore, I found him alone in his compartment looking out of the window at the river moving by. I knew he was seeing an even longer stream.

It was more than strange that he, Josephus Daniels, who had been born before Lincoln's funeral, should be riding on the speeding train headed homeward, or at least southward, from the great funeral at Hyde Park. He had seemed old—and a little old-fashioned—beside Franklin Roosevelt when he had brought Roosevelt to Washington as Assistant Secretary and almost as a boy. Now Roosevelt was dead and he was very tired. It had been a long day. But it had been a real Roosevelt day. Franklin would have loved it. Somehow, as in so many things about Roosevelt, Roosevelt's funeral had seemed larger than life. In the crowded garden while we waited and the music of the Army band came with the cortège up the hidden road from the river, soft then louder in dramatic dirge, the funeral of Roosevelt seemed larger than death. There was the sense while the band came slowly and louder and louder up the hill under the trees as if something more miraculous than music might come into the crowded garden square where the grave was waiting.

The train which had come up slowly and proudly in the morning altered its pace and character as it rolled down the valley from Hyde Park. A kind of wake, which dignity in official grief had restrained before, began in the compartments of some of those most hurt. There were signs of a new decisiveness among those who in death and change were most hopeful. Outside, some small crowds of the curious watched in Beacon and Peekskill, where so many had watched in the morning. The train moved, scarcely slowing, through the towns. It slowed and stopped in the widening rail yards of the Bronx, and night came on as it moved again through the darkness and the lights of Jersey. There were no more stops, and some of the passengers were sure that for them and for much more this was the end of the ride. Others were clearly confident that for them, for their purposes and ideas, this was the beginning. My father knew that it was neither. The one thing of which he was sure was the inescapable and indestructible quality of the American revolution for people, which to so many seemed to hang only from

Roosevelt's shoulders, like the blue Navy cape he liked to wear in his portraits.

We had buried Roosevelt, not revolution in America. It did not serve Roosevelt, his purposes or his country to suggest that he had created something strange, rootless and merely Rooseveltian. The greatest men could be spared and the least might be needed—even an old tired man. That old man might feel like the oldest of the revolutionists. My father was sure he would not be the last. There was not much more that he could do. He had built Bryan's monument, not disturbed because some in merriment pointed out that Bryan stood in bronze with his back to a re-opened brewery. It was more important to Father that he had brought Franklin there to make the speech of dedication and repeat Bryan's words, "You may dispute over whether I have fought a good fight; you may dispute over whether I have finished my course; but you cannot deny that I have kept the faith." My father knew that, almost like Bryan at the last, he himself seemed not only old but sometimes irascible on the board of the Woodrow Wilson Foundation, where conservative directors occupied most of the other seats and suggested somehow that Wilson had been for peace but not for people. Wilson's memory seemed almost as lost in silk hat and striped pants as Bryan's in the symbols of the alpaca coat and the palm leaf fan. The one certain thing, my father knew, was that history would hide Franklin Roosevelt in strangeness, too.

If at the last of Bryan's life it had been hard for the young to understand how so many millions could in hope have followed him, it would have been incredible at Roosevelt's beginnings in national affairs as a charming young man with money, a great name and an attitude as well as a heritage which made him the epitome of his class, to suppose that millions of the same kind of men moving in the same directions would follow him. If Wilson had been betrayed by aristocratic tastes in conflict with his democratic mind, it was even more strange that Franklin had escaped a similar self-betrayal. The revolution which seemed to come to climax—and perhaps conclusion —by Roosevelt's grave was not the miracle of Roosevelt. Roosevelt was the remarkable, almost the fantastic, creation of the revolution.

That, of course, would be the idea of an innocent. And even as a petted old gentleman, as Roosevelt's Ambassador who had somehow not got lost in the mestizo subtleties of Mexico, and as an ex-Secretary of the Navy who had deserved the wry respect of the admirals, my father was an innocent. On the Roosevelt funeral train he seemed one, particularly beside the dark James Forrestal, who was the last man to hold the status Daniels had held as Secretary of the Navy. Franklin Roosevelt's cousin, Joseph Alsop, regarded Forrestal as a symbolic figure in the era of Franklin Roosevelt when "the innocence, and with it the naïveté" of earlier times had disappeared. Franklin Roosevelt symbolized the era of Franklin Roosevelt. His greatness did not lie in his agility, his cleverness, his sophistication, his charm or his realism. Sometimes Daniels loved him despite those things. He knew that Franklin's greatness came only when he embraced the ancient American innocence that it had a moral purpose for mankind. America could only hope to come to its proper strength and greatness in understanding of that purpose, too.

That purpose is not new nor naïve. It is still revolutionary. My father understood that even in 1776 Thomas Jefferson's declaration was the embodiment of ideas and aspirations which were old in the world when young Jefferson wrote them down. His words had stated the causes of the American Revolution, but they also stated the cause of man. Neither the ideas nor the revolution were American in either origin or object. They merely came through the funnel of the patriots at Philadelphia, and they were stated there not merely for the colonies but for Christendom.

That, of course, is not entirely clear. Indeed, the danger

to that cause greater than aggressive totalitarianism may be the little-stressed but widely-spread notion that, for most stirring peoples on old crowded continents, the American revolution is an irrelevancy. Freedoms may seem only luxuries to those still seeking—and not always finding—bread. Their revolt is against scarcity; to them American freedom often seems the luxurious growth of the uncrowded spaces, the unlimited resources, the untouched possibilities. The plenty in freedom of the American people may seem rather to be envied than imitated by peoples no longer apathetic in hunger but with no new continents on which to build their dreams.

Strangely, that notion is most energetically spread by some Americans with new pride not as a naïve people but as an elite nation and with new fear in a sudden fascination with geography and ideas. A nation, like a man, can prefer to seem anciently endowed rather than newly rich. An inheritor may feel a great necessity to guard his possessions with tenacity. In an age of jet planes Mr. Jefferson's "wide ocean" seems unfortunately obliterated. The truth is it was never there. It was during Jefferson's own lifetime—never since—that America was actually invaded, the White House and the Capitol burned. For most people there never was an easy American Eden. The truth, of course, is that it was a radical American revolt against scarcity where plenty was possible that made the story of my father's times—and Bryan's and Wilson's and Roosevelt's and our own.

That revolutionary movement in our own times was not merely against five-cent cotton and ten-cent wheat. It involved not only farmers raising less corn and more hell, but also those who came seeking the bright promises of freedom in America and found themselves imprisoned in American slums. Old and new Americans piled up against a closed American frontier beyond which there was no more free land. Too much of the unlimited resources had been grabbed by too few of the people.

Franklin Roosevelt was just beginning to be a politician in New York when almost a hundred and fifty girls were piled up and burned to death in the Triangle Factory fire because no laws required such safety precautions as doors which opened outward. There were thousands of landless in uncrowded America. There were children in the mills. The palaces of the millionaires grew in Newport and Dutchess County and in Washington in the same years in which unemployment was widespread and soldiers stopped the strikes which began in the plant where they built the Pullman Palace Cars.

The people accomplished their own revolution. No elite organized the American escape. It was often suggested that "gentlemen in politics," acting in "disinterestedness within a class orbit," might cure these things. There were some such. Franklin Roosevelt to begin with was such a young man. So was his cousin, Theodore. TR wrote the then Sir Edward Grey that he thought there was something to be said for government by a great aristocracy. But that there was, he thought, "nothing to be said for government by a plutocracy, for government by men very powerful in certain lines and gifted with the 'money touch' but with ideals which in their essence are merely those of glorified pawnbrokers."

Herbert Hoover was even less sure of a ruling class which many Americans so much admired. When the Wilson administration began in America, as he noted in his memoirs, in London the upper classes regarded talk of ameliorating the condition of the poor as "sheer wicked radicalism designed to destroy 'the Empire.'" In America the word was The Constitution—as interpreted by a court on which the elite desperately did not want a Brandeis.

It is not so easy to see the aristocrats now. The income tax has reduced their visibility. The old poor can ride in their new cars to get permanent waves, too. Perhaps the elite in America can best be identified now as those who regard themselves as realists. They are plentiful among the diplomats and the soldiers. They appear frequently among the politicians. Sometimes they only live in Washington and are quite realistic about the fact that they do not care what cause they serve so long as they can stay in Washington and be invited to the parties. Others are diligent about the affairs of the world—or their clients.

I set it down as my faith that only the visionaries, including such a great reluctant one as Franklin Roosevelt, have helped the people shape their security, and that those who most confidently regard themselves as realists have retarded it. The difference between the idealists and the realists is not only that between the visionaries and the technicians, between those who make democracy a career and those who keep it as a creed; it is also that between the faithful and the fixers. The worst "five percenters" have always been those willing to settle the promise of America—and its promises to the world—on a percentage basis which often in terms of cash or power or glory they pocket themselves in a process which they present as patriotism.

Even among the visionaries venerated by the elite, Edison while he lived looked—and often talked—like a rumpled Populist and Henry Ford was an obvious crackpot about peace and other things, too. Those who were not petted by the plutocrats (and/or pawnbrokers) fall more clearly into the visionary class. Bryan had led "the poor and the oppressed." Wilson, as his official biographer said, was elected by "the under men of the nation." Certainly Franklin Roosevelt, in 1932, was not elected by Americans rich beyond the possibility of emulation. They led a native radicalism still determined in America. And America needs nothing so much as that tough, native radicalism now. It can count on world leadership as a part of a world comradeship only as it steadily serves its own stated ideal of all men created equal . . . deriving their just powers from the consent of the governed—and aiming at rights which include not only life and liberty but even the happiness of men. Obviously only visionaries would contemplate such things; they are all that the innocent demand.

In the proof of the relevancy of the American model of democracy to the needs of the world, the revolution of this century is more important even to American security than the one of a century and a half before. The first stated ideals; the second demonstrated the increasing possibility of their fulfillment. That was a process important to all men. It was also the process in which Franklin Roosevelt did not betray a class but caught the vision of his country. It was a strange transformation for him, sometimes a difficult one. It is the transformation required of a rich, proud America with a great heritage, too. It will not fail despite the pawnbrokers, despite those Americans who move in the world confident that they are no longer naïve, talking of American "know-how" as if other people knew nothing. It will not fail because of soldiers or statesmen who operate with the idea that the end of isolationism is the beginning of imperialism. It will not fail because of those who feel that in order to garrison the world America must be made a garrison at home. Not even because of those who feel that liberties must be curtailed in order that liberty may be preserved.

America will be least naïve when it maintains its innocence. It will do that because across history and forward in history to the real New World the Americans, when they are not too fat or too frightened, are the most radical people on earth. They will make mistakes. My father's faith was built upon the understanding that the greatest men among them have their faults. He had not only witnessed those faults but felt the effects of them. Also, he was confident as witness that if Bryan and Wilson, even Franklin Roosevelt, had not taken their places at the front of the political parade others would have been there. It was the procession of the people in the demonstration of their radical purposes at home which now joins and justifies the radical hopes of men in the world. America has no greater business than the honest, the whole-hearted and, yes, the very humble presentation of its purposes and its proof. It took its purposes from the whole world; that proof rightfully belongs to the whole world now. The problem is not one of power but of partnership in hope and trouble, old aspirations and new possibilities.

My father spoke his concern about that in the last year of his life. What he said seems to me the essence of our heritage and the one basis of our hopefulness. He went down to Warm Springs in Georgia to say it. He was eighty-five at the time, and he spoke in front of the house where Roosevelt had died. He was glad, he said, that he could remember not only that Roosevelt was great but beautiful as well—and young. "How young and debonair, striding and strong he had been!" It seemed to him, he said, instructive to remember that he had come to Warm Springs in the 1920's "when the world also, which had been so strong, so beautiful in its purposes for democracy and for peace, was crippled with the paralysis of bitterness at home and abroad." The years had passed but again there seemed to be "more hate and confusion than love and purpose in the world."

"In the New World and Old World alike," he said, "recent allies of courage and sacrifice are made in their victory to seem implacable enemies across an impermanent peace. . . . A great and beautiful nation, equipped as no other nation ever was for the leadership of mankind, is a cripple also and once again. And in a sick world we seem more concerned with contagion than energetic in cure."

He spoke his faith almost angrily:

"We need not be the captive of our fears.

"Only the already lost can think of our future as besieged.

"We have more to give than to guard.

"Our powers are not weapons but tools with which to build the promise of democracy into the purposes of mankind."

His old voice did not falter but he paused to face the hesitation he knew was in so many hearts.

"Sometimes that faith is hard to hold," he admitted. "Even to an old man who has seen many years, these times seem dark. But this place is lit with courage. It is illumined with faith."

He was not afraid of radical change. It had been his life. Franklin Roosevelt had not been afraid of it. His young brashness was as important as his mature concerns. The one after the other was an omen, a fact, a basis for faith.

Perhaps my father was innocent to the end. He was not afraid. Indeed, though people were inclined to think of him not only as an innocent but as a helpless one, in those last years he traveled much alone. In the month before he died, he made the presentation speech at the award of the medal of the Woodrow Wilson Foundation to his old friend, Barney Baruch, as an "elder statesman," though Baruch was only seventy-seven. It turned out to be as much Father's party as Baruch's. He talked, of course, of Wilson that night and of himself.

"All of you have seen great war in your time. But an American has to be as old as I am to have shared its actual physical meaning in America. I was born in a town which felt the artillery of an enemy among its homes and shops. My own mother was a war refugee inside the United States. She marched penniless with three infant sons into a barren peace." He never forgot that woman, his mother, on that road. He never forgot the dead carpenter, his father, whom the war had flung behind them. He saw leadership always in terms of such people. Franklin Roosevelt and Woodrow Wilson were to him not only men much and strangely loved, but men who marked the hope of such a woman with small sons at her hands, moving toward some hope on a sandy road in Carolina in the 1860's. She was never merely his mother there and then. She was an eternal woman on all the roads in the world.

"This is not a time for discouragement," he emphasized again that night in New York. "This is the only sort of time which needs our faith. These dark years are brightly lit for those who understand that what Wilson left us was not merely a plan for peace, but the imperishable pattern of the courage with the faith, the sacrifice with the vision. He took his faith from the heart's desire of an unhappy world. But he added flame to that faith. The troubles which we face now would not have dismayed him. They will not dismay other living men who not only guard his faith, but keep his spirit now."

He did not remember either Roosevelt or Wilson lugubriously. He spoke faith out of a happy heart. After he had made that last Wilson speech in New York he went uptown to see his slightly younger brother before catching the train to Raleigh. He stayed longer than he expected. He was not letting himself be tyrannized by time. But when his brother rode down with him through Central Park toward the Plaza Hotel to get his baggage on the way to the train, time and traffic both caught them. The traffic did not move and the clock did. The cab driver was not encouraging. So Father paid him off and led his city brother walking and protesting through the dark park to a street beside it where they caught another cab. There was no time to stop for bags then. There was hardly time to get to Pennsylvania Station. The Plaza could send the bags. He felt triumphant over time as he boarded the train, an old man without bag or baggage but in high spirits going home.

He died a little more than a month later. He was not sick long. He was in fine fettle until the day they put him unwillingly to bed. My brother Worth, whom Father and Mother had meant to be a doctor from the moment of his birth, came home to be with him as his physician and comfort in the big house every day and every night. His other sons were there always, too. And the big door through which so many people had come to see him in his last years seemed to be continually letting in more. The fourth of the Democratic Presidents in his lifetime called almost every day to ask about him. Small city neighbors, thinking of the watchers as well as the sick, brought not only flowers but cakes. In the South outside, the January was like spring. The camellia bush below his window was in full bloom.

He would have enjoyed his funeral, too. The company would have pleased him, the dignitaries, the sailors and marines, the workmen, the politicians, the neighbors and his white and Negro friends. But he would have been uncertain whether to weep with her or laugh at her if he could have seen one well-loved small granddaughter, sitting between Mrs. Woodrow Wilson and Mrs. Franklin Roosevelt and requiring the handkerchiefs of both of them for her tears.

Index

341